"We live in a moment when the need for churches to innovate has become undeniable. Yet that innovation must carry forward the best of Christian traditions so that they might faithfully offer life, hope, and healing to the world today. This book distills enormous wisdom in an accessible and practical, yet intellectually rigorous, guide for all those seeking to lead the church to adapt and flourish in trying times. Scott Cormode speaks to the heart of the challenges facing the church and offers hopeful ways forward."

—**Dwight Zscheile**, Luther Seminary

"In recent memory, no book has been so timely as *The Innovative Church*. In the face of social upheaval, as demonstrated by such challenges as a pandemic and racism as unfinished business, the mainline Christian church needs to hear concepts and strategies not solely on innovation but also on our basic human experiences of 'longings and losses' that just may propel us to a way forward. Drawing on deep theological and biblical groundings, Cormode provides a field-tested method for innovation to emerge for our churches. This is a must-read book if we are to break the downward malaise that we are currently experiencing and emerge from our present crises with a future of hope."

—**Bishop Grant Hagiya**, resident bishop of the Los Angeles Area of the United Methodist Church

THE INNOVATIVE CHURCH

THE INNOVATIVE CHURCH

How Leaders and Their Congregations

Can Adapt in an

Ever-Changing World

SCOTT CORMODE

B
Baker Academic
a division of Baker Publishing Group
Grand Rapids, Michigan

© 2020 by Scott Cormode

Published by Baker Academic
a division of Baker Publishing Group
PO Box 6287, Grand Rapids, MI 49516-6287
www.bakeracademic.com

Library of Congress Cataloging-in-Publication Data

Names: Cormode, Scott, author.
Title: The innovative church : how leaders and their congregations can adapt in an ever-changing
  world / Scott Cormode.
Description: Grand Rapids, Michigan : Baker Academic, a division of Baker Publishing Group,
  2020. | Includes index.
Identifiers: LCCN 2020011044 | ISBN 9781540962263 (paperback) | ISBN 9781540963468
  (casebound)
Subjects: LCSH: Christian leadership. | Church management. | Church renewal.
Classification: LCC BV652.1 .C668 2020 | DDC 253—dc23
LC record available at https://lccn.loc.gov/2020011044

This book is about continuity across generations.

To my parents,
Dan and Ann

To my children,
Donley and Elizabeth

And, of course, to my wife,
Genie

Contents

Preface

Not long ago, I had a conversation with an innovation team from a large church in Texas. This was the first follow-up Zoom call after the four of them had traveled to Pasadena for an innovation summit. At the summit, the team learned about how to respond with agility to surprises and how to innovate in the face of social change—even unexpected social change.

"With all that has happened in the last two weeks," one of them said over Zoom, "our innovation work now feels like genius." You see, when they left Pasadena on Saturday, March 7, 2020, they expected to return to business as usual. By Tuesday, however, the vast implications of the spread of COVID-19 were beginning to be clear. By Thursday, the church had canceled its weekend services. By Friday, less than a week after the innovation conference, it was announced that we would all be sheltering in place. Of course, as I met with them, each one was hunkered down in their own homes, socially distant from everyone who was not immediate family.

The team reported a massive change of heart in their congregation. When they returned from the innovation summit, the ideas they proposed to the senior leadership seemed uncomfortable because they did not fit the way the congregation liked to do things. A week later, those same senior leaders were clamoring for new ideas. The team quickly decided that the experiments they hoped they could start in a few months would begin that weekend.

----------◆----------

This project started as many innovations do, with the realization of a connection between two unrelated conversations.[1] On the one hand, in the Christian world I was hearing an increasingly urgent appeal that our churches need to change—even as our congregations have no idea how to change. On the other hand, in the tech world I was hearing about innovation—and about the growing sense that, in the words of one early computer pioneer, "The best way to predict the future is to invent it."[2] So I began reading the innovation literature with an eye to how it might help us recalibrate the church for life in an ever-changing world. I wrote much of the book manuscript in the winter of 2015, thanks to a sabbatical from Fuller Theological Seminary and a grant from Fuller's Max De Pree Center for Leadership (with heartfelt thanks to Mary and Dale Andringa).

The usual process is to publish a book once the manuscript is complete. But I wanted to ensure that these ideas would be useful to the church. So, taking heed of the innovation insight about iterative learning, I spent the next four years road testing and refining the ideas and insights in this book with congregational leaders.

We implemented the ideas through three parallel innovation projects—each one funded by the generosity of the Lilly Endowment and administered with wonderful care through the Fuller Youth Institute. The three projects were Youth Ministry Innovation, Ministry Innovations with Young Adults, and Innovation for Vocation.

Over a hundred congregational teams participated in these three projects. The process for each grant project was the same. We invited congregations from around the country to create teams of three or four. The teams went through online training to teach them the meaning of innovation (chap. 2), transformational listening (chap. 3), and the importance of making spiritual sense of daily life (chap. 4). The teams then joined a collection of teams from other churches in Pasadena for a three-day summit that followed the Christian innovation process (chap. 6), seeking new and creative ways to get young people to participate in reinvented Christian practices (chap. 5).

Each team returned home with a prototype for an innovation project. They then spent ten weeks running an experiment that would implement their prototype. Throughout the process, we provided monthly coaching calls that allowed the leaders to reflect on what they were doing and what they were learning. In 2019, I revised the manuscript to reflect what we learned by working with these hundreds of congregational leaders.

A key insight of the book is that leaders don't have followers but do have people entrusted to their care—and leaders need to become who their people need them to be. This book has gone through the same process.

It started as a much more scholarly book, with long sections that carefully explained the development of its ideas. But after working with all those leaders, I have moved much of the scholarly conversation into the notes or jettisoned it altogether.[3] The people entrusted to my care are the readers of this book. And the fruit this book bears will be seen in the lives of the people who are entrusted to the care of those readers. As you read this book, do so not just for yourself. Instead, as you read, ask yourself how you might use the insights of the book to serve the people whom God has entrusted to your care.

I am putting the final touches on this manuscript as we are dealing with the unfolding effects of this global pandemic. I got a call from the congregation I refer to in chapter 10 as "Millennial Church." The chapter describes the congregation's fumbling efforts to come to grips with denial over social changes. The subject of the FaceTime call was about all the ways they were reviving the experiments that just last year seemed to be too much for them. The pandemic jarred them out of their complacency. Indeed, now they are clamoring for the very change they recently thought was unnecessary. If this pandemic teaches us anything, it is that we cannot stand still while the world changes around us. The future church will have to learn innovation and agility.

Acknowledgments

P erhaps the most enjoyable part of writing a book is getting to acknowledge publicly all the people you would like to thank. Let me begin by
expressing my gratitude for Fuller Seminary—both the people and the
institution. It has been my home for many years. Truth be told, it has been my
intellectual and scholarly home since even before the school employed me. I
like to say that I am theologically conservative and socially liberal, and that
I am socially liberal for theologically conservative reasons. I learned that at
Fuller. The seminary taught me to read the prophets who stood up for the
widows, orphans, and aliens in our midst. It taught me to listen to lament and
to see the sinners and outcasts with compassion. The emphasis in this book on
listening to the people entrusted to your care began when I was under the care
and tutelage of Fuller Seminary, and I am deeply appreciative. Specifically, I am
grateful to President Mark Labberton and to my colleagues (especially Todd
Johnson and Mark Lau Branson and the entire ministry division). Particular
thanks go to Mary and Dale Andringa, whose amazing support contributed
far more to this project than they will ever know.

I am grateful as well to the Fuller Youth Institute (FYI) for allowing me to be
a partner in the gospel. Thank you to Kara Powell, Brad Griffin, Steve Argue,
Jake Mulder, Caleb Roose, and Zach Ellis. I am particularly grateful for the
ways that our work together on the FYI leadership team (Kara, Brad, Jake, and
Steve) has modeled the kind of candor and commitment, the kind of courage
and creativity, that chapter 7 will call a "Braintrust." I am privileged to work
with you—and also the hundred or so congregations that came through four
years of innovation summits. I am likewise grateful to Fuller's Max De Pree
Center for Leadership, including Mark Roberts, Michaela O'Donnell-Long,
and Tod Bolsinger.

I am indebted to the Lilly Endowment for their generous and enlightened commitment to innovation. The three parallel projects (Youth Ministry Innovation, Ministry Innovations with Young Adults, and Innovation for Vocation) were the primary proving ground for this book, and the ideas in it would be considerably weaker were it not for the congregational interactions they made possible. Thank you especially to Kathleen Cahalan and the leadership team that oversees the parent program ("Called to Lives of Meaning and Purpose") overseeing Fuller's Innovation for Ministry project. Because of their support, I was able to present an early form of this work at Regent College and at the Virginia Theological Seminary. And thank you to Teesha Hadra and Jessie Duisberg for the tremendous work leading that project.

Many thanks as well to Dudley Rose and Laura Tuach, who decided to make a manuscript version of this book the primary textbook in their capstone seminar on innovation at Harvard Divinity School.

Thank you to the Academy of Religious Leadership and the *Journal of Religious Leadership*. You have been my primary scholarly dialogue partners for almost twenty years now. I am particularly grateful for the feedback on a paper that described a very early version of this work.

Thank you as well to the scholars and friends who read the entire manuscript. I completely revised the content based on your feedback. Thank you to Dwight Zscheile, Terri Elton, Emily Click, Steve Argue, Kara Powell, Brad Griffin, Jake Mulder, Greg Jones, Kathleen Cahalan, Nancy Going, Rhonda McEwen, Jessie Duisberg, Steve Davis, and Genie Cormode.

I am grateful to my congregation (La Verne Heights Presbyterian Church) and especially to our discipleship group (Johnny and Tanya Eveleth, Paul and Stephanie Boles, and Brian and Heather Mahaffey).

Two friends have been particularly kind in walking with me over the years, and they deserve special thanks: Emily Click from Harvard and Steve Davis of Claremont McKenna College.

And, of course, thank you to the three generations of family to whom this book is dedicated: my parents, my children, and especially my wife, Genie, who is God's great gift to me. None of this would have been possible (or worth doing) without you.

1

How the Church Is Calibrated for a World That No Longer Exists

Almost everything about the current experience of church was established in a bygone era: the way we worship, the passages of Scripture we cherish, and the people we expect to see. The basic contours of church have not changed, even as the world has been transformed. The church as we know it is calibrated for a world that no longer exists.

Erica knows this all too well. In 2018 she brought her youth ministry team from Florida to Fuller Theological Seminary for an "innovation summit."[1] Erica came to the summit bearing a burden: her young people needed help, she said, in navigating their way toward hope and joy in a world of suffering. But the old ways of doing church did not want to acknowledge her students' pain. The old ways of leading a youth group involved distracting young people and promising a world free from pain; they did not focus on seeking a God who meets us in our pain. As Erica listened to her middle schoolers (and their parents), she could see that young people today are far more anxious, busy, and stressed than they were in the past, but the expectations of church life were no different. The old ways of being church are not calibrated to speak to the circumstances that Erica's young people encounter each day.

The world has changed, but the church has not. The internet has transformed how people get information, social media has changed the meaning of community, and the post-2008 economy now expects more labor hours from the average worker. The basic assumptions about time, money, and community—and about membership, Bible study, and ecclesiology—have

1

all changed. But congregations act the way that they did before the climate changed, and congregants often wish that the world would just go back to the way it once was. The mental models that we Christians hold about the rudiments of church (about things such as worship, teaching, and fellowship) were formed in the mid-twentieth century, long before social changes transformed the meaning of almost every institution in society. As the theologian Dwight Zscheile wisely observed, "God's promises in Christ are steadfast, but the shape and future of the church in America is increasingly uncertain" in an ever-changing world.[2]

Indeed, the pace of change is accelerating. Something new rolls over us even as we are still reeling from the last thing. In the past, the church had time to adjust between changes. It could absorb the initial shock of social change, wait for things to settle into an equilibrium, and then learn from those who had already adjusted to that new reality. But the wait-and-copy strategy will not work anymore. For most of the church's history, Christians had up to a century to recalibrate in the face of a disruptive change such as the Industrial Revolution. Even in the twentieth century, the church typically had a generation to recalibrate to changes like the advent of the automobile or the rise of suburbia. But now, sweeping changes are happening years apart rather than decades apart.[3] There is not enough time between changes before the next wave hits. The wait-and-copy strategy will no longer work because we live in what one scholar has called "a world of permanent white water."[4] The next wave will always come before we have adjusted. We will need to learn how to live in an ever-changing culture.

Even if a church figures out how to respond to some social change, it faces another problem. Congregations are tempted to make a change and then freeze that change—to breathe a sigh of relief that says they never have to change again. Think, for example, about changes in how we worship. In the late nineteenth century, cutting-edge Protestant churches incorporated organ music into their services. This was a controversial move. Established theologians opposed what they called the "innovators" who were spoiling the plain worship of God with their ostentation.[5] Of course, by the twentieth century congregations had become so accustomed to organ music that there was an anguished cry when innovators replaced organs with guitars. Once a change has been legitimated, congregations often demand that the change become permanent, even when the culture has moved on to something else. Neither the wait-and-copy strategy nor the change-and-freeze plan will help us. Clinging to these strategies means we are dancing to the rhythm of a song that no longer plays. We need a way to recalibrate in order to keep from getting out of touch with the needs of the world. That will take innovation.

Innovative Congregations

A changed world demands innovation, and a changed religious world requires innovative congregations. But there is a problem. Most of the literature on innovation assumes that the best innovations will tear down the structures of the past and replace them with something better in just the way that the iPhone camera destroyed Kodak, and Amazon replaced Borders bookstores. "Cut the ties to the past," some say. "Burn the boats." But we Christians cannot do this. We are inextricably—and happily—bound to the past. We will never stop reading Paul's letters to the Corinthians, we will never stop loving our neighbors as ourselves, and we will never stop saying, "Jesus is Lord." We cannot abandon the past.

Every Christian's faith depends on the inherited Christian tradition. We receive the faith; we do not invent it. No Christian, for example, invents practices like prayer or beliefs such as "Jesus is Lord." We receive them—both from God and from those who came before us. We depend on the Christian tradition. Yet, as the theologian Gregory Jones points out, "Tradition is fundamentally different from traditionalism." He quotes the Yale historian Jaroslav Pelikan: "Tradition is the living faith of the dead; traditionalism is the dead faith of the living."[6] Although at some level we all know that the experience of Christianity has changed over the centuries (e.g., there are few current congregations that chant in Latin), our tendency is to believe that the present is better than the past and that the future should look about like the present.

All this makes new ideas look suspect. Yes, we must be grounded in the Bible as the authoritative witness to Jesus Christ, and yes, we must be anchored by the theological reflections of the historic Christian church.[7] Yet we cannot be shackled to the ways the gospel has always been presented. Christian innovation cannot abandon the past, but it must find new ways to express itself for the future.[8]

Thus, the question of congregational innovation comes into focus. How do we Christians innovate when our credibility depends on continuity with the past and honoring tradition? To put it another way, *How do we maintain a rock-solid commitment to the unchanging Christian faith while at the same time finding innovative ways to express that faith in an ever-changing culture?*

That takes us back to the image of recalibrating. But how do we recalibrate? We recalibrate according to a standard. If I want to reset my watch, I look up the time from a standard I trust (usually my cell phone). If I sing, I follow the beat of the musicians. If I plant crops, I wait for the proper season to harvest them. But Christian recalibrating is particularly tricky because we need to account for both the ever-changing culture and the never-changing gospel. We can do that using the dual standard of people and practices—that is, according to the longings and losses of the ever-changing people entrusted to our care and according to the practices that constitute the never-changing gospel. To do that, we must recalibrate our understanding of Christian leadership.

Planting and Watering

If we think the world is predictable, we establish fixed routines hoping to create guaranteed outcomes. This would make leading a church like operating an assembly line. With an assembly line, you plug the right raw materials into the right machine and you know that every time you get just what you want coming out the other side. If you see a deviation, you stop and make adjustments until you get the expected result. But the world is not predictable enough for us to operate as an assembly line; we don't even know what tomorrow will bring.

We will need to think more like farmers. Farmers organize their efforts around the seasons of the year. They know to expect that spring will bring rain and summer will bring sunshine, but they never know how much rain or how much sun. Farmers have calibrated themselves to know what they can and what they cannot do, just as Christian leaders must. We need to have a view of leadership that acknowledges that God's work is decisive, that nothing we do can accomplish what we value most.

One short verse of the Bible summarizes Christian leadership. At the fractured founding of the church in Corinth, "[Paul] planted, Apollos watered, but God gave the increase" (1 Cor. 3:6 KJV). In Christian leadership, God's action is the decisive work. Paul and Apollos tended the Corinthian crops, but God made them grow. The Christian leaders did indeed have work to do, but it only mattered because of what God chose to do. The distinction is important because the work of Christian leadership is planting and watering. Indeed, this is a book about planting and watering.

We Christians spend our days and nights like farmers; we are tending the people whom God has entrusted to our care. But we cannot make the people grow. We do not operate an assembly line; there is no guaranteed outcome. We nurture our people by creating an environment conducive to growth, then we hand our people over to God. Only God can give the increase. If we are to innovate our way into the world that just now exists, we will need to think like farmers.

My grandfather was what the Bible calls a steward. He farmed 140 acres of citrus trees for a landowner who lived far away. The Hollow Hill Farm was entrusted to his care. He devoted himself to his trees, and he wanted them to bear fruit. But every season, he knew that it was God who gave the increase. So, if God did the decisive work, what did my grandfather do? He managed the environment that nurtured the orchard. Like Paul and Apollos, he spent his days planting and watering. While he could not guarantee a harvest, he could control the water, the soil, and the temperature that encouraged growth.

A farmer will go to great lengths to maintain that environment. For example, there were winter nights when my grandfather stayed up all night trying to deal with the cold. In the Southern California valley where he labored, the temperature occasionally dipped below freezing and threatened to kill the trees entrusted to his care. On those nights, he set up between each pair of trees what were called "smudge pots"—tall, fat pipes filled with burning motor oil. As they belched a smelly haze, they kept the trees from freezing. Smudging was exhausting and dirty work. All night long, he made sure each inky mess continued to burn. In the morning, my grandfather was covered with an oily residue, but his trees had survived. (If you lead in Jesus's name, you too will have days when you find yourself covered in some sort of grime.) My grandfather was a steward with an orchard entrusted to his care. His planting and watering could not guarantee growth, but he could focus on creating an environment conducive for growth.

This idea that God does the decisive work changes the way we lead, and it even changes the way we see Christian practices like prayer. For example, I learned to pray differently when my wife, Genie, had cancer (cancer that was a lot more serious than either of us wanted to acknowledge out loud). I realized that at the time I had a fairly simplistic mental model of prayer, and I needed a deeper understanding. Sometimes I acted like I could obligate God, as if just the right prayer would control God so that God would do what I wanted. And sometimes I acted like it was just self-talk, as if all it did was make me feel better. I knew neither view was true, but I regularly acted as if they were. I needed an understanding of prayer that allowed me—like the farmer—to hand over to God the things that mattered most to me.

The insight came when I acknowledged that I was deeply invested in something I could neither influence nor control. I wanted to make my wife get well, but I could do nothing to guarantee the outcome I desperately desired. It was deeply disturbing. And, at first, that led to fatalism. I'd just say to myself that God would do what God would do and try not to think about what I could not control. It was a way of emotionally protecting myself while overwhelmed by the initial shock of her cancer.

But eventually I found a way to express faith rather than fatalism.[9] I created a little ritual where each day I would start the morning by handing Genie over to God in just the way that a farmer has to turn his trees over to God. I did it each day as I began my commute because that was usually the first time I was alone with God. I would say (often aloud), "God, if I could take control of this myself, I would. But I can't. I am left with no choice but to trust you. So, with fear and trembling, I hand Genie over to you." While I said it, I would often make a gesture with my hands of lifting something up to God, asking God to accept this most precious thing from me.

That was a decade ago (she is fine now), but it changed the way I pray. I now see prayer as handing over my loved ones and my fears to God in an honest statement of belief and unbelief. I say (often aloud), "God, if I could make it happen myself, I would. But since I cannot, I hand this person (or situation) over to you. I believe; help my unbelief." I recognize that I have a part to play when I pray in that I have to lift the person up to God, but it is God who does the decisive work. It would be a tragic mistake to think that my work was the most important part of prayer.

In a similar way, Christian leaders often make this mistake when they pursue Christian innovation. We cannot act as if our work is decisive, as if we could create a program or process that would guarantee our people will grow. When Erica came to Pasadena for the innovation summit, she had a wonderful sense that her people belonged to God and that only God could meet her people in their pain. But there are other Christian leaders who, often through a misguided sense of responsibility, search for the proper program, one that will be enough to ensure that their people will develop a life-altering faith in Jesus. It is too easy to forget that our faith is a gift of God. It is not the result of any program we create. All our work is planting and watering. Without planting and watering, the trees will not grow. We do what God asks us to do, and then we turn our people over to God—just as my grandfather handed his trees over to God.

My grandparents remained devoted to trees even after they moved off the farm. When they retired, they purchased the only home they ever owned—a tiny house with a dozen enormous citrus trees off to the side. It was not so much a home as a small orchard with a house attached. Even decades after they retired, my 103-year-old grandmother would regularly hobble out into the orchard with her walker to irrigate her trees. It was both a burden and a pleasure for her; it was who she was. Grampa smudged, Gramma watered, and God gave the increase. Even in retirement, they had an orchard for which to care.

Every Christian leader has people entrusted to their care. Perhaps you do not have a traditional orchard. Maybe you tend an urban community garden or care for ancient, splintered trees. You may have a grove with many trees or just a few isolated plants. But every Christian leader is a steward. Each of us plants and waters those entrusted to our care.

The Christian Innovation Questions

Innovation often comes not through new answers to old questions but rather from asking new questions about everyday experiences. When the renowned scholar Peter Drucker wanted to recast the work of business, he created five new questions that every enterprise needed to answer.[10] They are often whittled down to this common shorthand: Who is your customer, and what does this customer value? Because these questions were originally created for businesses, they assume a "customer" who will pay a fee in exchange for a product or service. We Christians need a different set of questions because producing a profit is not our goal; we do not need to know what the market will bear. Thus, we can create a set of questions that are similar to the Drucker Questions, questions that can guide Christians and Christian organizations in their pursuit of God's purposes.

The questions will guide our planting and watering, but they begin not with our efforts but with God's work in the world. Second Corinthians 5:19 says that God was "reconciling the world to himself in Christ" and has given to us the ministry of reconciliation. "We are therefore Christ's ambassadors" (2 Cor. 5:20).[11] We are invited to partner with God in the work that God is already doing in the world. That's what it means to be an ambassador. An ambassador[12] is someone who stands between two peoples[13] just as Jesus, the Incarnate Son, stood between God and humanity. An ambassador is a citizen of one country who goes to reside in another country with the expressed purpose of creating good relations between the two. Every Christian is called to be an ambassador. A Christian ambassador is a citizen of the kingdom of heaven who lives for a while as a citizen of this earth for the express purpose of creating good relations between the two. We Christians represent Jesus in different settings, at different venues, among different peoples. But ultimately each one of us is *called* to be an ambassador. We need a set of questions that will enable us to calibrate our work as ambassadors of God's kingdom in this world.

Allow me to describe the questions here, knowing that we will flesh them out over the course of the next few chapters.

Q1. Who are the people entrusted to your care?

Q2. How do those people experience the longings and losses that make up the human condition?

Q3. What Big Lies do your people believe that prevent them from hearing the gospel?

Q4. How do you make spiritual sense of those longings and losses?

Q5. How do you express that spiritual meaning as a shared story of hope?

Let us return to Erica, the youth minister who came to Pasadena to learn about innovation. As Erica worked through the process of innovation, she answered the five questions. The first three questions helped her stay connected to the ever-changing experience of her people, and the final two questions helped her construct a response that was anchored in the never-changing gospel. Let's look at Erica's response to each question. Together the questions allowed her to create *a shared story of hope to make spiritual sense of the longings and losses of the people entrusted to her care.* That is Christian innovation.

Q1. Who are the people entrusted to your care?

Christian leaders do not have "followers"—only Jesus has followers. Instead, Christian leaders have people entrusted to their care. There are three theological reasons for recasting the mental model of leadership to be about "a people entrusted to your care." First, it emphasizes God's role as the one doing the entrusting. Second, it emphasizes that we are stewards of people who already belong to God. And third, it says that the measure of good work is not my intentions but instead the effect my work has on the people entrusted to my care.

Too often churches pursue innovation for the wrong reasons. The goal cannot be "to save the church" or "to bring in young families" or any goal that focuses on the church as an institution. The goal of innovation has to be fixed on the people whom God entrusts to our care, and that means knowing who you serve.

Erica came to Fuller with a clear sense of who she was called to serve. Her first responsibility was to her youth group, especially the large percentage of middle schoolers. After that, she recognized an additional responsibility to the teens' parents and to the congregation as a whole. But from the start, Erica recognized that her calling was centered on the middle schoolers entrusted to her care.

Q2. How do those people experience the longings and losses that make up the human condition?

Leadership begins with listening.[14] The greatest act of leadership began with the greatest act of listening, when the Word became flesh and dwelt among us. He did not just walk in our shoes; he walked with our feet. Every time God entrusts a person to my care I have to begin by listening, because before I can invite a person into a new story I have to understand that person's particular backstory. I have to understand what matters most to them—what stories define them. Only then will I be able to invite them into a gospel story that gives them hope. Otherwise, I am just treating them as a stereotype.

What do we listen for? Sociologist Robert Wuthnow argues that the reason our current crop of congregations is in crisis is that we have been listening for the wrong things.[15] Most leaders listen to the things that are important to their congregations rather than to the things that are important to their people. We need to listen to the issues that matter most to the people entrusted to our care—issues such as work and money, or health and family. These are the universal issues that comprise the human condition,[16] and every person asks fundamental questions about life, death, relationships, and how it all has meaning. These are the things that keep people awake at night.

For example, I recently heard a sermon preached to a community that was going through a recent and devastating loss. Having heard about the community's pain, I expected the sermon to address the anxious mood of the congregants; instead, the preacher preached a doctrinal sermon about the confession of sin. He never mentioned the community's pain. The preacher did not think about the things that keep people awake at night. The week before his sermon, I am sure far more people laid awake thinking about their community's fearful situation rather than about unconfessed sin. I am not saying preaching on sin is wrong; indeed, it is one of the things that the church must discuss. I am saying that in this case it was tone-deaf. If you are waiting with a distraught family in an emergency room, you would not take that moment to talk to the family about unconfessed sin. It would be callous. Likewise, when people are fearful and struggling, our preaching and teaching need to address the things that keep people awake at night.

We often make the mistake of thinking that we listen so that we will know what to say. Instead, we should listen so that we will be transformed by what we hear. If I listen with real empathy to the longings and losses of my people, then it cannot help but transform me. But that requires us to be careful about what we mean by empathy.[17] Empathy requires me to call up within myself the feeling that I see before me. If you tell me a story of loss—say, you feel anxious about how to care for your ailing parents—I may not be old enough to have ailing parents, but I have worried about sick friends and family. Empathy requires me to do more than observe your pain; it asks me to call up within myself the feeling I had when I worried about a loved one. When you see in me that I have shared your feeling, that connection creates the bond we call empathy. We will call this "transformative listening" because the goal is for the listener to be transformed by what they hear.

Before Erica came to Pasadena, she engaged her team in a listening project. As they listened to their middle schoolers, they heard about the things that keep them awake at night: "school stress, fitting in, sports performance, social media, family dysfunction, homework," as well as what Erica's team came to describe as "sources of worth failures (predicted and experienced)."[18] The listening led them to see their people as anxious, busy, and stressed and to know that any innovation they proposed had to address the painful longings they heard.

Q3. What Big Lies do your people believe that prevent them from hearing the gospel?

Longings and losses are such a powerful and indeed overwhelming part of most people's lives that we tend to create ways to simply cope with the questions rather than find ways to actually address the human condition. Our people can feel overwhelmed by their longings and losses, and they often take refuge in Big Lies. A Big Lie is a distorted belief—a way of seeing the world that upholds a falsehood.

We are all familiar with Big Lies that compete with the gospel. Big Lies might include ideas such as these: "Money can buy happiness." "Look out for yourself first." "Greed is good." But the subtler Big Lies are often distortions that we have adopted in the church. We may not say these things out loud, but our behaviors show that we act as if they are true. For example, in my innovation work with congregations, we have seen Christians who believed (perhaps silently) that "Some sins are worse than others and they will define you, while some sins are excusable and they will not affect you" or "Not doing bad things makes up for not doing good things" or "Good Christians will be successful." Your people may not believe those exact Big Lies, but we all believe Big Lies that distort the gospel.

Indeed, the world around us often depends on such Big Lies. Think of the Big Lies at a shopping mall (e.g., "You are what you wear," "The customer is always right," "You are only important for what you can spend") or the Big Lies embedded in social media ("You are what you post," "Friendship is the same as having followers," and "Community equals attention"). There are even Big Lies that distort Christian practices (e.g., "Sunday attendance equals worship" or "The church exists to fulfill my needs"). Big Lies block us from seeing the truth of the gospel and prevent us from knowing the love of God.

As part of Erica's online preparation to come to the Fuller innovation summit, she listened not only to the longings and losses of her middle schoolers but also for the Big Lie that was underneath their anxious, busy, and stressed lives. At the core, she found that they were constantly asking themselves "Am I valuable?" This led her to articulate their Big Lie as saying, "Love is conditional." Although no one spoke the phrase aloud, the sentiment summarized the fear of conditional acceptance that nagged her young people each day. And she came to see that whatever innovation project she pursued needed to provide a spiritual antidote to that Big Lie. Ultimately, she said, she wanted the project to provide her young people with what she called a "grace-based identity" that would allow them to experience "being known and loved anyway."

Q4. How do you make spiritual sense of those longings and losses?

Every Christian leader is called to make spiritual sense.[19] Understanding the longings and losses of the people entrusted to our care is the necessary beginning, but it cannot be all that we do. We Christians will need to make spiritual sense of the longings and losses of the people entrusted to our care, and in doing so, we will join a great cloud of biblical witnesses. Throughout the Bible we see God's appointed leader explaining the spiritual meaning of the people's common experience.

Look at the way that Jesus taught. Jesus repeatedly reframed the very meaning of the law. For example, he said, "Let him who has no sin cast the first stone"[20] and punctured the self-righteous arrogance of a crowd that could no longer see its own sin. He also extended the law in new and uncomfortable ways, using the story of the good Samaritan to show that "love thy neighbor" extends beyond the comfortable confines of polite society. Jesus offered an interpretation ("The last shall be first") that refocused people's lives. They thought that power and prestige signaled God's blessing, but it was a Big Lie. Instead, he offered an image of a servant who dies on behalf of his people, saying to his followers, "Whoever wants to be my disciple must deny themselves and take up their cross and follow me" (Mark 8:34). Jesus made spiritual sense of the longings and losses of the people entrusted to his care.

That is exactly what Erica set out to do once she had recognized that her middle schoolers believed the Big Lie that love is conditional. She wanted to provide them with "an identity found in God, not conditional acceptance," one that gave them what she called the "liberating sense of being known and loved anyway." She decided to do this by focusing on the Christian practice of lament, because in lament we are invited to speak honestly to God—even if we are angry at God. By introducing her middle schoolers to lament, she taught them that God would love them despite the messiness of their lives.

Christian practices are particularly useful for innovation because they are both new and old at the same time. They are old because each practice has been an essential part of Christianity since its inception. They are new because the expression of each practice changes drastically over time. But, along the way, we have forgotten (or neglected) some practices. Recovering those practices can accelerate innovation. As part of the preparation for the innovation summit, we introduced Erica to several reinvented Christian practices, which included lament (we will meet these practices in chap. 5). In learning about lament, she was able to imagine ways to use this ancient practice to help her middle schoolers create a "grace-based identity" that refuted that "conditional acceptance" they experienced every day.

Christian practices are a way of planting and watering. They create an environment for growth. They represent the received wisdom of our forebears in just the way that smudge pots (and, now, wind machines) represent the received wisdom of the farmers that came before us. But do not think for a moment that this planting and watering can ensure growth. Only God gives the increase. Indeed, as Second Corinthians assures us, God works through our weakness. None of our inadequate planting and watering guarantees growth any more than the practice of prayer obligates God. We pray because God invites us (indeed, commands us) to pray. But, like all Christian practices, our prayers take us back into the hands of God. We plant and water through practices, but only God can give the increase.

In the same way, the Christian practice of lament allows us to express our honest emotion (even and especially if we are angry at God) and still, in the end, hand our lives back to God. Erica used a Mad Libs format to teach her middle schoolers to talk to God the way the psalms talk to God. She wrote a simple lament, using almost a Mad Libs style for each of the components:

- God, I don't understand _____.
- God, please fix _____.
- God, I trust you with my future even if _____.
- God, I will praise you even when _____.

That structure became the way that she would help her young people make spiritual sense of their anxious, busy, and stressed lives. She believed that if they could express themselves honestly to God, it would be "liberating and provide an honest connection" that would rebut the Big Lie of conditional acceptance that poisoned their lives. For weeks, Erica invited her middle schoolers to fill in the Mad Libs structure so they could express their pain to God. And, after the young people had spent enough time using the Mad Libs, they felt comfortable writing their own laments.

Q5. How do you express that spiritual meaning as a shared story of hope?

The ultimate goal of Christian innovation is to invite our people into a new story—a communal story, a hopeful story. How are people transformed? People do not latch on to a plan or an abstract statement of doctrine. That does not change them. Instead, people are transformed when they participate in a story—a story that sets them on a specific trajectory.[21]

Let us follow the model of Jesus. Jesus invited people into the stories we now call parables. He told the story, for instance, of a man beaten and robbed on the road to Jericho and of the Samaritan man who unexpectedly cared for him. In another parable, Jesus invited people to see themselves in a story about a young son who squandered his inheritance but who was embraced by his father on his return, and he asked them to examine whether they might be like the older brother who was insulted by his father's kindness. And Jesus repeatedly said, "The kingdom of God is like . . ." He did not so much define the kingdom of God with detailed teaching as invite people into a vision of what God intended, a vision where "the last shall be first," a vision presented through stories.[22]

Ella Saltmarshe has written about how stories enable people to change.[23] She explains that stories do three things—three things that we will need if we are to recalibrate in accord with both the ever-changing culture and the never-changing gospel. First, *stories help people make sense of their lives*.[24] Scholars tell us that data enters our senses as a jumble with little meaning. Our brains have learned, however, to organize that data into patterns. Those patterns are often stories.

Second, Saltmarshe describes how *stories bind people together* to create communities. She includes this wonderful quotation from the novelist John Steinbeck: "We are lonesome animals," he wrote, who "spend all of our life trying to be less lonesome." And that is where stories come in. We tell stories, Steinbeck goes on to say, "begging the listener to [say] 'yes, that is the way it is, or at least that's the way I feel.'" When listeners hear themselves in our story, they can reevaluate their own situation and come to the conclusion, "You're not as alone as you thought."[25] Shared stories create a connection. And that story-shaped connection builds community. Shared stories create hope.

Third, Saltmarshe says that we can use new stories to *reauthor the stories that define us*. We all tell ourselves stories—stories that define us. A defining story may be a personal narrative like "God can never forgive what I have done." Or it may be a cultural narrative like "Society has taught me to think of myself as inferior." Or it may be a theological narrative like "God keeps score, and I will never measure up." Those stories define us—and often cage us. One of the most powerful things a Christian leader can do is to offer someone a story that re-narrates their life—a story that replaces a Big Lie (like "God can never forgive me") with the truth of the gospel (like forgiveness is available "for all who believe" regardless of what they have done [Rom. 3:22]).

What, then, are the stories that define us as Christians? "I [am] crucified with Christ, and I no longer live, but Christ lives in me" (Gal. 2:20); "Deny [yourself], and take up [your] cross daily, and follow me" (Luke 9:23); "Love your neighbor as yourself" (Matt. 19:19). Each of these invites us to picture ourselves imitating the contours of the stories that Jesus told to his followers. We welcome this invitation, but, at the same time, we recognize that we need something more specific as we live our daily lives. That is where Christian practices come in.

Christian practices are ritualized stories.[26] They give a contour—a narrative pathway—for us to follow. Christians practice hospitality, for example. Hospitality has been a Christian practice since the days of the apostles.[27] And Christian hospitality means more than a potluck meal. It involves treating outsiders like they are insiders and offering outsiders the privileges (like sitting at table) that are normally reserved for insiders. If we want to reauthor our lives to match the contours of the self-giving Savior who calls us to deny ourselves, then we will find ourselves practicing a hospitality that asks for nothing in return. No reciprocity. No expectation of gratitude. The Christian practice of hospitality gives to others solely because we have received a free gift of grace from the God who loves us. We enact the faith by living out these practices, by conforming our lives to the practices that have characterized Christianity from the beginning.

I define vision as "a shared story of hope." Vision inspires people and entices them to participate in something that is larger than themselves.[28] To reiterate, people are not changed by plans or doctrines; rather, people are transformed when they connect with a story that compels them to alter their trajectory.

Sometimes that transforming can happen when the story finally names the deep difficulty that a person feels. I think that, for example, a significant part of Martin Luther King Jr.'s early success was not about offering a plan but rather about naming a dilemma. When he talked about what it meant to be trapped by Jim Crow laws, people recognized themselves in that story. And when it came time to offer a plan, that too came in the form of a story. Indeed, his "I Have a Dream" speech was a vision in the form of a story. His audience did not come to some intellectual decision that nonviolence was the best philosophy (although Dr. King himself had done just that).[29] They "bought into" the vision because they could picture it. They could see the story playing out. And they could see themselves in the story. Vision is a shared story of hope.

We Christians offer something more specific than "future hope." We offer a hope rooted in the gospel—rooted in the life, death, and resurrection of Jesus Christ. Christian hope is different from other kinds of hope. When you hear a person say, "I hope it does not rain," they are expressing a wish for the future. They may or may not have much reason to believe that their wish will come true. But that is what they want. Christian hope is different. Our hope is not in some*thing* (like the weather); our hope is in some*one* (our Savior). So Christian hope is more like a quiet confidence. It is the sense that all our eggs are in Jesus's basket, and that is just fine. And we communicate that hope by inviting people into stories, just as Jesus did.

And that is what Erica did with her middle schoolers. The most powerful part of the experience for the young people was writing their own laments. Their experience with the Mad Libs format eventually gave them the confidence to write what was in their hearts.

Erica engaged in Christian innovation. She focused on the longings and losses (Q2) of the middle schoolers entrusted to her care (Q1). She refuted the Big Lie that "love is conditional" (Q3) by allowing them to experience through lament the idea that "God knows you and loves you anyway" (Q4), which created for them a way of narrating their life (Q5) that said that, when they see themselves as God's beloved, they are free to be their authentic selves. The old model of being church told Erica that the way to minister to middle schoolers was to teach them to behave. This innovation, instead, allowed her to proclaim that "God can handle whatever they throw at God, and God won't run away; and that's our youth group."

2

The Meaning
of Christian Innovation

Ralph Winter was an innovator. In July 1974, Dr. Winter stood in front of perhaps the greatest gathering of missionaries in Christian history. The Lausanne Congress on World Evangelization gathered the leaders of missionary agencies from 150 countries. They saw themselves, quite appropriately, as descendants of a line that could be traced back to biblical times. The church, they knew, had been practicing foreign missions at least since Barnabas brought Paul to Antioch in Acts 11—back when the followers of Jesus were first called "Christians."[1] The mission leaders saw themselves as descended from the medieval monks who crossed borders to bring the faith to Scandinavia. They especially felt a connection with enterprises like Hudson Taylor's China Inland Mission. The mission leaders who came to the conference agreed on the past, but they were divided about the future.

Some of the leaders had come to the conference ready to proclaim that the era of missions had ended. Such leaders pointed to the fact that now churches were in almost every country in the world. They believed that any further effort for foreign missions would be little more than an imperialist attempt to control the indigenous churches. Others believed that, although the gospel was planted in almost every country, the wise and mature Christians of the West could not abandon the fledgling churches they had planted any more than the apostle Paul could abandon the churches he founded on his missionary journeys. When Ralph Winter came to the Lausanne Congress, the pressing question for mission leaders was whether the missionary enterprise should cease or continue. He told them it should do neither. Instead, he said that they should *reinvent the practice* of missions.

Ralph Winter needed to change the mental model that most mission leaders held about the very nature of the missionary enterprise. At the time, the most cherished passages for mission leaders were variations on the parting words of Jesus. The Gospel of Matthew (28:19–20) records Jesus saying, "Go and make disciples of all nations"; Luke (in Acts 1:8) says that his followers should be witnesses "to the ends of the earth." The missionaries at the conference all agreed that the church had finally fulfilled the mandate. But they disagreed on what the next step should be. Winter began by telling them that they were all mistaken, even where they agreed. "A serious misunderstanding has crept into the thinking" about missions, he said, "based on the wonderful fact that the Gospel has now gone to the ends of the earth." Even though there are now disciples in all nations, it is a misunderstanding, he said, to think that "Christians have now fulfilled the Great Commission."[2]

Winter then reinterpreted the most cherished biblical texts on missions and, in so doing, transformed the missionary movement. He said that Christians misunderstand the Great Commission's mandate to preach the gospel to every nation because they misunderstand the word "nation." In the Bible, a nation is not a country with geographic boundaries and government oversight, he said. If that is what the Bible means by nation, then indeed the gospel has been preached to every nation. Winter said that the word "nations" refers instead to ethnic groups or cultural groups and that a nation-state might have many of these groups residing within its borders. He gave examples of nations like Pakistan, where there was indeed a national church but where "97% of the population is not culturally near this church." And he described the Church of South India, where "97% of its members come from five of the more than 100 social classes (castes) in South India."[3] Winter showed that a simple misunderstanding of the word "nation" had led mission leaders to a serious misunderstanding of the Great Commission. So he set out to change their mental model of the word "nations" and in so doing to recalibrate their understanding of global missions.

Once Winter had named the problem with how the assembled missionaries understood Matthew 28, he showed that the solution to the problem lay in the other cherished missions passage. He described how Acts 1:8 develops along concentric cultural circles—expanding from a city (Jerusalem) to the surrounding region (Judea and Samaria) and into the world. "You will be my witnesses in Jerusalem, and in all Judea and Samaria, and to the ends of the earth," it says. According to Winter, Jesus was "not talking merely about geographic distance but about cultural distance" in showing how the gospel would spread. Winter described in detail the ways that the geographically near Samaritans were culturally distant from the Jews (indeed not just distant but also separated by what Winter called "walls of prejudice"). Likewise, Winter showed how contemporary cultures like the Naga people of northern India followed a model similar to the concentric circles of Acts 1:8. The Naga church ministered to their people in their own language (what Winter called E1 evangelism, analogous to "Jerusalem"), and they ministered to neighboring Naga peoples who spoke sister languages (E2 evangelism, analogous to "Samaria"), but if they wanted to minister to people in faraway parts of India, they would have to do cross-cultural evangelism (what Winter called E3, analogous to reaching "the ends of the earth"). Winter eventually coined the term "unreached peoples" to describe groups that have never had a culturally near experience of the gospel. That notion of "unreached peoples" animates evangelistic missions to this day.

When the Lausanne Congress convened, many mission leaders were calling for a moratorium on world missions because they claimed that the "missionary mandate was complete." Winter transformed their mental model of world mission by recasting it as cross-cultural mission—to reach each of the ethnic groups that comprise what Jesus called the "nations." *Winter innovated within the bounds of the Christian tradition.* He reinvented a traditional belief (the Great Commission) embodied in a traditional practice (missions) by giving his people a new way to see it—and thus a new way to see themselves. When the conference began, the leaders wondered if they should abandon their task. By the time the conference ended, they had committed themselves with unprecedented vigor to renew the task. And Winter made that happen by reinventing a Christian practice.

Winter's idea was an innovation in Christian missions. Since that time, mission agencies have stopped thinking of the "nations" as political states and started thinking of them as people groups. Twenty-five years after Lausanne, *Time* magazine said, "Ralph Winter revolutionized what remains (even today) the true lifeblood of Evangelicals—missionary work overseas."[4] He offered a new idea, which changed the way missionaries saw themselves and their world, and he created avenues to action that the missionaries would not have otherwise seen. Ralph Winter was a Christian innovator.

----------●----------

Ralph Winter innovated about two generations ago. Let us look at a more contemporary situation to see what is at stake for us today. Imagine a conversation between coworkers. In this case, the coworkers happen to be computer programmers. But they could just as easily be the custodians who clean the programmers' building, or retirees ruminating over coffee at Dunkin' Donuts, or even teens chatting between classes.

Let's start with Gina, who is a Christian. In the adjacent cubicle is a young man named Duc, who is in his first job after college. His immigrant parents sacrificed much so that he could get his degree. Let us say that Duc confides to Gina that the long hours at work and the distance from friends and family make him feel lonely and unloved. At an appropriate point in their conversations, Gina compassionately talks to Duc about the death and resurrection of Jesus. She tells him that God, in his great love, sent his Son to live and die as one of us so that Duc might be connected with God and with other people. Gina tells him that instead of feeling unloved and lonely, he can experience the hope of love and community. Up until this point, it sounds just like many evangelistic conversations that we Christians have been having for generations. But what happens if that gospel does not sound to Duc like hope? Perhaps he tells Gina that death seems terribly harsh and then asks her, "Can't we talk about Jesus without all this stuff about his death?"

This is the moment when we see how Christian innovation must be different from secular innovation. If Gina were a secular entrepreneur, she would listen to her "customer," find out that Duc finds Jesus's death distasteful, and innovate a new gospel that no longer needs to talk about the shame of sin or the ugliness of death. But she cannot do that. We are permanently, inextricably (and blessedly) bound to the death and resurrection of Jesus Christ. Gina cannot innovate a new gospel for Duc. But neither can she simply repeat to him the old ways of stating the good news; the world has changed, and she cannot pretend that our explanation of the gospel can remain static, like the rigid back of a Puritan pew. Yet Gina can innovate: find a new way to connect that unchanging gospel to the present experience of this person whom God has entrusted to her care.

Thus, Gina shows us how the needs of our current era require Christians to unite innovation and tradition—that is, to create a sparkling new future that honors the past. To put it another way, the heart of this book and this chapter asks one question: How do we maintain a rock-solid commitment to the never-changing Christian faith while at the same time creating innovative ways to express that faith to an ever-changing culture? If we are going to recalibrate the church, we need to engage in *meaning-making innovation*.

This chapter's discussion of meaning making is part of a four-chapter trajectory. These chapters (2–5) will together take up the question: What is the goal of recalibrating the church? This chapter will explain what we mean by Christian innovation and what it has to do with recalibrating the church. By the end of the chapter, we will conclude that *the goal of Christian innovation is to create shared stories of hope that make spiritual sense of the longings and losses of the people whom God has entrusted to our care.* The next three chapters will unpack that statement by describing (1) how we can understand those longings and losses, (2) how we can make spiritual sense of them, and (3) how we can create shared stories of hope for our immediate future by recovering (or reinventing) historic Christian practices. Together these chapters will give us a goal to pursue as we seek to maintain a steady commitment to the never-changing Christian faith yet at the same time present that gospel in an ever-changing culture.[5]

Now that we have seen the progression of the next few chapters, let us focus on the argument of this chapter. The purpose of this chapter is to describe the meaning of Christian innovation—to describe the work that Christian leaders need to do if we are going to recalibrate the church. The chapter will ultimately show that Christian innovation happens when we make spiritual sense of the longings and losses of the people entrusted to our care. To reach that conclusion, this chapter will explain the following:

1. the concept of mental models, how they come to us as stories, and how they dictate our behavior;
2. that the Christian tradition (to which we maintain a rock-solid commitment) comes to us as a series of beliefs wrapped in contemporary expressions—and how we need to preserve the traditional beliefs and recalibrate the contemporary expressions; and
3. that Christian innovation is the innovation of meaning—and how that allows us to reinterpret ancient practices (often by changing mental models).

So let's start by looking at mental models.

Mental Models

The best leaders change the way we see the world. They do this by changing what are called "mental models."[6] Mental models are the categories we use to make sense of the world. We take them for granted. For example, picture an automobile. Go ahead, conjure up the image in your head. Some of you may picture a Volvo and others a Buick. But no matter what make and model you picked, it's likely that each of you pictured it having four wheels, a windshield, and a steering wheel. Why? Because a car *should* have four wheels. If I showed you one of those concept cars with only one front wheel, you would likely say to yourself, "I don't know what that is, but it's not a car." Your mental model of a car includes it having four wheels. A mental model is the image we carry in our heads of how something *should be*.

That's a rather innocuous example. So let's consider a different one. What's your mental model of a preacher? Ask a group of seminary students what a preacher should be, and you'll likely get many answers. One might say, "A man standing in the middle of a stage with a black Bible open in his left hand as he talks through a passage verse by verse." That's one way of being a preacher. It's probably not the way everyone would preach. But think about that student. If all she has ever seen is an open-Bible guy, she is likely to think that all other ways of preaching are as strange as a three-wheeled car.

Later I am going to argue that the essence of Christian leadership is to transform people's mental models so that *God's people use Christian categories to make sense of their lives*. That is what I will mean by "making spiritual sense." But before I do that, I want to give a more concrete example of transforming mental models. Let's look at Jesus, as portrayed in Mark 8.

The center of Mark's Gospel turns on Jesus's recalibrating the disciples' mental models and then showing how that recalibrated understanding changes the way they act in the world. The Gospel of Mark is constructed so that the first half builds steadily until a turning point. After that turning point, the rest of the story aims at the cross. That turning point is the encounter at the end of Mark 8.

Starting at verse 27, Jesus talks to the disciples about the mental models that the crowds have used in trying to make sense of Jesus. Jesus asks his disciples, "Who do people say that I am?" And they answer him, "John the Baptist; and others, Elijah; and still others, one of the prophets." In other words, Jesus asks, "What mental models do people use to make sense of me?" People are not sure what to make of Jesus. So they reach back into history to look for precedents. They look for a mental model that would fit their understanding of Jesus. Indeed, God's people have a word for someone who speaks for God, who makes them uncomfortable, and whom they will ultimately ignore and kill. That word is "prophet." So that is how the crowds interpret Jesus: they call him a prophet.

Then Jesus becomes more personal and asks what mental model the disciples themselves use when they interpret Jesus. "He asked them, 'But who do you say that I am?' Peter answered him, 'You are the Messiah'" (NRSV). The disciples have decided that Jesus is more than a prophet. They have decided that "Messiah" is the best mental model to use in interpreting Jesus's ministry. They have the right mental model for interpreting Jesus. Or so they think. That's because the next step of growth for the disciples requires Jesus to transform the meaning of this mental model.

Jesus knows that the disciples have the wrong mental model; what they understand by a messiah is not what he intends to be. They expect him to be a king who will sweep away the Romans and set up a kingdom that will conquer its neighbors. But Jesus does not intend to be the king that the disciples hope for him to be. So he explains to them what *he* means by accepting the term "Messiah." "Then he began to teach them that the Son of Man must undergo great suffering, and be rejected by the elders, the chief priests, and the scribes, and be killed, and after three days rise again. He said all this quite openly" (Mark 8:31–32 NRSV).

Jesus offers a new mental model for interpreting this fundamental identity called Messiah. He describes the Messiah as one who suffers. But the disciples do not react well to Jesus's attempt to teach them. Peter finds this new mental model so offensive that he tries to correct Jesus. "Peter took him aside and began to rebuke him. But turning and looking at his disciples, he rebuked Peter and said, 'Get behind me, Satan! For you are setting your mind not on divine things but on human things'" (8:32–33 NRSV). Jesus pushes Peter and the disciples to accept this new mental model. He wants them to see the Messiah as one who suffers in order to redeem rather than one who conquers in order to reign.

But Jesus was not done transforming their mental models. To see what was at stake, we need to skip ahead a couple of chapters. In Mark 10, the disciples James and John ask to sit at Jesus's left and right "in your glory" (Mark 10:37). This statement further reveals how integral this idea of a reigning king was to the disciples' mental model of a Messiah. They pictured Jesus, in his glory, as a king like David. And they thought that king would have a palace. In that palace, they thought there would be a throne room, with a large throne where the ruling Messiah would reign. Next to that throne would be a little throne on each side of the Messiah's big one. James and John were asking to occupy the two little thrones beside Jesus.

The organizational scholar Ronald Heifetz says that "people don't resist change; they resist loss."[7] In Mark 8, the disciples (in the mouth of Peter) were resisting Jesus's attempt to change their mental model of a Messiah because they had something to lose. And now we know what they were afraid to lose. He was not just changing their mental model of what it means to be a Messiah; he was also changing their mental model of what it means to be the disciple of a Messiah. That change was going to cost them something. It was going to cost them their little thrones. A reigning ruler could offer them little thrones, but a suffering redeemer would offer them only sorrows. Then Jesus drove the point home.

He made it clear to them what this new mental model of "disciple" was going to cost them. "He called the crowd with his disciples, and said to them, 'If any want to become my followers, let them deny themselves and take up their cross and follow me. For those who want to save their life will lose it, and those who lose their life for my sake, and for the sake of the gospel, will save it. For what will it profit them to gain the whole world and forfeit their life? Indeed, what can they give in return for their life?'" (Mark 8:34–36 NRSV).

Jesus asks the disciples not only to change the most important mental model that they were using to interpret Jesus (i.e., the Messiah) but also to change the mental model that they were using to interpret themselves (i.e., the Messiah's disciples). Jesus expects all of their actions going forward to be different as they live out this new mental model. The Gospel of Mark pivots on this passage. After this passage, everything in Mark's Gospel points to the cross. Once Jesus announces this new mental model, the entire story becomes about living out the new meanings of Messiah and disciple. The disciples do not fully understand the implications of these new mental models until the Spirit comes at Pentecost. But the faithfulness of their actions after Mark 8 depends on their coming to grips with these new mental models. Jesus, then, is our example of what it means to lead by *transforming people's mental models*.

These transformed models change the way people act in the world. When the disciples thought that the Messiah was sent to reign, it was appropriate, for example, for a pair of disciples to ask to sit on little thrones. It was also appropriate to expect that the last thing the Messiah would do was to experience the public shame of a humiliating death on a Roman cross. But if the Messiah has come to suffer in order to redeem, then it makes sense that a disciple of that Messiah would also live a life of service on behalf of others. In other words, changing the mental models that the disciples used to make sense of Jesus and the mental models they used to make sense of themselves transformed the actions that the disciples tried to achieve in society, with God's help. If a Christian leader transforms people's mental models, then the people's actions will change as well.

Let's look at a more contemporary example. Martin Luther King Jr. created a pathway for African Americans that did not exist until he introduced it. He did it through what we have been calling "meaning-making innovation." Before Dr. King, African Americans had two options while living under the oppression of Jim Crow: they could erupt in violence, or they could lie down in pain. Dr. King gave them a third option; he planted the seed of nonviolence in the South. Beginning with the Montgomery bus boycott in 1955–56, he created a new way to respond.[8] Dr. King gave his people a new way to see the world and a new way to interpret their circumstances.

His first appearance as a public figure—indeed, the first great speech of the civil rights movement—occurred on the first night of the boycott. As he stood in the pulpit that Monday night, the wider society was telling Dr. King's sisters and brothers that what they were doing was wrong. He reminded them that the prevailing mental model had them believing they could either be good Americans or good Christians—but not both. Good Christians stand up for justice, this mental model asserted, but good Americans obey the law. Anyone who wanted to fight the injustice around them had to break the law (and perhaps even disobey God) because fighting for justice surely meant violent protest. That night Dr. King changed the way they saw themselves and what they were doing. He told them that they were being good Christians *and* good Americans. Also, he assured them, they would do both what Americans had always done and what Christians had always done. American citizens, he said, obey the law, just as Christians stand up for justice. So he told them that they would obey the law *and* they would stand up for justice. Then he gave them an idea they had never heard. He told them about nonviolent protest.[9]

Before Dr. King, his people could either lie down to obey the law in pain or stand up to seek justice through violence. Dr. King's people did not need the physical inventions that we normally associate with the word "innovation." They needed, instead, a new way to see the world—*new meaning that paved a new avenue for action*. He showed them how nonviolence allowed them to act both as justice-loving Christians and as law-abiding Americans. This meaning-making innovation does not abandon the past. It usually involves reconfiguring an idea that has already existed. Martin Luther King Jr. married the Old Testament language of justice from the past with Gandhi's twentieth-century language of nonviolence, thereby creating a third way that his people had not considered. That is Christian innovation.

I want to emphasize three things about mental models because they will be important as we innovate our way forward. Mental models dictate behavior. Mental models often come to us as stories. And, because mental models dictate behavior, changing the story dictates new action.

First, *mental models dictate behavior*. If we are going to recalibrate the church, we will want to recalibrate more than how the church talks. We will want to change people's actions. The most powerful way to change how people act is to change how they see the world—that is, to change their mental models. When Jesus's disciples believed that a messiah was a conquering king, they believed that they should receive the honor and good life that are due to the closest advisers to a king. But when they came to understand (only after

God's intervention at Easter and Pentecost) that Jesus came to suffer and die, then they started acting differently in the world. They started expecting that they too would suffer. They stopped trying to avoid suffering. John (who once asked Jesus for a throne) could stand before the council in Acts 4 with the expectation that he and Peter would land in jail, because they knew that their Messiah had experienced the same thing.

Second, *mental models often come to us as stories*. People look for the story that makes the most sense of a situation. "Cultural frameworks," the sociologist Ann Swidler has said, "tend to be organized around imagined situations."[10] For example, my church is large enough that I sometimes see a child crying in the social time after worship. When I meet a crying child, I try to figure out what the situation means. Usually I observe the parent's face to get a clue. I can often distinguish an angry parent from a concerned parent. When I see an angry parent, I often read the situation as "the child has done something wrong and is now crying because she is in trouble." When I see a concerned parent, I look for further cues like a scraped knee. Then I might conclude that the child fell down and injured herself. But notice how much the very language I use to explain the sense-making process presumes a story. In the first instance, I did not say simply that the child misbehaved. I drew it out so that it composed a scene. The child got caught and is now crying because she is in trouble. It falls naturally into a scene from a larger story. Likewise, when I describe a child scraping a knee, I harken back to all the times when I scraped my knee as a child and all the times I hugged my daughters when they scraped their knees. The story has a background, and it has connotations (e.g., scraped knees are not serious injuries). The most natural way for me to make sense of a new situation is to put it into a story.

This story-shaped logic applies even when people are engaged in what would appear to be abstract thinking. Swidler interviewed people about the concept of love. She found that they did not display the deductive process that one usually associates with rational thinking. We tend to think that, at their best, people use abstract ideas like beliefs and values to come to some pristine conclusion and that they then apply that abstract conclusion to the specific situation at hand. Swidler found that such is not the case. "People are little constrained by logic," she found. And that's why "logical deduction rarely influences social action directly."[11] Instead, people tell themselves stories. Several key narratives repeated themselves in her interviews. In some cases, people defined themselves over against the paradigmatic stories. For instance, many people claimed not to subscribe to the "Hollywood ideal" of marriage, which seemed to be that a couple falls madly in love, overcomes some obstacle, and then lives happily ever after. The respondents used this image to say that love is hard work. But they did not offer a principle or a generalization. Instead, they told the story of the Hollywood ideal and then added that love is not like that. There were also paradigmatic examples that served as positive ideals.

Yet Swidler found something even deeper. Stories were not just illustrations. People constructed their ideas about love by playing out stereotypic scenes in their heads. For example, they talked about balancing individual needs against the needs of the other person. Swidler concluded, "Their cultural understandings of love are organized not around the logical coherence of a single image, metaphor, or theory of love but around a core situation or problem."[12] That is, as people worked out strategies for dealing with similar situations, they came to similar generalizations about love. Mental models often come to us as stories.

Third, *changing the story changes behavior*, and it does so because it changes the mental model that dictates action. That is why all this discussion—of mental models, of meaning making, and of stories—is so important to our recalibrating the church.

The way to change a person's behavior (or a congregation's behavior) is to change their mental model by changing the story they tell themselves. We have already seen how Dr. King changed people's mental model and enabled a healthier way to interact with the world, now let me give two powerful examples of how changing the story we tell ourselves changes our mental model and creates new behavior.

First look at the work of the design firm IDEO.[13] Regularly IDEO receives difficult assignments, some of them literally a matter of life and death. One assignment involved children and MRI machines. Children were often terrified by the narrow spaces and loud banging that MRI scans entail. They almost always had to be fully sedated to hold still for an MRI. Then IDEO was commissioned to create a new kind of MRI machine for children, one that did not require children to be sedated.

The expectation was that they would design a new device, a new machine, what we will call "product innovation." But they discovered that they did not need to make a new machine; they needed to make new meaning by using a new mental model.

They started by listening with empathy to the children they hoped to serve. From a child's perspective, the MRI is scary—cold and metal, cramped and loud. But they also observed children in other settings. For example, kids regularly enjoy loud movies and often clamor to go on scary rides at Disneyland. That is when they realized that the children did not need a new machine. They needed a new story—a new way to make sense of the cold metal and cramped spaces.

of buying and selling—where everything has a price. Its rules dictate your expectations and actions.

For example, suppose I am looking for a shirt at a store. I have a mental model of what a store should be (e.g., the prices should be fixed and easy for me to locate) and what I expect from a clerk (e.g., that part of the job is to answer my questions). But the trip to the store shapes me further. It teaches me to see human encounters as an exchange and to see people for their role (rather than through a relationship). It even teaches me how to react when someone does not meet my expectations. I am far more likely (I am chagrined to admit) to get angry at a clerk or at a company than I am to become cross with my family or friends. For example, I recently called my cable company because my internet went out. It took me five calls to get through. When I finally spoke to a person, I was angry. Now, I know that this call-center technician was not to blame. But I was impatient and short with her because I saw myself as participating in a business liturgy. My mental model was that I was the "customer" and she was not so much a fellow human made in the image of God (as the Christian liturgy would teach) as she was the representative of a company that had taken my money but provided poor service.

"Every liturgy constitutes a pedagogy that teaches us to be a certain kind of person,"[20] writes Smith. The liturgy of commerce taught me to be a stereotypical annoyed (and annoying) customer, and it competed with the liturgy of Christianity that teaches me to be an ambassador of the God of grace. One reason our churches get stuck is that we are conditioned to use the wrong mental model. We adopt secular liturgies and replace Christianity with Christendom.

Christian Innovation Involves the Innovation of Meaning

Christian innovation cannot be exactly like secular innovation, yet Christians can learn from secular innovators. Before we say how Christian innovation is different, it would be helpful to trace the development of innovation as an idea. This will help us clarify our mental model for "innovation."[21]

"Innovation" has come to mean at least five things for secular scholars.[22] The fifth of these concepts is most germane for Christian innovation, but we should look briefly at all of them because they often confuse Christian leaders. First, there is *product innovation*. This is the mental model most people carry when they hear the word "innovation." Like Thomas Edison inventing a light bulb or Apple inventing the iPhone, innovation sometimes refers to devices. This has little connection with the kind of Christian innovation that will recalibrate the church.[23]

Second, there is *process innovation* such as Henry Ford's revolutionary assembly line or "the Toyota Way," a process that transformed how manufacturers approach quality.[24] Yet changing our methods will not likely recalibrate the church.

Then there is *internet innovation*, where the result is to create an app or a website such as Uber or Google Earth. But if we don't change the content of our messages, simply delivering sermons over the internet will not transform us.

There is also *social innovation*, a term that has two competing definitions. Gregory Dees defines social entrepreneurs as people who pursue change in the name of a social value, either using the resources at hand or embedding the change agency in a for-profit company.[25] By contrast, Roger Martin and Sally Osberg argue that social entrepreneurs are people who take "direct action . . . to transform the existing system."[26] This kind of innovation has attracted some attention from Christians because some leaders see it as a way to do good in the world and possibly a way to bring the gospel message into a new structure.[27] That is really a wonderful thing. But the goal for this book is to change how we communicate the gospel to the people entrusted to our care. Changing the structures that carry that gospel will solve a different (and important) set of problems, but it will not recalibrate our churches away from a world that no longer exists. None of the first four definitions of innovation will enable us to recalibrate.

These four ways of constructing innovation do, however, share common themes, particularly in the ways that the secular literature has approached the problem. They are strongly influenced by Joseph Schumpeter's idea of "creative destruction,"[28] and they argue that innovation is "disruptive"[29] and "discontinuous."[30] This is why most secular ideas about innovation involve replacing one (presumably obsolete) thing with another thing, whether it is a device, a process, an app, or a social system.[31] Indeed, Christians reading about these kinds of innovations might naturally be inclined to abandon the past, which, we have agreed, we Christians cannot do. So we will need another mental model for innovation.[32]

There is a fifth way to think about innovation, one that is more compatible with Christianity's commitment to embodying tradition. There is the *innovation of meaning*, or what Paul DiMaggio has called "cultural entrepreneurship."[33] A Christian leader's task is to make spiritual sense of the lives of the people entrusted to their care. This is how we enable spiritual growth. We provide our people with the categories—in the form of both doctrines and stories—that they need to narrate their lives. And the most powerful kind of innovation is not a new device or a new website: it is a new interpretation, a new way of seeing the world.

This is what innovation scholar Andrew Hargadon means when he says, "Innovative [organizations] can succeed not by breaking away from the constraints of the past . . . but instead by harnessing the past in powerful ways."[34] Very little meaning making involves creating a completely new idea. The innovation we call the Reformation, for example, was not built on a wholly new idea; it came from a new reading of Paul's Letter to the Romans. It created new categories (e.g., justification by grace through faith alone) and gave people a new way to narrate their lives (e.g., "I am saved by grace"). This is "meaning-making innovation." Ralph Winter's insight, likewise, was an innovation because he gave new meaning to the word "nations." However, Winter would have argued that, instead of giving new meaning, he restored the meaning that the word carried all along—just as Luther would have argued that he restored the proper emphasis in Romans on justification by grace through faith. But to their audiences, it was an innovation, an innovation of meaning. We need to learn more about this type of innovation because from this point onward, when this book refers to "innovation," it will mean "meaning-making innovation."

Hargadon's approach to explaining innovation is quite different from the approaches of scholars of innovation who advocate abandoning the past. His approach can help us create innovation that honors the Christian tradition. Hargadon believes that innovation is usually about creating new meaning that requires new cultural tools. This is even true when he talks about inventors such as Thomas Edison. Having been influenced by Swidler, Hargadon explains why and how that process of creating new cultural tools works, and he shows how to construct organizations that take advantage of that knowledge. He calls the process "recombinant innovation."[35] Hargadon builds this process around the cultivation of new cultural tools,[36] especially tools that connect to the past. Innovative organizations "succeed not by breaking away from the constraints of the past," he says, "but instead by harnessing the past in powerful ways."[37] This is good news for those of us whose credibility depends on fidelity with the past.

Hargadon begins by showing where people get their cultural tools, knowing that people who will innovate new tools need to know how tools are created. Those tools come from the networks that surround every person. All people are embedded in networks of ideas and relationships.[38] Although some of these are formal networks that are defined by organizational structure (like an organization chart), they are not as important to Hargadon as are the networks that shape ideas, and especially mental models.

He is more interested in interactions that influence how people see the world. For example, if I read the same blog every morning but talk to my boss only once a week, then that blog may be more influential than my boss, or it may be more influential on a wider range of topics than are interactions with my boss.[39] Either way, I am embedded in a network of relationships, ideas, and interactions. From these networks I glean the set of choices for interpreting the world, choices that Swidler calls a tool kit.[40] Christian innovation is about creating new choices for people, choices that allow them to follow Jesus *and* to address issues in their lives.

We tend to think of innovation as being about the creation of something that did not exist before. That can certainly be true. But in the world of Christian organizations, we are unlikely to create something out of nothing. We will create something by using the raw materials of our traditional faith to innovate this new set of choices for interpreting the world. Indeed, innovation will likely come from mixing and matching ideas that are already present with new situations,[41] thereby making new spiritual meaning for the people entrusted to our care. Ralph Winter did not invent the practice of sending missionaries to other nations, but he did reinvent the meaning of missions. In the same way, Martin Luther King Jr. did not invent the idea of nonviolent protest. He borrowed it from Mahatma Gandhi and introduced it to a people who experienced it as an innovation. Each made meaning by combining or recombining ideas to create something new.

Perhaps another example will help us see what Hargadon means by meaning-making innovation. Think, for example, about the "seeker-sensitive service" that became popular in evangelical churches over the last generation. The seeker-sensitive service was not something new under the sun. It was an adaptation of something that had existed for centuries—the Christian practice of worship. The new thing, however, was that this service of Christian worship was designed so that it would make sense to people who were not already familiar with the contours of Christianity. Yet not only that: this innovative service was also calibrated to address the needs (the longings and losses) of a particular people, those who do not know Jesus but may actually be interested in him. The service came about because some Christians decided that there was a particular people entrusted to their care: those who do not yet know Jesus. The service was not all that new. It included elements that had been present for generations. But it felt new to people who were used to the traditional way of doing things. Indeed, it not only felt new, but it also felt to many of them as if it were not quite right. It was new and different, and "new and different" worried some people. That is why the seeker-sensitive service started out as such a controversial way to conduct a worship service. Now it is an acceptable part of the American Christian repertoire. How did it move from controversial to common? How did this Christian innovation take hold?

Sociologists have a term for what happened with the seeker-sensitive service. They say that the service had to be "legitimated." In the public mind, it had to move from being illegitimate (i.e., an expression of the Christian practice of worship that was inappropriate because it did not fit their mental model of worship) to being legitimate (i.e., an appropriate expression of that practice because the mental model of worship had now expanded). This builds on Ann Swidler's extremely influential work on culture as a tool kit.[42]

Swidler argues that we humans have only a limited set of options when we try to engage in action. Culture provides only enough tools to fit on our tool belt. We can only carry on those actions that culture deems appropriate (i.e., legitimate) for that moment. It would not, for example, be culturally appropriate for me to offer a turtle dove as a sacrifice to God as part of my Sunday morning worship—even though it appears that for many years God's people were instructed to do just that. We Christians have agreed that animal sacrifice is no longer necessary because Jesus, our high priest, is himself the once-and-for-all sacrifice (cf. Heb. 5–10, esp. Heb. 7). Likewise, until recently it would have been inappropriate (not legitimate) for Christians to "speak in tongues" when they prayed, or for Christians to gather in mixed company for a Bible study in a college dorm room, or for churches to send teenagers to a foreign land on a weeklong mission trip. But each of those forms has recently been legitimated. They are, in Swidler's terms, now part of the cultural tool kit that is available for Christians who wish to take action in the world.[43] This pertains to Christian innovation because *the cultural tool kit available to contemporary Christians is constructed to support the tasks of a previous era, the era of Christendom.* We are trying to make do with the tools we have, even though we are taking up tasks for which we do not have the proper tools. The process of Christian innovation will involve legitimating new cultural tools.

Legitimation is not a well-reasoned process for people. When I first experienced "seeker-sensitive services" back in the early 1990s, I had my doubts. It did not seem legitimate because my mental model said that a worship service needed certain mandatory elements—especially some kind of confession of sin. It also seemed overly commercialized to have a "food court" selling sandwiches in the middle of a church campus (it all smacked of money changers to me). I also worried because many of the congregations I knew that were engaged in seeker-sensitive services did not allow women in leadership.

Then I had an odd experience. I was going to be traveling to another part of the country for work. One of my friends said that I should attend her sister's church. So I contacted her sister and arranged to go to church with her. It was one of the nation's most well-known seeker-sensitive churches, where it just so happened that my friend's sister was the first woman to sit on the board (because the congregation was making a conscious effort to include women in leadership). The day before I was going to go, I discovered that an old friend would be in town that day. We arranged to go to a ball game together, but I explained that I was going to this church first. My friend said that he would tag along to the church, and then we could go to the game. I foolishly had not thought to invite my friend to church because he is not a practicing Christian. But as we drove to the church, he explained that he was open to what he called "the spiritual." He loved the experience; he sang, he prayed, he did what seekers are supposed to do. Then after the service, in the dreaded food court, I saw person after person come to our table and talk with us. It was like taking the whole congregation out for a meal. They chatted, they did church business, they talked about concerns for ailing friends, they may even have prayed for one another. In that experience I realized that all three of my delegitimating expectations were doused. I was experiencing hospitality and *koinonia* in a food court while sitting between a female leader and a satisfied seeker. Yet somehow something in me wanted to complain. It just did not *feel* right. It was not what I knew, what I was taught in seminary. It did not fit my mental model for how worship should look. The experience had answered all my objections, yet I was uncomfortable. Eventually I got over it, but the point remains: changing mental models is difficult.

---------- • ----------

Peter Drucker says, "Innovation in any one knowledge area tends to originate outside the area itself."[44] We cannot tweak our way to innovation. We are still tethered to the Bible and to the historic faith. So our goal is not to expand beyond the historic faith but rather to understand that historic faith in a new way. We need new mental models to engage in meaning-making innovation. Let me conclude with one last example.

The American church has been stumbling into the same mistake that the Detroit automakers made in the 1980s. It has to do with mental models. In the 1980s, "Detroit believed that people bought automobiles on the basis of styling, not for quality or reliability."[45] They had the survey data to back it up. Americans reported that they cared more about how a car looks than how it runs. That gave the automakers a mental model of the consumer—and of themselves—just as the disciples had an inaccurate mental model of Jesus and of themselves. According to a prominent study at the time, Detroit assumed that it was "in the business of making money, not cars" and that "cars are primarily status symbols." They did not care much about the quality of the cars, and they assumed that consumers did not either. These assumptions set them up to be surpassed competitively by Asia-based companies like Toyota, which emphasized the quality of a car rather than its looks.

Here is the part that is crucial for churches. "The problem with mental models lies not in whether they are right or wrong—by definition, all models are oversimplifications," Peter Senge says. The problem is that we do not examine them because *we take mental models for granted*. Detroit did not just acknowledge that Americans care about styling. They totalized the idea. "They said, 'All people care about is styling.'" Detroit took people at their word, assuming that persons understood their own mental models. "Because they remained unaware of their mental models, the models remained unexamined. Because they were unexamined, the models remained unchanged." That meant that "as the world changed, a gap widened between Detroit's mental models and reality," leading them to make poorer and poorer decisions. Detroit had a faulty view of itself because it had a faulty view of the American people, and they became mired in a business model calibrated for a world that no longer (and perhaps never) existed.

Lest you think that the problem of unexamined mental models applies only to businesses, let us look at the church. Robert Wuthnow argues that the American church is suffering because it has an incorrect view of itself and of its people. The clergy who speak for the church, Wuthnow observes, hold a mental model that compartmentalizes life. They proclaim a gospel that speaks only to spiritual issues but never touches on the problems of daily life. Although written in the 1990s, Wuthnow's critique feels eerily current. "In recent years," Wuthnow notes, clergy "take up the issues supplied by the media and become embroiled in culture . . . rather than speaking to the concerns that face parishioners in their daily lives"—lives filled with the "pressures of working harder to make ends meet, worries about retaining one's job, lack of time for one's self and one's family, marital strains associated with two-career households, and the incessant demands of advertising and the marketplace." The solution is for congregations to recalibrate their mental model of what it means to be church in order "to preserve the sacred teachings of their traditions, [by] making them relevant to the strenuous, pressure-filled lives" that their parishioners lead.[46] Like the Detroit automakers, we in the church have defined ourselves incorrectly. Detroit thought that its job was to make money, not cars. The church too often thinks its job is to build up the church rather than to make spiritual sense of everyday life. We need to recalibrate.

In this chapter, we have seen many examples of how to innovate by changing mental models to make new meaning. Jesus transformed the disciples' notion of the kingdom of God in Mark 8 by changing their mental model of a "messiah." Ralph Winter transformed the practice of world missions by changing the mental model surrounding the word "nations." Martin Luther King Jr. enabled African Americans in the South to be, at the same time, law-abiding citizens and justice-seeking Christians by introducing the idea of nonviolence. The design company IDEO enabled children to endure MRI tests by using a story structure to transform a scary procedure into a playful adventure. The Colombian government used messages from home to change wanted criminals into wanted children. Martin Luther sparked the Reformation with a new way to make sense of the book of Romans. And the seeker-sensitive service recast the practice of worship and thereby made room for people who did not have much experience with Christianity. In each case, the innovation was neither a product, a process, a social program, nor an app. The innovation came as a new way to make meaning. Meaning-making innovation is the means for recalibrating the church.

How, specifically, do we recalibrate? How do we create meaning-making innovation that addresses the concerns of daily life? Doing that will require two tasks because we will need to calibrate ourselves according to two standards. To understand daily life, we will need to calibrate ourselves to the ever-changing culture. And to make spiritual sense of that daily life, we will need to calibrate ourselves to the never-changing gospel. Now we turn to the specific question of how to recalibrate.

3

Leadership Begins with Listening

Catherine was there thirty-five years ago when her congregation was founded, although she was only in kindergarten at the time. She grew up thinking that every Sunday began with setting up chairs and sound equipment—the first year in a garage, then in a school cafeteria, and on into a warehouse, before the church finally had a place to call its own.

She and her church friends used to think that there were always three generations: the kids, the adults, and what she called the "geriatrics." All throughout her twenties, Catherine thought of herself as part of the "kids" generation because it was the "adults" who ran the church. She got married in her mid-twenties, was thrilled when two wonderful children came rather quickly, then was devastated when her husband walked away. Now her kids are eleven and thirteen, and her parents are in their seventies. One day she turned to a friend after church and said with dismay, "*We're* the adults now."[1]

Catherine feels responsible for things she cannot control. She remembers when the congregation was growing and the biggest problem was finding room for all the children. Now she knows that the church has waned. There are fewer people, it is true. But of greater concern is the fact that there is less energy and little urgency. Everyone seems to be a little tired. You could describe Catherine's extended family and her congregation in similar terms: the older generation is slowing down, and Catherine's generation is paddling hard just to keep its head above water.

Catherine works as a department manager for a store that sells bed and bath supplies. She started out running the cash register and was soon promoted because of her hard work. The first thing in the morning, she gets her children off to school. She tries to make sure they have a good breakfast, but sometimes that means they end up munching on a bagel as she drives them to the middle school, where they are in the eighth and sixth grades.

Then Catherine goes to her store. She does not officially start work until nine, but she is usually there a little after eight. Even then, there is not enough time to take care of all the paperwork from the corporate office before the other employees show up at 9:30. The store manager likes Catherine a lot. In fact, she treats Catherine like the de facto assistant manager. That means that Catherine receives a lot of praise and trust. But it also means that she ends up doing a lot of work that is not technically in her job description. Catherine hopes (indeed expects) that someday she will have her own store.

The bulk of the day goes by quickly: managing employees, receiving shipments of new stock, and dealing with customers. Catherine does not feel as though she has much time to think. She just responds to whatever happens next. The feedback she gets from others tells her that they see her as a mother figure—the one they go to when they need someone to help them solve their work problems or even just to listen to them talk about their lives outside of work.

Catherine arrives home around 6:30. Because her lunch break consists of a diet bar gulped down with a Coke Zero, she has worked almost straight through for ten hours. She throws together some dinner and gathers the kids to eat at seven. Ideally the kids have already done their homework. But middle schoolers rarely do anything without adult supervision. So she spends the next hour or three urging them to finish their homework, shower, and get to bed at a decent hour.

She falls in bed at ten o'clock. You may think that would be the best part of her day. But it is the part she dreads. That's when she thinks about the fact that she barely makes enough money to pay the bills (her ex-husband contributes nothing). Catherine spends more than half her salary on a two-bedroom apartment. When she gets her own store, that will mean more money, she tells herself, but more hours as well. Where will she find the time? She feels guilty that she is not saving for her kids' college and that she has no money put away for retirement. And she worries about needing life insurance in case something happens to her. All the while, she wonders about her own parents. Indeed, she thinks that her mother's lifetime of working on her feet is what made her health fail, and Catherine wonders what will happen to her own health when she is their age.

Catherine does not have time to take her kids to the church youth group. She only gets alternate weekends off from work. But she tries to get them to church about twice a month. She prays and asks God to reach them. Her congregation was really helpful to her when her husband left her with two kids under five and no job prospects. But she worries that the kids don't seem to have enough church in their lives to hear much about Christ's love. "I want them to have more God in their life."

---------•----------

Leadership begins with listening. That is the main point of this chapter. When I teach on Christian leadership—whether it is with seminary students or at speaking engagements among laypeople—I tend to start the same way no matter what the topic. I make sure that when people walk into the room, they will find the same message written in big red letters either on the whiteboard or on a PowerPoint screen. It says simply, "Leadership begins with listening."

This is not the stereotype of leadership. If you were to gather, say, the sixth graders at Catherine's children's school and ask them what it means to be a leader, they might well decide that "a leader is someone who tells people what to do." It is a good definition for how our culture understands leadership (i.e., it reflects our mental model of leadership). We tend to think of leaders as being people who speak. I of all people need to recognize how I have contributed to that stereotype, since I wrote a book about what Christian leaders should say when they speak.[2] So I will grant that speaking is important.

But something comes *before* speaking. Leadership begins with listening. I say this phrase perhaps fifty or more times during a ten-week class. Often my initial response to a student question will be to say, "Where do we start? Leadership begins with listening." Then we will talk through the ways leaders must listen before they can speak or act.

I have apparently done this so many times that it has become part of my identity as a professor. A while back, I ran into a former student in an airport, far from home. He obviously recognized me but did not immediately greet me by name. Instead, he walked straight up to me, pointed at me, and said, "Leadership begins with listening." Everything that we do as Christian leaders flows from there.

You will recall that we have five questions that will help us recalibrate the church. I list the five below as a reminder. As you read them, especially notice the first three. They are about listening.

Q1. Who are the people entrusted to your care?

Q2. How do those people experience the longings and losses that make up the human condition?

Q3. What Big Lies do your people believe that prevent them from hearing the gospel?

Q4. How do you make spiritual sense of those longings and losses?

Q5. How do you express that spiritual meaning as a shared story of hope?

We will take up the first three questions in this chapter and the final two in the following chapters.

In this chapter, we will focus on how the first three questions deal with listening. The outline of the chapter poses three questions:

1. Who do we listen to? (to God, and to the people entrusted to our care)
2. What do we listen for? (for longings and losses, and for Big Lies)
3. How do we listen well? (with empathy)

The primary reason we listen to our people is that they deserve to be heard because they are made in the image of God. They bear that image in the world, and the work we do as Christian leaders must honor the spark of God embedded in each person we encounter. But there is another reason to listen, one related directly to recalibrating the church.

We listen so that we will be transformed. Before we can recalibrate the church, we must ourselves be recalibrated. We Christian leaders must so immerse ourselves in the needs of the people entrusted to our care that they change us. The daily difficulties of our people pull us out of our own selfish pursuits and remind us anew that we in the church exist to serve the people whom God entrusts to us—to love those neighbors as we love ourselves. We ourselves must be transformed before we can ask other people to change. Indeed, we do not lead on behalf of our own interests and agendas. We listen in order to be transformed by what we hear. *Innovation begins with transformative listening—with listening that will transform the hearers.*

Who Do We Listen To?

Listening to God

Leadership begins with listening. That means listening to God and listening to the people entrusted to our care. The bulk of this chapter focuses on listening to other people. But before we explore that, it is crucial to emphasize that every person who leads in God's name must begin work with a willingness to be transformed—with what Anne Streaty Wimberly calls a "radical openness to God and to one another." Wimberly explains that, in our busyness, we often are caught up in our own way of seeing the world—in our own agendas, commitments, and opinions. We get lost in our need to serve ourselves. She calls for "unbiased silence aimed toward radical openness to God."[3] We listen to God through Scripture, through songs, and through sitting in expectant silence. This listening precedes all action. And it leads us to listen to the people whom God calls us to serve.

Listening to the People Entrusted to Our Care

Christian leaders do not have "followers";[4] only Jesus has followers. Instead, Christian leaders have people entrusted to their care. There are three theological reasons for recasting the mental model of leadership to be about a people entrusted to our care. First, it emphasizes God's role as the one doing the entrusting. The 2 Corinthians passage (5:18–20) that names each of us as ambassadors begins by emphasizing that God was in the world, "reconciling the world to himself" in Christ Jesus. Everything we do derives from what God has done, is doing, and will do. By entrusting those people to us, God calls us to imitate God by caring for them.

Second, it emphasizes that we are stewards of people who already belong to God. The people entrusted to our care are *God's* people, made in the image of God. They are not my people, made to accomplish my goals. I cannot treat them like tools that I can wield to my own devices. And I cannot treat them as stereotypes whom I can comfortably ignore. They belong to God.

Third, it says that my intentions are not the measure of good work. It is the effect my work has on the people entrusted to my care. My grandfather the citrus farmer recognized, as a steward, that the trees did not belong to him and that his labor would be measured by the fruit his trees produced. He stood between the owner and the trees. In the same way, a Christian leader recognizes that God may have called Paul to plant and Apollos to water, but the Corinthians were not Paul's people nor were they Apollos's people. The people belong to God, and God is the one who gives the increase.

Thus, God calls leaders not to a task but to a people.[5] *My purpose derives from my people and not from my passions or my plans.* The needs of my people define the work that I do as a leader. And, if my passions or my plans for my congregation are different from the needs of my people, then I have to allow the needs of the people to overrule my hopes and my plans. I had to learn that lesson in my own life. I'll tell you what I mean.

God gave me daughters. Long before I was married, I pictured someday playing basketball with my children. I am passionate about basketball; I still play twice a week. The fact that I happened to fall in love with a tall woman only heightened the hope that I would someday teach my children to play basketball. The fact that my children were girls was not a problem. I would have been happy to teach them basketball.

But it was not to be. My two daughters looked at their mom and they looked at their dad, and they decided that Mom was much more interesting (I agree). Mom knits and sews and bakes; Mom is a computer programmer. My girls have no interest in sports. Instead, they like fashion and food—and science.

What did I do when the needs of my children conflicted with my passions and with my expectations about fatherhood? I had to follow the interests of the children God entrusted to my care. I needed to cultivate strengths that did not come naturally to me. I had to adopt their passions; I could not force them to follow mine. That means that when we talk together about fashion, I can now participate in a conversation about pencil skirts, ruched sleeves, and boyfriend jackets (although my girls were not likely to wear all three at the same time). And I can talk about jewel tones and "cutting along the bias"—although it still amuses them that I cannot distinguish warm colors from cool colors. If my girls had chosen basketball, my wife would know the proper way to hedge a pick-and-roll. Instead, I can extol the virtues of *addi Turbo* knitting needles. I don't care much about fashion, but I am passionate about my daughters.[6]

These are the people whom God has entrusted to my care. I did not pick them; God gave them to me as a gift. And that gift created an obligation for me. I had to become who my daughters needed me to be. So my calling to be a father and my passion for the daughters entrusted to my care required me to develop "passions" that did not come naturally. It is not about me. It is about the people entrusted to my care. *Your calling is not about you; it will require you to become who your people need you to be.*

Listening to the people entrusted to your care is the first step of innovation. Even secular companies recognize this. For example, years ago Google decided to expand its work beyond simple internet searches. But it had to decide which projects were central to its work of innovation and which ones were considered peripheral.[7] The company settled on a single phrase that guided each decision: "Focus on the user."[8] Google did not ask about making money; Google did not ask about what skills or passions its people might have. It planted its flag by serving the people who use its website. Each Google innovation kept coming back to the user.

In the same way, Greg Jones of Duke Divinity School argues, "In our thinking as well as our living, we are oriented toward our end, our telos:

bearing witness to the reign of God. That is what compels innovation."⁹ We bear witness to what God is doing for and with the people entrusted to our care. We stand like an ambassador between God and our people. Everything ambassadors do relates directly to the people they are sent to serve. All that we do in Christian innovation serves those people whom God has entrusted to our care.

Listening to the Tumbleweeds

Who, then, are the people entrusted to our care? Sometimes they are the people we choose to serve; thus a pastor is called to a congregation or a retiree volunteers in a homeless shelter. Often they are the people planted right next to us—perhaps in the cubicle across the aisle or in the apartment across the hall. But other times they roll into our lives like tumbleweeds.

I really like this image of tumbleweeds that God blows into our lives. Let me give you a couple of examples. A few years ago, I got an email from my alma mater. The college wanted to send someone by to see me. I knew this person was likely a fundraiser, and I really did not want to talk to him. But the seminary where I teach was doing its own fundraising, and I thought it might be interesting to see how another school did it. So the young fundraiser showed up at my office and told me what was happening at my former school.

Then, just as he was about to leave, he looked around my office and casually said, "You have a lot of books about God. Do you mind if I ask you about God?" What was I going to say? "Of course, I'll talk to you about Jesus." So we talked about his struggles and his questions. And I invited him to come back. Over time, he returned about once a month to "talk about God," and he eventually joined a church and was baptized. At some point, I had to recognize that, even though he was a tumbleweed that blew into my office without warning, he was now one of the people whom God had entrusted to my care. I bore a responsibility for him.

A similar thing happened to my wife. She was at an evening meeting of Bible Study Fellowship, and a woman in her small group needed a ride home. It was on my wife's way, so she took her. And then the next week, and the next, and the next. And as they drove, my wife discovered the woman's needs. So she began to help. This was a tumbleweed that God rolled into my wife's life. Soon that woman became one of the people entrusted to my wife's care.

Anyone who is paying biblical attention to our conversation will realize that we have stumbled into one of the most well-known gospel stories. When we ask "Who are the people entrusted to our care?" we end up mimicking the young lawyer's question to Jesus, "Who is my neighbor?" Our calling is nothing more (and nothing less) than loving the neighbor whom God plants nearby.

We must define our neighbor the way that Jesus did. In the parable of the good Samaritan,[10] the priest and the Levite are so wrapped up in their own business that they never acknowledge the needs of the hurting man: they decline to be a neighbor to the wounded man; they never acknowledge him as their neighbor.[11] In the same way, we in the church can get so caught up in our own agendas that we neglect to listen to the people entrusted to our care. If leadership begins with listening, then we must be neighbors and listen to the people whom God has placed nearby.

Let's be more specific. We started the chapter by looking at Catherine, the single mom. Who are the people entrusted to her care? Catherine has a family. She is entrusted with the care of her two children and (increasingly) with her aging parents. She is a manager at the bed-and-bath store. So she has employees (and, to some extent, customers) entrusted to her care. She used to help with the children's ministry at church and still feels a connection to those kids—even if she has no time to volunteer.

Increasingly, she expresses her love for her neighbors by looking after the younger employees at the store. They come to her for advice about both work-related issues and their personal lives. And she quietly calls the women who work the floor at her store her "flock." That's what it means to have people entrusted to your care. But as we move forward in talking about innovation (about recalibrating the church), we will have to move beyond the individual level. We will need to identify the people entrusted to a congregation's care.

Catherine may have many people entrusted to her care, but Catherine herself is entrusted to the care of her congregation. The congregation's leaders bear an obligation to her and to her children. Even if her need to work prevents her from attending church as regularly as she clearly would like, the church bears an obligation to reach out to her—to listen to her, to understand Catherine on Catherine's terms. Catherine is entrusted to the care of her congregation.

Who are the other people entrusted to the care of Catherine's congregation? Her congregation is filled with good people, most of whom have been Christians all their lives. So at some level, the church needs to see itself as serving those people's needs. But it must be more than that. The congregation is in a town that is 40 percent Hispanic. Yet almost everyone in the congregation is white. If you ask the congregants in Catherine's church why there are so few Latinos, they point out that Hispanic people are traditionally Roman Catholic. That is true. But most do not attend church, and lapsed Catholics still need to hear about the love of Jesus. Catherine's church knows it needs to reach out to all its neighbors, but it does not know how to do that. People like Catherine do not know what to say. Well, it turns out that the next step (the next of our five questions) is about what to say—or more importantly, how to listen before you speak. The next step toward Christian innovation is listening.

What Do We Listen For?

Listening to the people entrusted to our care is indeed the first step in transformative listening (the kind of listening that will transform us). That first step causes us immediately to ask, "But listening for what?"

First and foremost, if we are going to listen in order to be transformed, we must listen to the longings and losses of the people entrusted to our care. This is the pivot point for all of our innovation efforts. We Christian leaders know that the world has changed. But this allows us to be more specific. *The changes that matter most—the ones that demand a gospel response—are those that affect the longings and losses of the people entrusted to our care.* So we begin there.

But once we have understood the idea of longings and losses, we begin to see that there are places where our people feel especially trapped. Some aspects of life typically create problems for our people. So we will need to listen carefully to those areas. Specifically, we need to listen for what we will call the Big Lie. But all that listening starts with the longings and losses of the people entrusted to our care.

Listening for Longings and Losses

We will eventually want to invite people into the gospel story. But before I can invite a person into a story, I need to understand that person's own story. I must understand what matters most to them, what stories define them. Only then will I be able to invite them into a gospel story that gives them hope. Otherwise I am just treating them as a stereotype.

The sociologist Robert Wuthnow argues that the reason our current crop of congregations is in crisis is that we have been paying attention to the wrong things. We may have been listening, but we have been listening for the wrong things.[12] Most congregations, he says, are more concerned with the culture-war issues of (other people's) morality and the minutiae of doctrine (paying attention to the small issues of theology that separate Christians rather than the large concerns of theology that unite us). Wuthnow does not say that such values and beliefs are unimportant. Quite the opposite. He says that what we believe is so important that it must be connected to the lives that people lead each day.

We need to listen to the issues that matter most to the people entrusted to our care—issues such as work and money, or health and family. The way I describe it is this. There is a moment when you lay your head on the pillow at night; you are not yet asleep, and the worries of the day come rushing in upon you. Do you know that moment? That is when the issues that matter most to you jump into your mind. Some issues are aspirations—things you long for. Some issues are fears—things you are afraid you might lose. Before we can engage in Christian innovation, we must listen to the people entrusted to our care until we know their stories. These are the things that keep people awake at night.

There is a name for these issues, the ones so important that each human being faces them. The Western tradition describes these hopes and fears as "the human condition," and we will call them "longings and losses." The questions that characterize the human condition ask about what makes life worth living and why living a worthy life is so difficult. Some questions are about purpose and meaning: Is this all there is? Does anything I do really matter? Is life really worth the pain? And, for people of all ages, what do I want to be when I grow up? Other questions deal with the need for community: Does anyone really know me? Would people like me if they really knew me? How can I be in community without losing my individuality? And how can I be an individual without succumbing to the inevitability of isolation?

The Fuller Youth Institute summarizes longings and losses by saying that every young person (indeed, any person of any age) is regularly dealing with questions of identity, belonging, and purpose.[13]

Other human-condition questions deal with basic human fears, such as the fear of death, the fear of condemnation (am I really good enough?), and the fear of shame or guilt. Intrinsic to the human condition are the difficulties of working out basic human struggles (as with work, with family, with health, with finances—and the role conflict that these basic struggles create when they compete with one another). Every person deals with these questions because each of the questions goes to the heart of being human.

Oftentimes people find it too overwhelming to talk about "the human condition." It feels too esoteric or abstract. Indeed, most people living in the world do not lie awake contemplating "the human condition." Instead, they lie awake thinking about the things that make up the human condition—perhaps about their children or their parents, a problem at work or at school, or anticipating a hoped-for lunch with a friend. Some people struggle with questions about safety or hunger;[14] others deal with health or finances.

Every person has longings that define them—hopes, dreams, and aspirations. Some of these are big. For example, I may hope for health for my children, or I may aspire to some accomplishment. Or they can be more immediate. I may hope for a successful meeting with my boss or anticipate that this weekend I will finally get the rest that I crave. On the flip side, many of my losses are about longings that have been denied. I may hope for health for my loved ones and experience loss when a loved one passes away. You may hope for a good meeting with your boss and experience loss when he treats you badly.

Have you ever lain awake at night, replaying in your mind a meeting at work or a conversation with a friend? Have you ever lain there kicking yourself over what you said? Have you ever spent fifteen minutes figuring out what you should have said? Think about how much it would change the way you lead if you knew what stories your people played out in their heads as they lay awake at night. Transformative listening involves being transformed by these intertwined longings and losses that make up the human condition.

Perhaps some examples are in order.[15] Indeed, for this generation the most resonant examples of the longings and losses that make up the human condition come from Pixar movies.[16] (In chap. 7 we will think about how Pixar makes a deliberate effort to understand longings and losses. Then we will investigate what the firm's organizational culture can teach us about congregational culture.)

When I teach about longing and loss, I show my students the first segment of the movie *Up*, and I invite students to listen for what keeps the characters awake at night.[17] The sequence begins on the steps of a church chancel as a couple happily marries. Without words, the segment tells that couple's story as they set up a house, long for children, discover they cannot conceive, deal with the heartbreak, plan for a vacation adventure, use the vacation money instead to buy the necessities of life, live together, work together, grow old together, and are ultimately parted when the wife becomes sick and dies. The four-minute sequence ends on those same church-chancel steps with the husband bereft after his wife's funeral. After I show the segment to my students, I have them list the longings and losses covered just in this short sequence: children, companionship, productive work, adventure, love, and so forth. These are the things that every human being longs for, and these are the things that create mourning every time a human being loses one.

Another Pixar movie dealing with the human condition is the Oscar-winning short film called *Bao*; it's about an aging Chinese immigrant mother. The movie starts out with a fantastical situation. We later come to realize that the situation is actually a dream that she has while napping one afternoon.

In the dream, the aging woman is making Chinese dumplings (called *bao*). Her husband does not seem to have time for her. He reads his newspaper, gobbles his meal, and wordlessly scurries off, briefcase in hand. As the woman continues preparing the dumplings, one of the dumplings comes to life (as can happen in a dream or a cartoon). The dumpling sprouts legs and arms and rewards her with a big smile. The woman and the come-to-life dumpling become friends. She takes the dumpling-child shopping at the grocery store and to tai chi in the park. And she protects him when he tries to wander off. Over time, the dumpling-child grows into a rebellious teen and eventually a young adult—old enough to date a woman who is clearly not Chinese. Soon he insists on marrying the white woman. He packs a suitcase and heads for the door. In a fit of desperation, the woman scoops the dumpling-child up, plops him into her mouth, and swallows him whole. When she realizes what she has done, she is devastated, and we see her mourning the separation from her dumpling-child. But the short animation does not end there.

We see the woman napping, and then in the background we see the outline of her actual son—who in fact does look a bit like a dumpling. That's when the audience realizes that the mother was dreaming—dreaming about her precious son (her dumpling), who has indeed married an Anglo woman. But the dream has taught her a lesson. She decides, after the dream, to accept the newlyweds. The short movie ends with the family making dumplings together.[18]

The movie has won many awards—not just for its animation (although I am sure that is fine) but especially for its resonance. The movie invites us into a story that taps into the longings and losses of the human condition. Every parent knows the temptation to overprotect a child. And every child knows what it's like to want to grow out from under a parent. The impulse is part of what it means to be human. It just so happens that this movie shows what that looks like for immigrant families; it plays out a little differently for immigrants. But everyone experiences the longing to individuate and the loss that comes with individuation. And everyone recognizes the bittersweet experience for a mother whose dumpling of a son grows up and leaves the house. She longs for her child to be mature enough to stand on his own, and then she mourns the loss that comes when he is mature enough that he no longer needs her for daily living. It is part of the human condition.

The human condition is that every person in the world experiences those longings and losses. It is our shared story. And the gospel is God's response to the human condition. If we are to proclaim a shared story of gospel hope, we need to recognize our own shared story of pain, our shared story of longing, and our shared story of loss. *The gospel is God's hopeful response to our shared story of longing and loss, and that gospel is what turns our common experience into a shared story of hope.*

We in the church tend to think that the human condition is simply about the need for forgiveness—as if being forgiven will remove the longings and losses that make being human so complicated. But even after redemption, we live in the interim. We are stuck in this time. We long for the healing of all creation, and we suffer losses because creation remains (for now) tainted with sin. Those longings and losses permeate our lives. They define us. They are what it means to be human.

That is why Jesus came to live among us—to experience what it means to be human. It was the greatest act of listening in history. He came to literally inhabit our story. The apostle Paul talks about how an ambassador stands in the middle. The book of Hebrews puts it a different way. Jesus our mediator is the high priest who stands between God and humanity. But he is not just any high priest.

Jesus is a high priest who (according to Heb. 4) knows our weaknesses. He too would anxiously stay awake; in the garden of Gethsemane he prayed all night (Mark 14:32–42). Jesus knows not just the longings but also the losses of what it means to be human. When Lazarus died, Jesus wept. Jesus knew that he would raise Lazarus. So why the tears? Because he was human. Because he felt the pain of loss. Because he felt empathy for Lazarus's sisters, Mary and Martha. *The Word became flesh and dwelt among us to experience the depth of longing and the agony of loss*—to understand people by being a person.

Like an ambassador, he came and dwelt among us in order to make reconciliation possible. That reconciliation cost him something. Jesus not only gave up his life on Good Friday but also each day lived the same longings and losses as the people he came to save. Jesus, who was fully God and fully human, each day experienced the longings and losses of the human condition.

Leadership begins with listening—listening to the longings and losses of the people entrusted to our care. There is a reason why our innovation must begin with empathetic and vulnerable listening. *We leaders need to be transformed by identifying with the heartfelt longings and the heart-wrenching losses that our people experience every day.* If we live with our people's pain, as Jesus lived with ours, we will not settle for just talking about doctrine. We will instead talk about how our beliefs respond to the daily lives of the people whom God entrusts to our care. The unchanging gospel message is the most powerful thing on earth. It is the most powerful message on earth because it is God's answer to the human dilemma that every person experiences. Jesus died so that we might have life—and live that life abundantly.

This takes us back to the need to recalibrate the church. Our congregations are ailing because we approach congregational questions from the perspective of the organized church and not from the perspective of the people who make up the church. Let me illustrate what I mean by returning to Catherine the single mom.

Catherine feels trapped. She is trapped by the long hours she needs to work just to feed and house her family. She is trapped by the time it takes to be a good mother to adolescent children and to be a good daughter to aging parents.

When I ask seminary students or pastors to read Catherine's case, they often respond with judgment rather than with empathy. They look at things from the congregation's perspective rather than looking at Catherine's experience. They blame her for not getting her kids to church. But they do not think of any options to offer her for how to make that feasible. They want to tell her that good church people bring their kids to church. Then they conclude that, if Catherine is not bringing her kids, she is deficient. They think their job is to motivate Catherine, not to help her. But they can think that only because they fail to hear how the situation pains Catherine: it keeps her awake at night. If they had taken Catherine's perspective, they might brainstorm ways the congregation might help her get her children to church. But they only see the church's side of things.

If we are going to recalibrate the church, we must listen so hard that we are transformed by our people's longings and losses. We must understand our people's stories—identify with our people and see things from their perspective. That will change our ability to innovate a gospel message that responds to those longings and losses. At Pixar, they often remind themselves of a quote they attribute to Mister Rogers: "There isn't anyone you couldn't learn to love once you've heard their story."[19] Hearing their story means knowing their longings and losses—how they participate in the human condition.[20]

We must understand their story because our calling is to love them. We are ambassadors to a people whose lives are defined by their longings and losses. Therefore, any attempt by Christians to innovate must respond to those longings and losses.

Listening for the Big Lie

The human condition is such a powerful and indeed overwhelming part of most people's lives that we tend to create ways of coping with the questions, especially ways that are inadequate to the task of addressing the human condition. I have learned a lot on this point from a presentation made at the installation of Fuller Seminary's fifth president, Mark Labberton.

When President Labberton was inaugurated, he chose to use the occasion as an opportunity to elevate voices that the seminary would not normally hear (an example of "Leadership begins with listening"). So he invited speakers from around the globe to speak to the seminary about the needs of the moment from their social location. There were Christian speakers from Africa, Asia, North America, South America, Europe.

One speaker, Aaron Graham from Washington, DC, was asked to speak from the perspective of an urban church planter. His first point fit nicely with what we have said so far. According to Graham, the way to grow a church that can transform a city is to begin by listening to the context—to listen to the lives of the people entrusted to one's care.[21] Then he went on to describe what his congregation listened for in the lives of the people who began attending his new church. For the most part, these were idealistic young transplants who had come to Washington to work in government offices. In terms of longing and loss, they longed to change the world, but they were experiencing long hours and heavy burdens as a tremendous loss.

At this point in his presentation, Graham introduced a device that he learned from a Fuller professor named Alexia Salvatierra.[22] Early in the civil rights movement, the leading organizations sent young people into Southern communities and asked them to listen (another example of "Leadership begins with listening"). They already knew a lot about the Southern longing for equality and the loss of rights. These Christian ambassadors were taught to listen for what the leaders called "the Big Lie." They were also tasked to come up with a spiritual response to that Big Lie. Eventually, these leaders came to codify the Big Lie at the heart of Jim Crow as saying, "Some lives are worth more than others."[23] Without that Big Lie, all of the oppressive Jim Crow system falls apart. The spiritual response to that lie, they decided, is to say, "Everyone is created in God's image; therefore, all are equal."

Graham took inspiration from this cycle of listening and spiritual response. He asked his congregation to listen to the people entrusted to their care—these lonely idealists who had come to Washington. Here is how Graham's congregation came to articulate the Big Lie that they heard. These young people believed that "we can change the world apart from community." The people entrusted to Graham's care, he said, were educated but unfulfilled; they had "amazing résumés but felt alone." This lie captured both the longing and the loss that defined Graham's people.[24] They longed to make a difference, but they felt the acute loss of community. The Christian truth that countered the Big Lie is that the Holy Spirit binds Christians together in community. Aaron Graham's ability to minister to the idealistic government workers entrusted to his care turned on his ability to counter the Big Lie that trapped them.

A Big Lie is a massively distorted mental model. From the last chapter you will recall that mental models are the stories we tell ourselves about how things are or how things should be. Sometimes we hold them in story form, and other times we make summary statements that encapsulate those model-defining stories. For example, Jesus tried to instill in his disciples a mental model for the kingdom of God. He did that both by telling many, many stories (i.e., parables that begin with the phrase "The kingdom of God is like . . .") and by providing summary statements that encapsulated those stories (such as "So the last shall be first, and the first shall be last").

Meaning-making innovation often happens when we replace an outdated and deficient mental model (a Big Lie) with a statement or story that more accurately captures the truth of the gospel. Let me illustrate by going through some of the examples of meaning-making innovation we encountered in the last chapter. After that, we can look at some examples of how Jesus destroyed Big Lies. Finally, we will look at some of the Big Lies that trap "good" churches and prevent them from moving forward.

In the last chapter, we discussed Ralph Winter and Martin Luther King Jr. Dr. King built what became the first great speech of the civil rights movement around countering a Big Lie. The Big Lie was that African Americans in the South had to choose between being a good Christian and being a good citizen. A good Christian stands up for justice, and a good American citizen obeys the law. So the Big Lie was that there was no way to stand up for justice while obeying the law. He countered that lie by explaining nonviolent protest. Ralph Winter stood before the assembled missionary community, which believed the Big Lie that having Christians in every country in the world fulfilled the Great Commission to "make disciples of all nations." He countered the lie by offering a new explanation of the biblical word "nation," an interpretation consistent with the original meaning of the word.

Likewise, Martin Luther countered two intertwined Big Lies: the lie that being obedient to the law defined a Christian, and the lie that the Roman Catholic Church had the authority to decide who kept the law. Luther countered those lies by citing Paul's message to the Romans as the primary Christian belief, often summarized as "justification by grace through faith alone" (cf. Rom. 3:24–25). In all of these cases, the Christian leader engaged in meaning-making innovation by countering a Big Lie with a new understanding of the truth of the gospel. In doing so, they were following Jesus's example.

Jesus spent much of his ministry upending Big Lies. In Mark 8, the disciples believe the Big Lie that a messiah is a military ruler. Jesus explains, instead, that the Messiah will suffer, die, and rise again. In the parables, the Big Lie is the idea that those on top deserve to be on top and will remain there. Instead,

Jesus says, "The last shall be first." In the Sermon on the Mount, Jesus frames a series of Big Lies about the law by saying (six times), "You have heard it was said . . ." or the like. And each time he corrects the lie with the phrase "But I say . . ." (Matt. 5:21–48 NRSV). In his encounters with the Pharisees, the Big Lie is the Pharisees' idea that following the rules equals obeying God (and the companion lie that the Pharisees' rules equal God's rules). Jesus countered these dual lies by focusing on the spirit of the law. In each case, Jesus built up the faith by tearing down Big Lies.

Indeed, this last example is especially important for Christians living in American churches. We are often like the Pharisees in believing the Big Lies. Here are some Big Lies that are common in American congregations. There are Big Lies about *identity*, such as "Some sins are worse than others, and they will define you"; "Some sins are excusable, and they won't affect you"; and "Not doing bad things makes up for not doing good things." Or Big Lies about *belonging*, such as "Believing the right things separates people into insiders and outsiders," and "God likes insiders better." Or Big Lies about *purpose*, such as "Mission means doing things to and for people, not with them";[25] "When I do hard things, I deserve to be celebrated"; and "Believing the right things about mission is the same as doing them." We even have Big Lies that are distortions of Christian practices, such as "Sunday attendance equals worship," "Reading my Bible equals discipleship," "Going on a mission trip equals doing mission," and "You can 'love your neighbor' without knowing anyone who is not like you." All of these are Big Lies—Big Lies that many of us cherish.

In fact, behind all bad theology is some Big Lie. Behind every misunderstanding of the church is a Big Lie. Behind every misaligned congregation is a Big Lie. We have calibrated our churches for the Big Lies. And any attempt to recalibrate the church will require us to understand the Big Lies that imprison us. Leadership begins with listening, and that means listening for the Big Lie.

We can see that commitment to Big Lies in people's responses to Catherine's story. I mentioned earlier that I share this case study with my students and that their tendency is to scold Catherine rather than to respond with empathy. The reason they do this is because Catherine, her congregation, and even my students all buy into the same Big Lie.

The lie is *individualism*. Each of them believes that any response to this situation will require Catherine to do the changing. But I believe that it is the congregation that needs to change. They need to see Catherine as part of the body of Christ—a body that is bound together. When Catherine's children were young, she brought them to the church to be dedicated (this church baptizes only adults). And when they were dedicated, both the parents and the congregation took vows that they would work to raise these children to love God and follow Jesus. They may proclaim a theology that says, "We are all connected in the body of Christ," but the theology that they practice attaches the caveat that only Catherine is responsible for her children. Together they form a Big Lie that says, "The church is not responsible for raising the children entrusted to its care."[26]

Now let's say that the congregation recognizes the Big Lie and decides to act differently. What would this look like in Catherine's situation? The congregation need look no further than its own history. When Catherine was in middle school, her parents did not drive her to the youth group. A high school senior named Jane would come around in an old station wagon and pick up Catherine and her brother (as well as many other students) to take them to youth group. Today's seat-belt laws might prevent a contemporary Jane from picking up as many students as yesterday's Jane did, yet the congregation could easily take responsibility for ferrying Catherine's middle schoolers to and from youth group. Change would require the congregation to confront its Big Lie of individualism, holding that "the congregation is not responsible for the children entrusted to its care."

This section of the chapter has focused on what we listen for. We listen for the longings and losses of the people entrusted to our care. And we listen for the Big Lies that trap them. But there is one more question we must ask: "How do we listen well?"

How Do We Listen Well?

We listen well when we listen with empathy and when we listen across differences. Let us take these skills[27] one at a time.

Listen with Empathy

Empathy is feeling with people. Feeling with people requires me to connect with something in myself that has felt what the person in front of me is currently feeling. I need not have been in that exact situation before, but I need to identify with the universal thing that they are feeling—the thing that all humans feel. I may not be a fifteen-year-old girl who was just dumped by her first boyfriend, but I have had my heart set on something only to have it crushed unexpectedly. I may not be an eighty-year-old husband sitting with his hospitalized wife, but I have been terrified and worried—and powerless—all at the same time. Listening requires empathy.

Empathy is different from sympathy. Sympathy is feeling something about someone else. It is abstract and detached—and a bit self-centered in that it's about how their situation makes me feel and not about how their situation makes them feel. Empathy is feeling *with* that person. It is personal and engaged. Scholars identify four components of empathy: (1) seeing things from the other person's perspective (e.g., for a fifteen-year-old, a breakup can seem like the end of the world); (2) staying out of judgment (e.g., I don't get to say that it is silly to care about a breakup so much); (3) recognizing the emotion in the other person (e.g., I need to understand that the fifteen-year-old is feeling rejected, embarrassed, and crushed); and (4) communicating my understanding (i.e., it does not do any good if I think or feel all these things but do not communicate them).[28]

The difference between empathy and sympathy has to do with the effect each one has on the person in pain. "Empathy fuels connection," according to Brené Brown; "Sympathy drives disconnection." And "what makes something better is connection."[29]

Sympathy keeps the other person's pain at arm's length, while empathy allows that pain to call up in me a similar experience of pain. It is that feeling shared between people that creates connection. Think of Jesus bending down to talk to the woman caught in adultery (John 8). He does not just scribble on the ground; he is also putting himself at her level. While bent low next to her, he says, "Let him who has no sin cast the first stone" (8:7). Then he stays bent down at her level—literally sharing her lowly state. Only after the crowd disperses does he straighten up to pronounce judgment: "I do not condemn you." He literally takes her perspective—her lowly view of the world. Empathy is feeling with someone, not just feeling about them.

"*Empathy is a vulnerable choice*," Brown reminds us, "because in order to connect with you I have to connect with something in myself that knows that feeling."[30] Let me confess, empathy is hard for me. I often want to settle for impotent sympathy because I don't want to remember that I too often felt terrified and powerless. I don't want those feelings intruding on my day. Empathy makes me vulnerable because it pierces the shell that I maintain to protect myself from pain. But the only way to be truly empathetic is to feel the pain *with* someone. And the connection that makes empathy so powerful requires me to have your pain conjure up my pain.

There is no connection without that vulnerability. But I am sad to confess that I regularly settle for sympathy rather than empathy. Sympathy makes *me* feel better, but empathy makes *you* feel better. Empathy creates the connection that reaches through your pain. There is one more thing we have to say about the connection between empathy and vulnerability.

Empathy cannot want control. This is a particularly hard lesson for me as a dad and as a pastor. If I am listening to my daughter or to someone in my church tell me a story, and if I want them to do something, then I am not listening for the purpose of understanding them. I am listening in order to find ways that I can get them to do what I want them to do. On the other hand, if I choose to listen with empathy, I am vulnerable. I risk not getting the outcome that I want. And that is why a lot of people cannot bring themselves to practice empathy. They are afraid that they might lose something. But if we are to follow Jesus's example, then we must risk empathy. Empathy cannot want control.

This point is particularly important for those of us interested in recalibrating the church. The most powerful stimulus for such recalibrating is when we are transformed by listening to the longings and losses of the people entrusted to our care. But *the moment we want control—and especially the moment that our fears demand control—we lose the ability to feel with people and we shut them down.* Let me give an example.

A few years ago, I was working with a church in the Pacific Northwest. Most of the members of the congregation were well over sixty-five, yet there was a small but vibrant contingent of younger adults. The congregation's leadership (its pastor and its board) decided that they wanted to make the congregation more welcoming to younger adults. So the congregation engaged in a listening exercise designed to get at the longings and losses of the people in and around the congregation. As part of it, a group reported on conversations with the younger adults.

One young man, whom we will call Zack, reported on what he thought was an important insight: the issues that the church counted as important felt out of touch to people his age. He gently suggested that some other issues were a regular part of conversations among Zack's age group and might feel not just out of place but even threatening to the older adults in the congregation.

One older woman compassionately asked for an example. Zack said he felt uncomfortable even giving an example because he thought that the phrases might set people off. The compassionate woman pressed him ("Tell me more . . .") and empathetically told him that the whole point of the project was to listen to things the church needed to hear.

So Zack took a deep breath. Then he said that a normal conversation among people his age might include the phrase "gender fluidity." Someone immediately said, without judgment, "I'm afraid I don't know what that means." So Zack started to explain the term and why it expressed a longing or loss for his people.

But before he could really get started, an elder cut him off. "That sounds like something that is the culture of this world," the elder erupted. "There are two worldviews opposing each other—the kingdom of God and the culture of this world." At first Zack thought he might get to explain himself after the elder had ceased his interruption. But the elder spent fifteen minutes railing about how dangerous it was to adopt "the culture of this world." He just kept talking until Zack gave up any hope of explaining himself.

Zack had begun by reporting that there were phrases so threatening that he feared his congregation could not handle them. Before he could finish explaining what he meant, the elder proved his point. Zack's intention had not been to advocate for "gender fluidity" or to oppose it. He was making a more basic point.

He worried that, if he invited people his age to visit the congregation and to talk about what kept them awake at night, then the congregation would have such a great need to control the conversation that the congregants would not be able to listen with compassion. Because the elder proved him right, neither Zack nor any of his friends ever really offered anything substantive to the strategic conversation again. It was not safe. Empathy cannot want such control of others.

Empathy is inviting. The opposite of shutting down a conversation is to invite it to go deeper. The Fuller Youth Institute summarizes the commitment to listening with the phrase "Tell me more . . ."[31] Whenever a Christian leader does not know what else to say, whenever I hear someone start to reveal something that is hard, whenever someone says something that hits me, the simple response is an invitation: "Tell me more . . ." All leaders need to put themselves in positions where people are telling stories from their lives. This gives leaders a holy opportunity to invite those people into deeper conversation. Even if leaders find that what a person says is disturbing (such as the elder who could not stomach even the phrase "gender fluidity"), the best instinctive response is to invite the person to say more. And that leads us to the next characteristic of empathy.

Empathy is never judgmental. The prevailing stereotype of the church out in the culture is that we Christians are judgmental. For example, one survey found that almost nine out of ten young adults who do not go to church see Christians as judgmental.[32]

We see exactly what judgmental means when we contrast Jesus with the Pharisees. Jesus had compassion on people, even when they were wrong. He was gentle with the woman at the well (John 4) and the woman caught in adultery (John 8). Notice that, in both encounters, Jesus did not ignore sin. But he was gentle and kind. The Pharisees, on the other hand, were condescending and ruthless. That is, unfortunately, how many people outside the church experience those of us who represent Jesus. They see us as judgmental.

But there is likely a reason why we Christians end up acting like Pharisees: we insulate ourselves from other people's pain because empathy makes us vulnerable.

Empathy will transform us. If we allow the longings and losses of our people to seep into our souls, then they will call up similar emotions within us. We will begin to identify with the hopes and the fears that our people feel every day. We will see things from their perspective. And then we will no longer be able to sit in condescending judgment. By feeling with people, we step into their shoes. And that will transform us.

So we must listen with empathy. Empathy is feeling with someone. Empathy is a vulnerable choice. Empathy cannot want control of others. Empathy is inviting. Empathy is never judgmental. If you practice this kind of empathetic listening, empathy will transform you. The first step in listening well is to listen with empathy.

Listen across Difference

The second step is to listen across difference. The celebrated Nigerian novelist Chimamanda Adichie describes what she calls "the danger of a single story." She depicts how easy it is to treat people as stereotypes. For example, she describes the reaction of her roommate when she started college in the United States. The American roommate assumed that, because she was African, she could not speak English (yet English is the national language of Nigeria) or use a stove. The roommate "felt sorry for me," Adichie says, "even before she saw me. Her default position toward me, as an African, was a kind of patronizing, well-meaning pity. My roommate had a single story of Africa: a single story of catastrophe."[33] Adichie then goes on to describe how she herself was guilty of the same prejudice when she made assumptions about a servant working in her Nigerian home. In each case, *someone who is different is just a stereotype until we take the time to listen to their story.*

The antidote to the prejudicing single story is, of course, listening to many stories—especially stories from people who are not like yourself. That may mean doing homework before bumbling into embarrassing attempts at listening to the kinds of people you have never encountered. It is important, for example, for Anglo congregations to listen to the experience of African Americans. But before they do, they might want to read a bit about the experience of African American men,[34] women,[35] and young people.[36] That would go at least a step toward understanding[37] how little those congregations know before they put people in the awkward position of having to correct the most basic misunderstandings.

Listening across difference will do at least three things that will help us recalibrate the church. First, listening across difference will change who we see as the people entrusted to our care. Second, listening across difference will create the kind of empathy that will transform us—as opposed to the kind of listening that confirms how we were right all along. Third, listening across difference will change whose story we privilege. Let me give one example that illustrates all three of these points.

Last November, the pastor of my church decided that it was important for our suburban congregation to listen to the experiences of people who are not like us. So he invited three preachers to speak to us on three consecutive Sundays. One was Asian American and two were African American. After each worship service, he invited people to stick around for a forty-five-minute question-and-answer session. During one of those sessions, a congregant told a story to the rest of the congregation.

June has been a member of our congregation for years. Many people in the congregation knew her when she was a teen. She and her husband have four children. Two are biological and two are adopted. Their adopted boy happens to be of African descent. June told the story of shopping with her children. When she shops with her blond boy, she told the congregation, women will sometimes come up to him and start a conversation. They remark how cute he is. Their first reaction to him is a smile. When she shops with her black child, she continued, those same women shy away from him. They don't comment on him. Their first reaction is often to scowl and clutch their purse. Same mother, same family. Drastically different treatment.

Here is what is so important about that story. It changed the congregational conversation about race that November. Why? One well-meaning woman in the congregation told me, "I did not know why we were talking about race. I guess it is important for the national scene. But I never thought it was our issue. But then I heard June's story, and I realized that it has to be our issue because it affects one of us."

Notice all the mental models (and Big Lies) embedded in that one small quote. The woman assumed that it would be "our issue" only if it "affected one of us." She defined "us" narrowly as the people who presently attend the church. Or, to revisit the point of this section, listening to June's story (or better yet, seeing the world through her black son's eyes) changed the woman's notion of the people entrusted to our care. Listening to someone who is different (even though they are one of "us") created a kind of empathy. She could picture the pain June felt watching her child be instinctively rejected. Listening changed the story that she privileged. She thought that only the stories of people like "us" are part of our story. But seeing things through someone else's eyes changed the way she listened to the subsequent preachers at our church. There is one other thing to say about listening across difference.

Listen with the goal of accommodation rather than assimilation.[38] In assimilation, the burden is on you the outsider to change if you and I are going to share a culture. In accommodation, the burden is on me the insider to change. So, for example, I was talking to my pastor last week about a family that has recently started attending our church. They happen to be recent immigrants from China and had never encountered Christianity before they came to America. So they are having trouble distinguishing which habits of our congregation are American and which are Christian. (For example, we would say that the practice of worship is Christian, but the style of music we sing is American.) So my pastor asked me to help find a seminary student from China who might begin to meet with this family to teach them about Christianity. The fact that the burden of finding such a guide fell to the church and not the recent immigrant family is an example of accommodation. But it cannot stop there. If the congregation wants to be truly accommodating, the pastor will also meet privately with the Chinese seminarian to receive lessons on how to make changes in order to be more welcoming to the immigrant family. This would be new territory for our congregation because, although many nonwhite people do worship in our midst, our dominant way of doing things is the way white churches act. In other words, we have expected anyone who is different from us to change to be like us. In accommodation, we need to change. In assimilation, they need to change.

Let me give one other example. I used to know a pastor who would regularly say to his congregation, "We cannot invite children to church and expect them to act like adults." He would say this whenever a child would be loud or disruptive. And he would say it with a welcoming smile. It became such a common phrase that whenever a child acted out, someone would repeat the phrase to the embarrassed parent. The sentiment is the essence of accommodation. We cannot expect outsiders to act like insiders. If there is anyone who needs to change, it should be the insiders. We must listen so we can practice accommodation.

And, if we are going to listen in order to be transformed (which is the kind of listening that enables innovation), then we will need to listen across difference. It will change who we see as the people entrusted to our care, it will create empathy for people who are not like us, and it will enable us to see other people's stories as more important than our own. Empathetic listening is a necessary precursor to innovative recalibration.

Let us go back to Catherine, the single mom. For example, a leader at Catherine's church might be listening to her story. "Tell me more about why you felt so sad when you realized that 'we are the adults now.'" Or, "Tell me more about what you remember about growing up in this congregation." Or even, "Tell me more about what it's like to feel responsible for yourself, for your kids, and for your parents." Indeed, there are lots of times when all I know to say at the end of someone's story is "That sounds really hard. Tell me more about that."

--------●--------

We now know both the reason for Christian innovation and its purpose. Christian innovation is necessary because the church is paying attention to the wrong questions. It is calibrated to serve a world that no longer exists. So the purpose of Christian innovation is to create a shared story of hope that makes spiritual sense of the longings and losses of the people entrusted to our care.

When Ralph Winter addressed the Lausanne Congress in 1974, the people entrusted to his care were not just the missionaries gathered there. We always innovate on behalf of the one whom the Bible calls our neighbor. The people entrusted to Winter's care were the billions of souls living without the gospel. He looked at their longings and losses. They longed for the peace that can only come from Christ, but they were no closer to receiving God's invitation than they had ever been. The cultural distance meant that there would be no one coming anytime soon to bring them the gospel. But Winter knew that he had to convince the gathered missionaries to change their thinking. That drove him back to the Bible. It caused him to reexamine the Great Commission with the longings and losses of the unreached world in his mind. Thus, he made spiritual sense of the situation for the Lausanne Congress. He told the mission leaders that the "nations" to which Jesus called them were not nation-states but cultural groups. Winter illustrated it by telling stories that they would recognize, such as stories from missions in India. Then he invited them into a shared story of hope for the future. He reminded them of their rallying cry: "the evangelization of the world in this generation." Winter told them that the old story (the one in which nations mean countries) would never help them reach the people who longed for the gospel, much less do so in this generation. But then he offered them a new story. If the mission agencies changed their mental model to focus on people groups, then they could mobilize their efforts with the hope of every person having a church in their own language and culture. Then, and only then, could they hope to evangelize the world in this generation. Ralph Winter's Christian innovation created a shared story of hope for the future that made spiritual sense of the longings and losses of the people entrusted to his care.

Earlier in the book, we encountered five questions that will guide us through Christian innovation. Let me remind you of the five questions.

Q1. Who are the people entrusted to your care?

Q2. How do those people experience the longings and losses that make up the human condition?

Q3. What Big Lies do your people believe that prevent them from hearing the gospel?

Q4. How do you make spiritual sense of those longings and losses?

Q5. How do you express that spiritual meaning as a shared story of hope?

In this chapter, we have examined the first three questions through the eyes of one woman (Catherine). We saw that (Q1) Catherine and her family are people entrusted to her congregation's care. We saw that (Q2) Catherine longs to have "more God" in her children's lives. She feels loss as well: not enough money to save for college or for retirement, and worries about her parents. And we saw that (Q3) the church believes a Big Lie about her, that "the church is not responsible for the children entrusted to its care." All of these questions spin out of the idea that leadership begins with listening.

But leadership does not end with listening. Once we have listened with empathy to the people we serve, we need to figure out how to provide a gospel response to the longings and losses we hear. That is where the next chapter begins.

4

Making Spiritual Sense

The last chapter was about answering the first three innovation questions, and together those answers keep us in sync with the ever-changing people entrusted to our care. This chapter and the next will enable us to answer the final two questions, and together they will keep us anchored by the never-changing gospel.

The overarching goal of the chapter is to show how to make spiritual sense of those longings and losses that we so carefully listened to in the last chapter. The chapter will explain how to make spiritual sense—and it will introduce three ways to do it: (1) planting language, (2) changing mental models, and (3) reinventing Christian practices. We will spend the bulk of our time focused on the third point. Indeed, you could summarize the thrust of the entire book succinctly. We *will recalibrate the church by reinventing Christian practices. These reinvented practices will create shared stories of hope that make spiritual sense of the longings and losses of the people entrusted to our care.*

To see what is at stake, let us begin the chapter by practicing what we preach. We begin with listening. Specifically, we will describe a common issue that comes up when we pay attention to the longings and losses of the people entrusted to our care. Once we have explained what we have heard, we will use that issue as an example throughout the chapter for how to make spiritual sense of the issues that arise when we listen to our people. The issue is loneliness.

In contemporary society there is an "epidemic of loneliness."[1] About one-third of adults over fifty in the US report feeling lonely.[2] And in Britain, over ten thousand people a week call the Silver Line, a call center for older adults who crave human contact.[3] This rampant loneliness poses a major health threat. It "can shorten a person's life by 15 years, equivalent in impact to being obese or smoking 15 cigarettes a day."[4] Loneliness is common, and it is dangerous.

And it is not just a problem for elderly people. Gen Z (the young adult generation) is the "loneliest generation."[5] Indeed, in a study of over twenty thousand Americans, "more than half of Gen Zers identified with 10 of the 11 feelings associated with loneliness."[6] Over a third of high school seniors say they "often feel lonely."[7] Loneliness is also a problem for mothers[8] and in the workplace.[9]

Every time you listen to the people entrusted to your care, there is a good chance that you are listening to someone who is lonely.[10] But they likely won't come out and say it. For example, among the ten thousand calls a week to the Silver Line, "only rarely will someone speak frankly about loneliness."[11] There is such a negative connotation about being lonely that people will not admit what they are feeling.

That means you will need to learn to listen for the feelings behind what they say. Think back, for example, to Catherine, the single mom from chapter 3. She spends her days caring for others, hopping from one needy person to the next. But she never talks about someone who takes the time to listen to her—not even her boss. If she were one of the people entrusted to my care, I'd be thinking that she is probably lonely. And I'd be wondering how to make spiritual sense of the loneliness.

What It Means to Make Spiritual Sense

Every Christian leader is called to make spiritual sense.[12] Understanding the longings and losses of the people entrusted to our care is the necessary beginning, but it cannot be all that we do. Knowing someone's pain only helps us if we do something about it. We Christians will need to make spiritual sense of the longings and losses of the people entrusted to our care. Doing this will allow us to join a great cloud of biblical witnesses.

From the earliest biblical times, God has called leaders to speak in God's name to God's people about the things that matter most in life. These leaders provided a divine perspective on the daily dilemmas that the people faced. Moses, for instance, proclaimed to the people in Egypt that God had heard their cries when their greatest longing was to be released from bondage. Then at Sinai, he gave them the law as a framework for interpreting life as God's chosen people. Finally, as he prepared to hand leadership over to Joshua, Moses told the people who stood on the banks of the Jordan River that they had a choice between life in the land that God promised and death in fearful wandering—and he urged them to "choose life" (Deut. 30:19). At each of these critical moments in Hebrew history, God's appointed leader explained the spiritual meaning of the people's common experience, such as their losses under Pharaoh and their longings for a homeland.

When Moses told the Hebrews that God had not forgotten them, he was making spiritual sense. The people had been telling themselves a story that made sense of their lives: "We are no longer God's chosen people." Moses told them it was a Big Lie and offered them a better way to see the world.

God's leaders continued to make spiritual sense once the people had taken possession of the land. There the judges reminded the people that their only hope lay in the God who brought them out of Egypt and not in being like other nations. Samuel the judge told them that they longed for the wrong thing when they clamored for a king. Yet God gave them a king. But Yahweh did not make the king the only leader of God's people.

The prophets explained God's interpretation of national events to succeeding generations and instructed the kings when they strayed.[13] Nathan, for example, helped David see his sin for what it was. Elijah and Elisha told the people that a wicked king was no reason to turn to false gods, who would only let them down. Jeremiah warned the people of God's coming judgment and led them in lament when that judgment came crashing upon them. And Haggai called on the returning exiles to stop focusing on their own selfish pursuits long enough to rebuild God's temple. In each case, *God's leader gave a divine perspective for God's people—providing a story that reinterpreted their lives.* That's what it means to make spiritual sense of the longings and losses of the people whom God had entrusted to their care.

The apostles likewise sent epistle after epistle to newly formed churches, thereby helping them understand how Christians should interpret their longings and losses amid Greek culture. Should Christians purchase meat that had been sacrificed to idols? Did Christians in Asia Minor and nearby Europe bear a responsibility for the poor in Jerusalem? These are the kinds of everyday questions that the apostles addressed. God called these people as leaders so that they would teach the church how to use Christian categories to make sense of their daily lives. Indeed, *this act of interpreting daily life was the primary way that the apostles and prophets guided the people of God.* The apostles led the fledgling churches entrusted to their care by making spiritual sense.

This work of interpretative leadership functioned at two levels. On the one hand, the apostles directed specific churches on how to handle specific circumstances. On the other hand, this act of making spiritual sense created a precedent for the whole church.

For example, the primitive church wondered about how to help the Greek-speaking widows who lost everything when they converted to Christianity. So the church appointed "the seven" (Acts 6) to embody the Christian commitment to hospitality and *koinonia*. The apostles thus gave the church a mental model for guiding its action. They could easily have said that the preaching of the gospel is so important that the church can neglect the widows. But instead, the church created a division of labor. Some Christian leaders (i.e., the apostles) devoted themselves to preaching; others (i.e., "the seven") gave themselves to the care of the poorest and most vulnerable people entrusted to their care. That act of dividing the tasks grew into a theological understanding of the church as a body with many gifts (e.g., 1 Cor. 12). Meanwhile, these seven then became the model for the church office of "deacon" (1 Tim. 3). The apostles led by making spiritual sense, for example, of one group's losses (i.e., the Greek-speaking widows) and in so doing created an innovation that spread out to the whole church. This is Christian innovation. It happened when Christian leaders made meaning.

In this day of bureaucratic organizations and nondirective therapy, we tend to forget that the first duty of a Christian leader is to provide a Christian perspective, an interpretative framework for people who want to live faithful lives. We wrongly expect Christian leaders to be either hierarchical authorities who control their congregations or egalitarian enablers who just support their staffs. And we call that leadership. But the authoritarians cannot mobilize God's people (at least not for long), and the enablers are ultimately ineffectual. We settle for these poor shadows of the leadership we see in the secular world. Thus, we tend to forget that *Christian leadership is fundamentally an act of theological interpretation*—and that *Christian innovation is fundamentally an act of creating new theological interpretation*.

The purpose of Christian leadership is to make spiritual meaning. Just as the prophets showed the Hebrews where God was at work in their world, so a Christian leader should help God's people see how to interpret their daily lives from God's perspective. Just as the apostle Paul reinterpreted basic tasks such as buying meat to eat, so a Christian leader today leads by shaping the ways God's people interpret everything going on in their worlds.

The stereotype of a leader is a person who tells people what to do. But the best leaders rarely need to order people around. Instead, *the best leaders give people the tools to think for themselves*. Then those leaders point people on a path forged by those new ideas. That's what Martin Luther King Jr. did when he inspired America—white and black—to civil rights. And that's what Jesus did when he preached the Sermon on the Mount. The best leaders make spiritual sense of the longings and losses of the people entrusted to their care.

Once we can talk about the human condition of the people entrusted to our care, we will eventually want to create a theological response. But before we can do that, we need to make a transition between life as people describe it and the theological issues that are the soul of the matters making up their experience of the human condition. Let me give you an example.

The biblical book of Philemon follows the pattern we have been describing. Paul leads by bringing spiritual meaning to a very real (and complicated) situation from daily life. The letter has three major characters: Paul the apostle, Onesimus the slave, and Philemon the slaveholder (from whom Onesimus has escaped). We know something about how the three relate to one another. Both Onesimus and Philemon are fledgling Christians, entrusted to Paul's care. What are the longings and losses of these people? Onesimus longs for freedom and wants to be right before God, yet being right before God seems to come at the cost of admitting that he ran away. Philemon has lost a slave and wants him back, but he also wants to be right before God. These longings and losses create some role conflict. Philemon is a slaveholder and a Christian, just as Onesimus is a runaway slave and a Christian; these roles are in competition. And there is one more role in play here: Onesimus now appears to work for Paul.

All of this creates a presenting problem: Should Onesimus return to Philemon? There is a deeper issue, of course, about the relationship between slavery and Christianity. But Paul does not take up that issue. He believes that the deeper question is this: Does one's role in society define questions of identity, belonging, and purpose? Specifically, does Onesimus's social role as a slave create his identity in society, structure his relationship with Philemon, and define his purpose?

Paul then takes the question to its spiritual destination. He frames it as a theological issue. Which is more important, he asks, the social perspective that defines the relationship between Philemon and Onesimus as master and slave, or the spiritual relationship that defines them as brothers in Christ? Ultimately, this is a question of role conflict. The roles of brother-in-Christ and slave-in-bondage are in theological conflict. And Philemon believes a Big Lie: that Philemon does not need to treat Onesimus as a brother since he is a slave. So Paul destroys Philemon's Big Lie with the truth of the gospel. Paul makes it clear that brotherhood in Christ supersedes the master-slave relationship. And he "asks" Philemon to act accordingly (1:21). Paul frames his request with a reminder: "You owe me your very self" (1:19).

Notice how Paul creates a new mental model for Philemon. Philemon's mental model of Onesimus, that "he is a runaway slave," dictates the action that Philemon thinks he should take. But Paul recasts the mental model of

Onesimus. Paul suggests that Philemon's mental model of Onesimus should move from "runaway slave" to "brother in Christ." Once Philemon adopts this mental model, Paul believes that Philemon has but one course of action. He needs to allow Onesimus his freedom and send him back to serve alongside Paul. The apostle makes spiritual sense of the situation by providing a theological framework (a Christian mental model) for interpreting the matter.

Paul starts (Q1) with the people entrusted to his care, both Onesimus and Philemon. And (Q2) by looking at the longings and losses of each party in the drama, he is able to frame the problem as a theological issue. Paul then (Q4) makes spiritual sense of the problem by explaining how to understand the issue, using Christian categories (i.e., brothers in Christ) rather than the (Q3) Big Lie that is obvious to the world (i.e., to see them as master and slave). Once Paul has made spiritual sense of the problem, the innovation is obvious.

The idea that Christian brotherhood supersedes slavery in the Roman Empire was an innovation. And that innovation became (Q5) a shared story of hope for Onesimus, for Philemon, and for the whole Christian church. Paul innovated by making spiritual sense of the longings and losses of the people entrusted to his care.

The central task for a Christian leader is to make spiritual sense. The most powerful way to make spiritual sense is to change the mental models of the people entrusted to our care—that is, replace their Big Lies with the truth of the gospel. This is how Christian innovation happens. The question, of course, is how a leader might do this. Let us now look at three ways to make spiritual sense. Each one is a way of changing the mental models of the people entrusted to our care.

Making Spiritual Sense by Planting Language

One way to make spiritual sense is to "plant language." Christian leaders plant language about God. They water it and nurture it. Then they turn their people over to God, who gives the increase as the new vocabulary bears fruit in their people's lives. If we know that all humans regularly face the longings and losses of the human condition, then we need standard answers to the questions our people will regularly face. It is far more powerful to introduce people to the language before they need it. Then our people are already primed to use that language. Let me give you a few brief examples to illustrate what I mean.

I worked with a pastor who would regularly say on Sundays to his smug suburban congregation, "God meets you in your brokenness." This seemed a bit strange to them because they did not think they were broken. But, of course, the pastor would spend his weekdays meeting with congregants who were discovering just how broken they were. The ready-made language gave them a way to handle their pain; his stating it ahead of time gave them an invitation to visit him when they discovered that brokenness.

Likewise, the pastor of my own church planted language when we put up a new building for youth and children. The congregation decided we would do the work ourselves. And Pastor Steve attended all the building committee meetings. He rarely spoke up. But at each meeting he would remind the people, "If we put up the building and divide the congregation, we have failed." There was surprisingly little conflict until the very end.

A controversy arose over the carpet color. The youths' side of the meeting wanted one color, and the children's side wanted another. All Pastor Steve had to say at the contentious meeting was the same: "If we put up the building and divide the congregation, we have failed." So each side agreed to compromise. The fact that he had been saying the same thing for so long gave it legitimacy. The people had already decided to agree to his statement. If he had waited to bring it up until there was a conflict, people might have taken it personally. But the fact that he had already planted the language allowed it to blossom at just the right time.

Sometimes planting language allows people positive options when they do not know what else to do. Let's say, for example, that a tragedy happens in your community—perhaps a fire, a shooting, or a flood. And let's say that your congregation regularly sings the praise song "Blessed Be Your Name,"[14] which includes the lines "When the darkness closes in, still I will say, 'Blessed be your name.'"

Now picture how having that vocabulary at the ready would affect your congregation. It would give the pastor something to say when talking to the congregation about the tragedy. But, more importantly, it would give your people something to say to God when they pray. When your people don't know what to pray, when they lie awake at night wondering how to make sense of their lives, they need a prepared vocabulary for making spiritual sense of the things that matter most in their lives. They need someone to plant language that will bloom at just the moment they need it.

Let me give one more specific example. Behind many longings and losses is a basic question of fear. I have come to believe that behind our fears—behind the fears that we all experience as part of what it means to be human—is one question: "Can God be trusted with my future?" The single question summarizes a clutch of questions: Does God love me? Is God strong enough to change my future? What if God does not give me what I ask? All of them combine to create the bigger question. Any time my people's longings and losses describe their fears, I know that, at some level, they are asking, "Can God be trusted with my future (and the future of the ones I love)?"

We Christian leaders need to plant vocabulary that addresses this question, whether our people are asking the question aloud or not. Can you see how a gospel-infused story of hope is the natural antidote to fears about whether God can be trusted with my future? This has fairly straightforward implications. For example, when I preach at my church, I regularly include in my sermon the phrase "God can be trusted with your future." I'll usually throw it in toward the end and then add a sentence or two from whatever I have been saying to tie the sermon to the idea that God can be trusted.

I do this because long ago I read Max De Pree's famous dictum: "The first responsibility of a leader is to define reality."[15] As a leader of my church, I want the people entrusted to my care to live in a world defined by the fact that they can trust God. So I make a point to link whatever I am teaching to the deeper idea that they can trust God.

Here's what happens. When the people entrusted to my care encounter difficulty in life—a son is in the hospital, a mother is struggling with depression, a retiree is anxious about money—when my people fret about the future, they have a phrase to go back to and a place to which they can return. "I may be terrified," I want them to say, "but I know one thing: God can be trusted with my future." That's why we plant language.

Indeed, the way I have written this book is designed to plant language that will change your mental models. There are phrases that I repeat again and again: "The people entrusted to your care." "Leadership begins with listening." "The church we know now is calibrated for a world that no longer exists." Each chapter contains these phrases (or an equivalent). At first it might appear that I am a poor writer who does not know that he is being redundant. But I see that repetition as planting and watering. I keep repeating the phrases that will change your mental model of Christian leadership. I believe that if I can sufficiently plant these phrases—plant this vocabulary—into your brain, it will change the way you encounter your work and the people entrusted to your care. Just as Jesus spent much of his ministry repeating stories about the kingdom of God, so I will regularly repeat ideas and phrases so that the vocabulary can take root in your view of yourself. One way to make spiritual sense is to plant language.

Making Spiritual Sense by Changing Mental Models

It is tempting to think of meaning making as a rational process in which observations lead to conclusions, which lead to action. But it turns out that people do not always follow an orderly or deductive formula when figuring out what a situation means. Instead, people engage in what Karl Weick calls "soliloquies." These are internal conversations that allow people to talk themselves into an interpretation of a given experience. The conversations play out in people's heads as they work to assign meaning in a new situation. This led Weick to conclude that "soliloquies define cognition."[16] But those soliloquies are not well-reasoned arguments. They are stories. *We reason by telling ourselves stories.* Let me explain.

Perhaps the easiest way to explain the stories we tell ourselves is by telling a story. Have you ever been in the middle of a conversation and said something stupid, but you can't quite tell what it is? A few years ago, I was teaching a class when I realized that all the women in the class were angry. They had their arms folded and their faces pinched. What did I do in that moment? I kept lecturing—but in the back of my mind I was playing out what I had said for the last few minutes, wondering what had offended so many people. Then I realized that the class was getting worse. I could see that some of the men were glaring at me with their arms across their chests.

So I decided to stop and make the problem discussable.[17] "What stupid thing did I say this time?" I asked. No one talked, they just gave me puzzled looks. "I can tell you are angry; look at you, hunched in your chairs and with your arms crossed; what did I say that made you so angry?" All at once the class erupted with the same answer, "We're not angry. We're cold." I looked up at the digital clock (which had a thermometer) to see that it was fifty-six degrees in the classroom. It turns out that the heating and cooling system was reversed, and instead of heating, it was blowing cooled air into an already-cold room.

Suppose I had not known to ask my students why they were angry. And let's say that I went home that night and told my wife the story. We would have played the lecture out in our discussions and would have "figured out" what I had said that made them angry. We would have found something because I was sure there was something to find. The story that I told myself would become, for me, the facts. I did just what Weick said I would do. I had a conversation in my brain where I tried to figure out what story made the most sense of what I saw. Then I acted as if that story was the truth.[18]

To learn how to guide our people in making spiritual sense, it is best to start with how people make sense of any situation. I see a roomful of students with their arms crossed. How do I decide what that means? You see that your teenage son is not yet home at midnight. How do you decide whether to be worried, angry, or pleased? You discover that your mother needs surgery. How do you decide if God can be trusted with her future? Or you listen to a political candidate who claims to be a Christian. How do you decide whether to celebrate his faith or condemn his hypocrisy? Daily life is filled with those decisions. That is why making spiritual sense is such a powerful way to lead.

We have already seen that we can innovate by changing the mental model a person uses to make meaning. But now we see something new. *Changing that mental model often involves changing the story that people tell themselves.* Let us return, for example, to Jesus's conversation with the disciples in Mark 8. Jesus changes the mental model that the disciples held about the meaning of the Messiah. Now we can see that the disciples carried that mental model as a story. It was the story they told themselves about Jesus and about their place as his disciples. They believed that the Messiah was going to raise an army that would conquer the Romans and rule the region the way King David had once ruled. *They did not have an abstract definition of the Messiah. They simply had the story*—a story that was a Big Lie.

When Jesus refuted their mental model, he did not offer a new definition. He offered a new story—one where the Son of Man must suffer, die, and be raised in three days. He planted the vocabulary; he planted the story. At that time the disciples did not really understand the new story. They even rebuked him for it. But then, after Pentecost, that new story that Jesus had planted bore its fruit. The story made sense of their experiences. They adopted that story as the definition of the Messiah. Notice how *this new mental model (this innovation) moves from a faulty story to a gospel story—from a Big Lie to a story that is centered in the truth of the gospel.* Jesus innovated by changing the story the disciples told themselves.

To recap, we have learned that the most powerful way to lead is by making spiritual sense. We can make spiritual sense by planting language, such as "If we put up the building and divide the church, we have failed." We can make spiritual sense by changing the mental models, especially the stories that we tell ourselves, as Jesus did when he replaced the story of the Messiah as conquering king with the story of the Messiah as the one who suffers to redeem. We are still searching for a way of making spiritual sense that will help us recalibrate the church—that will create innovative ways to embody the never-changing gospel for our ever-changing people. That is where "Christian practices" will help us. Indeed, we will devote the rest of this chapter and all of the next to discovering how we might use reinvented Christian practices to innovate our way forward.

Making Spiritual Sense by Reinventing Practices

Christian practices are embodied beliefs, enacted stories. (By practices, we mean things like prayer, worship, almsgiving, and evangelism.) When I worship God, I am acting out with my body what I already believe in my heart. Likewise, when I give alms, I am living out what has been a part of the Christian story since the faith began.

Let me explain how practices embody stories. Suppose I read in Scripture about "the widow's mite" or I recall how the apostle Paul collected money for the poor in Jerusalem from the fledgling churches in Asia Minor.[19] I know from those stories that the compassionate giving of money to aid the poor is part of what it means to be Christian. I can look at any time in Christian history and find Christians giving money to aid the poor. The idea of almsgiving does not come to me as an abstract concept with a clear definition. It comes to me as a bundle of stories. Over and over I hear how Christians gave. Thus, I come to believe that I too should give. Indeed, my very giving (my engaging in the Christian practice) is nothing more (and nothing less) than my imitating the stories I have heard. I enact the stories. I bring them to life with my body. We have seen how mental models come to us as stories. The same is true for practices. We hear the stories. We see them lived out in other people's lives. And we imitate what we have seen. We enact the practices.[20] Practices are ritualized stories—that is, ways of acting out the faith according to well-worn narrative pathways.[21]

In this conversation about practices, the rest of this chapter will take up three tasks: (1) we will explain the characteristics of Christian practices, (2) we will describe how to reinvent practices, and then (3) we will give an example of a reinvented practice. The purpose of all of this is to recalibrate the church by using reinvented practices to create shared stories of hope that make spiritual sense of the longings and losses of the people entrusted to our care.

Characteristics of Christian Practices

It is true that we usually encounter practices as stories. But if we are going to employ Christian practices as one of our standards for Christian innovation, then we will need to be careful about definitions and know exactly what we mean. Knowing the characteristics and the parameters of Christian practices will give us an advantage when we want to consider how we might use a specific practice to address the needs of the people entrusted to our care. Such clarity is particularly important if we wish to reinvent historic Christian practices for the current world. Being clear on the definitions will thus allow us to know what parts of a practice must endure and what parts we might trim away as we recalibrate.[22]

Our many-layered understanding of social practices draws on the writing of a philosopher named Alasdair MacIntyre, who laid out his ideas in a book called *After Virtue*.[23] His formal definition is too esoteric for our present purposes. We will describe Christian practices[24] this way: (1) They are actions that Christians have repeated for generations; indeed, they constitute the faith. (2) A Christian practice is an end unto itself, not solely a means to a larger end. (3) A Christian practice has standards that must be preserved. (4) The form of a Christian practice can change over time.

First, *Christian practices are actions that Christians have repeated for generations*. Practices[25] are communally defined by a tradition and historically rooted within a tradition. An individual cannot, acting alone, invent a practice or engage in the practice alone.[26] It does not become a practice until it becomes a regular part of the life of a community. This criterion separates the usage we will adopt for the term from the common parlance on, for example, spiritual practices. More individualistic concepts have erupted in American society: in some religious environments it has become fashionable to separate spirituality from religion—with the specific implication that spirituality does not depend on tradition in the ways that religion does.[27] Indeed, some people denigrate "religion" because they think it is tantamount to adhering to someone else's form of spirituality. By contrast, I argue that faith is a profoundly communal endeavor. When we pray or when we worship, we never stand alone. We are connected to the people of faith who have prayed to and worshiped God for thousands of years. This is what Craig Dykstra means when he says, "*The past is embedded in the practice*."[28] This connection with the tradition and with the past is necessary to hold in check the human tendency for self-absorption. Attempts at practices that fail to include the community of faith have no checks and balances. I believe that the human capacity for self-delusion is so profound that we need those restraints if we are going to do anything more than worship a projection of ourselves.[29] Practices must be communally defined and historically grounded.[30]

Think, for example, about hospitality. Hospitality as a Christian practice is different from secular hospitality. Secular hospitality is about entertaining. We have friends over for a meal. Or we might think about the "hospitality industry," which is the collective name for hotels and restaurants (i.e., places where we exchange money for lodging and food). Christian hospitality, on the other hand, involves treating outsiders like insiders. We offer meals to strangers and not just to friends. We welcome people for free rather than charging them a fee. But it should go deeper than that. We should invite them to *participate* in ways that are reserved for insiders. Hospitality is rooted in the Christian tradition.

This emphasis on the rootedness of practices is part of what makes them so useful as a standard for innovation. Mark Labberton, the president of Fuller

Seminary, has regularly said that his goal is for the school to have *"roots in orthodoxy and branches in innovation."*[31] Without roots in the Christian tradition, our attempts at innovation will be blown to and fro. The potential of hospitality as a source for innovation depends on its rootedness in the Christian tradition. Hospitality was important to God's people in the Old Testament, in the New Testament, in the early church, and in the medieval church. We draw on models from that tradition, and we have precedents to study from our forebears.

For example, the medieval church regularly interpreted the parable of the good Samaritan as a story about hospitality. The Samaritan was the only one in the story, they would say, who understood the obligations that one person has to another simply because that person is also made in the image of God. The priest and the Levite who pass by the wounded man fail to see the obligations that they owe to him. Then, in the kind of reversal that Jesus often found so powerful, the outsider (the Samaritan) treats the injured Jewish man as his brother—even though the Jews in Jesus's audience would not recognize the Samaritan as an insider. In other words, when the representatives of the faith did not recognize the bonds of community, the one outside the community stepped in. This is clearly a story about hospitality.

Yet the medieval church took the meaning a step further. In the story, the Samaritan takes his wounded brother to an inn and entrusts him to the innkeeper's care. By the time of the Reformation, the standard way to interpret the parable was to see the inn as a metaphor for the church. This is why, for example, what is likely the most famous painting of the parable (Rembrandt's *The Good Samaritan*) depicts the Samaritan handing the injured man over to the innkeeper.[32] For much of the church's history, Christians believed that a central role for the church was to provide hospitality for the sick and suffering. That hospitality included both physical and spiritual care. The two were not so separate as they are today. Understanding the role of hospitality in the Christian tradition will provide one of the roots that anchors our innovation. In fact, Christian practices are so deeply rooted in the tradition that, some would say, they can define the faith.

When we talk about these Christian practices, we mean the practices that scholars call "constitutive practices." There are *certain practices that constitute the faith*. To be Christian is to engage in these practices, and to engage in these practices is what it means to be Christian. They form our identity as Christians, they show the world who is part of the community of faith, and they explain the reason we exist as Christians. There has never been a time when there was such a thing as a Christian who did not engage in these practices. Indeed, if such a person failed to engage in such practices, we would say that they were not acting as a Christian.[33] Practices such as showing hospitality, expressing gratitude, and keeping the Sabbath are intrinsic to being Christian.

Second, *Christian practices are ends unto themselves.* They are not means to some greater end. For example, singing is not a Christian practice; worship is. The purpose of singing in church is the worship of God. Let me explain the difference. Not long ago, the Broadway show *Hamilton* became a phenomenon. Especially among young people, there was a fervor about the musical. It spoke to them and it spoke for them. I was at a wedding reception recently where the DJ played a song from the musical that begins with the lyrics "To the bride; to the groom." Immediately a group of twenty-somethings jumped to their feet and started singing along. They had an almost religious fervor as they lost themselves in the song; it expressed a deep and heartfelt emotion. But none of us would confuse that with the worship of God. In like manner, many people describe seeing the play on Broadway with reverence: they talk about how it affected their soul.[34] But none of us would confuse that with the worship of God either. Singing itself is not worship. It is a means to an end, but it is not the end itself.

The flip side is just as important. Worship is not a means to a greater end. We do not need to justify it; it is automatically good. If you worshiped correctly, then you did something good. There is no need to explain any further. The same is true for almsgiving. If you gave money from your heart to help a poor person, it is automatically good. There is no need to justify it. But what if later you discover that the person was not poor or that they used the money to do bad things? It does not matter. At the time, you were enacting the Christian practice of almsgiving. You were embodying the same story that motivated Christians for thousands of years. Engaging in a Christian practice is not a means to a larger end; the practice justifies itself.

The reason that practices justify themselves is that they have what scholars call "internal goods" and embody a virtue. We can distinguish internal goods from external goods. External goods are the collateral benefits that accrue from a practice—the by-products that can sidetrack us from the reasons we pursue the practice in the first place. Mother Teresa gaining prestige in the world or a university making money are examples of external goods. Mother Teresa did not help the poor to gain prestige; a university's reason for being is education, not profit. Those external goods come from doing the practice, but they are not the beating heart of the practice. Internal goods are the things that embody the cardinal virtues of a practice; they achieve the ultimate ends of the practice. Every practice points to some virtue and thereby enacts some ultimate good so intertwined with the practice that excellent participation in the practice is tantamount to embodying the virtue.[35] Every practice is built on a foundation of those same virtues that it intends to embody.

Oftentimes practices represent a bundle of internal goods. They stand for the appropriate way of aligning those goods so as to enact the Christian faith when faced with a particular kind of situation. For example, several internal goods are associated with the Christian practice of hospitality. The practice involves treating outsiders like insiders by offering to the outsider (without fee or expectation) the privileges that usually accrue only to insiders. It also involves an openhanded generosity, an attitude that others come first, a commitment to dignity for all people, and a sense of gratitude for what God has done. Our Christian tradition recognizes that the stranger in our midst creates a particular moment of decision for God's people. It would be tempting for us to stray from the parameters of the faith in dealing with the situation. So the tradition has constructed a stock response. When faced with the stranger, we are to practice hospitality. It is the Christian thing to do. And we are to do it with generosity, gratitude, and in a way that preserves other people's dignity. Practices represent Christianity.

But they do more than that. *Practices embody beliefs*. The theologian Miroslav Volf describes the connection by saying that we need to talk about both "belief-shaped practices" and "practice-shaped beliefs." Neither the beliefs nor the practices make sense without reference to the other. We recognize that we practice what we believe, but we also know that, for most of us, we practice what we do not fully understand. "Christian practices come first," Volf reminds us, "and Christian beliefs follow."[36] *Practices embody—and enflesh—Christianity.*

Yet it goes deeper than that. Practices do not just embody Christianity; they also constitute it. "Christianity cannot be explained or understood without reference to a distinctive cluster of practices," Brad Kallenberg writes. "In order to participate in . . . Christianity one must necessarily participate in these practices. To put it another way, to participate in the community is to participate in the practices."[37] There is no meaningful separation between the Christian faith and the practices of the Christian faith. We express our faith through the practices, and engaging the practices constitutes expressing the faith. That is why they are called "constitutive practices." They constitute the Christian faith.

Notice what is missing from the list. There is no mention of an instrumental goal. The goal of hospitality is not to provide a meal or to give shelter. Those are only pleasant by-products. If we are openhanded and treat people with dignity, they will receive the meal, the shelter, or the welcome they need. Yet we must focus not on what we provide but on *how* we provide it. I am not saying that the end product is irrelevant; I am saying that it is too weak a goal to serve us. We can too easily turn the practice into an exchange if we focus on the outcome and not on the process. To put it another way, if we focus only on the outcome, then the external goods will come to dictate how we provide the care. That is why every practice has certain standards of excellence built into its historical development. Participation in a practice only embodies the internal goods of that practice when it adheres to the practice's standards of excellence.

Third, *Christian practices have standards*. The standards of excellence are the markers that separate productive participation from destructive participation in the practice. Perhaps the easiest way to explain this is to look at practices outside of Christianity. Kallenberg uses the example of chess,[38] and Jeffery Stout uses the example of baseball.[39] These illustrations are particularly helpful because the end goal (what scholars call the *telos*) is so clear. The goal of chess is to win the game; the goal of baseball is to win the game. But the reason why they are great examples is that there is a right way to win and a wrong way to win. In baseball, for example, there are ways to pursue winning that draw attention to yourself and away from the team. If, say, I hit a home run, I can run around the bases calmly or I can whoop and holler and draw attention to myself. At one level, there is no difference because it is the home run that matters toward winning the game. But at another level, I am tearing down the team (and thus endangering future wins) when I draw attention to myself. The standards of excellence are about the right way to do things.

These standards become particularly important when the end goal is harder to quantify than a win or a loss. When I provide hospitality, my goal is to welcome the stranger so that I treat the outsider like an insider just as God has treated me. There is no direct measure of "welcoming."[40] Indeed, the virtues that sustain hospitality (virtues like generosity, placing others first, and gratitude) are even harder to measure. That is why the standards of excellence often come to us as stories of what to do when common situations arise. In baseball, if there is a runner on second base and less than two outs, even a Little Leaguer knows that it is better to hit the ball to the right side of the diamond (even if you make an out) than it is to hit the ball to the left. The situation is so familiar and the story so common that there is a name for it: "hitting behind the runner." That is just "good baseball." Likewise, we know that Christians are supposed to feed the hungry, clothe the naked, and visit the prisoner. It is part of good hospitality. Notice, as well, how the entire tradition would agree that it is better to hit behind the runner or to clothe the naked. Kallenberg summarizes the points we have made: "Practices are human activities" producing "goods that are internal to the activity," have "standards of excellence without which internal goods cannot be fully achieved," and are extended throughout the system.[41]

Fourth, *the form of a Christian practice can change over time*. Practices endure, but the form may look quite different throughout history. Look at the Christian practice of almsgiving. In Jesus's day, there were beggars on the street, and the most obvious way to give alms was to put coins in their hands. This continued to be the case for hundreds of years. But nowadays, the best way to give alms may not be to put money in someone's hand. It may be to write a check to a social service agency like the Salvation Army, which can provide goods and services to homeless persons. None of us would say that almsgiving must involve coins in hands.

That points out an important caveat to our understanding that the form of a practice can change over time. As practices change, it is tempting to make mistakes.[42] Two important mistakes come to mind. One common mistake is to allow external goods to become more important than the purpose of the practice. The other is to distort the virtue that the practice embodies.

Let me illustrate by going back to our check-writing almsgiver. Writing a check is neither good nor bad in itself. But there are temptations. For example, if I write a check to a nonprofit or church, I can obtain a receipt. That receipt may allow me to write the donation off my taxes. The tax write-off is an external good that accrues to me as a by-product of my almsgiving. There is nothing wrong with an external good so long as it does not become a reason for giving (as opposed to a pleasant by-product). So, if I give money to lower my taxes, I no longer am practicing almsgiving. The motivation must be to respond to the need of the poor. That point is closely tied to the virtue I am embodying. When I give alms, I embody the virtue of compassion. I feel empathy,[43] and that causes me to respond by giving. But for many givers, the inconvenience of empathy proves too much.

Thomas Jeavons and Rebekah Burch Basinger have shown that contemporary givers find it convenient to write checks because then they never need to deal with poor people. The authors argue that contemporary almsgiving should include "genuine participation"[44] with the poor because it is hard for a person to give from a place of empathy (recall: empathy is feeling with) if that person does not interact with the people for whom they are to have empathy. If we are going to reinvent a practice, we must be careful to ensure that the new form of the practice continues to embody the virtue and to be an end unto itself (rather than a means to a more self-serving end). We understand that the form of a practice can change.

Reinventing Practices

We now know that the form of a practice can change over time. And that is a really powerful insight. It gives us the ability to respond to the ever-changing needs of the people entrusted to our care. Let me explain.

We have already seen some of the good reasons to reinvent practices. Practices embody the Christian tradition. They constitute faithful living, and they endure through generations. But they allow something more.

Samuel Wells uses the analogy of improvisational comedy to talk about how Christians live holy lives in an unpredictable and difficult world. Wells explains that most people misunderstand how improvisational comedy works, just as most people misunderstand how Christian practices work. Most people think that someone doing improv should try to be funny and that the funniest people are the ones who come up with clever retorts. But that is not how improv works.

Improvisers are taught to give their full attention to listening to their partner or to the scene around them. There is no time for an improviser to think of something clever. That is, they are taught what to notice (their partner) and what to ignore (their own urge to be funny). Instead of being clever, an improviser is taught to be "obvious"—where "obvious" means to be so transparent that she can say whatever comes into her head without having to filter it.[45] Once she has developed the habits of *listening* to and of agreeing with (indeed, over-accepting) the *story* that her partner is living, then her partner can trust her to blurt out whatever comes out of her cultivated instinct.[46] If my improv partner says, "Look at the monkey in the tree," then I turn and look, and that leads me to comment as if there is a monkey in the tree. Listening dictates my action.

Wells argues that improvisation is similar to the Christian life. Christian "ethics is not about being clever in a crisis but about forming a character that does not realize it has been in a crisis until the 'crisis' is over." That is why "the Bible is not so much a script that the church learns and performs as it is a training school that shapes the habits and practices of a community." When the church has been soaked in these habits, "this community learns to take the right things for granted, and on the basis of this faithfulness, it trusts itself *to improvise within its tradition.*"[47]

This improvising is what we mean by innovation that honors the Christian tradition. Such "improvisation means a community formed in the right habits [can] trust itself to embody its tradition in new and often challenging circumstances."[48] Christian practices give a person the agility to invent new ways of expressing the Christian tradition. This happens not by being clever but by being so soaked in the tradition that improvised innovations can erupt spontaneously.

Notice how this is so revolutionary—so innovative—that it changes the very goal of Christian discipleship. Think, for example, of youth ministry. Much of youth ministry is built around teaching young people what to do in predictable situations when they are tempted to sin. It is designed to *prevent* young people from doing things—especially the things that their parents want them to avoid. This is what Dallas Willard condemned as "the gospel of sin management" (which is no gospel at all).[49] It assumes that copying (some of) Christ's behavior will make a young person like Christ. But it does not teach virtue; it only teaches someone to avoid vice. If we are going to form young people to be like Jesus, then we need to cultivate instinctive virtue in them— the ability to allow virtuous behavior to erupt spontaneously from within.

Example of How to Reinvent Christian Practices

This is where all the vocabulary that we have been sowing finally bears its fruit. The best way to reinvent practices is to follow the innovation questions that we established in chapter 1. We will move through the first four of those questions now to explain how doing so enables us to reinvent a practice (leaving question 5 for the next chapter). Because every experience of a practice is deeply contextual, we will focus on one practice (hospitality). Normally we would focus on one congregation. But since this work is supposed to be an example for many congregations, I will describe a composite congregation—in this case, a suburban congregation comprised mostly of white worshipers, many of whom are over sixty. I have worked with so many congregations from around the country that fit this description that no one of the churches I have worked with will feel like they are on display.

Q1. Who are the people entrusted to your care?

This congregation has two answers to the question. One is factual and the other is aspirational. In fact, the people entrusted to the congregation's care are the people who come to the church to worship. Most of the congregants are in the middle class and white—and those who are not white have assimilated to white culture. Some folks work in professions; others work in blue-collar occupations. Many are retired, with a fair number of widows. The aspirational answer, however, is that the congregation would like to reach out to its neighbors. A few years ago, the church board used some online resources to do a demographic study of their area. They discovered that a lot of people in their area did not go to church and that many of them were not white. There were also more young families in the area than were represented in the congregation. The board had several meetings to discuss the data and decided to make an official commitment to reach out to the community. But not much has come of it.

Q2. How do those people experience the longings and losses that make up the human condition?

Longings and losses are the things that keep our people awake at night. There are many longings and losses alive in American congregations. The Fuller Youth Institute, for instance, likes to talk about identity, belonging, and purpose. But I will return to an issue that we discussed earlier: loneliness.

The British government made headlines when it appointed a Minister for Loneliness.[50] Why? Repeated medical studies showed that large portions of the population are lonely and that loneliness is correlated with heart disease and stroke.[51] Meanwhile, in the United States, National Public Radio reported on a study done by Cigna Health Care: according to Cigna president David Cordani, "Half of Americans view themselves as lonely."[52] This is an issue that affects teenagers in school, retired people, and middle-aged folks who are still working.[53] It cuts across races and classes. So it is safe to say that within any American congregation, there is likely a group of people whose loneliness keeps them awake at night. If we phrase this issue as "longings and losses," we could say that loneliness is a significant loss and that those people long for community.

Q3. What Big Lies do your people believe that prevent them from changing?

In this case, we will focus on the Christian practice of hospitality because it seems deeply connected to the kind of community that is missing for lonely people. Hospitality is important for a congregation that wants to reach out to its neighbors. So we can rephrase the question to ask, "What Big Lie do your people believe about the Christian practice of hospitality?"

There are likely many Big Lies that people believe about hospitality. But let us focus on just three. The first Big Lie is that hospitality is about food. Many Christians would limit their understanding of hospitality to helping with a potluck dinner at the church, or perhaps to inviting someone to dinner at their home. This lie takes the wide and deep idea that hospitality represents in Scripture and narrows it so that it is an exercise in domesticity. When Jesus ate with sinners, it was not the eating that offended the Pharisees. The dinner table was simply the location. They were offended because Jesus treated as insiders some people whom the Pharisees saw as outsiders. It is easy to think that a potluck supper open to anyone is the extent of hospitality. But that is like saying, "Because we did not prevent them from coming, they should feel welcomed."

A second Big Lie that Christians regularly believe about hospitality is this: "To belong, you have to become like us." It is the essence of assimilation to say that outsiders need to change if they expect to be welcomed. Yet the biblical examples we have of hospitality repeatedly emphasize that the host should do the changing. In our congregations, it is quite common to expect people to dress like us, to talk like us, and to act like us. This is like saying, "Being like us is the best way (the only way) to enter the kingdom of heaven."

The third Big Lie is about how people respond to our initial invitations to hospitality. It says, "Hospitality is only for people who deserve it, and especially not for people who are 'bad guests.'" This is a lie because it makes the offer of hospitality contingent on the outsider expressing gratitude for receiving the hospitality. This makes the outsider's gratitude—an external good in that it is not the purpose of engaging in the hospitality—more important than the insider's expression of care through hospitality. We practice hospitality because we are imitating the God who shows us hospitality. We can only complain about "bad guests" if we choose to forget that we are the bad guests who regularly take God's hospitality for granted. God decided to treat us like insiders even though we did not deserve it ("while we were still sinners," Paul writes in Rom. 5:8). If we practice hospitality only with those who are properly grateful, we make ourselves into the unforgiving servant whom Jesus condemned in Matthew 18. We choose to forget how much God has forgiven us as we magnify how much we are caring for someone else. Any right reckoning of what God has done (of the price that Jesus paid) requires us to seek the outsider in just the way that Jesus came for us.

Q4. How do you make spiritual sense of those longings and losses?

To make spiritual sense, we need to do two things at the same time. First, we will seek to respond to our people's loneliness and open ourselves to our neighbors by engaging in the Christian practice of hospitality. And second, we will do so in a way that refutes the Big Lies.

How might we begin this task? The first step is to reexamine the Christian practice from a biblical and historical perspective. We can look at Abraham's hospitality in Genesis, or Rahab's welcoming the Hebrew spies in Joshua, or perhaps the ways that prophets like Elijah and Elisha cared for vulnerable families (in 1 Kings 17 and 2 Kings 4, respectively). We can look at how Jesus gave and received hospitality with outsiders (and how the righteous followers of God condemned him for it). We can look at how Christians throughout history have extended hospitality—and we can look at the mistakes Christians made in not extending hospitality.

That allows us to come up with the summary statement that might go something like this. Hospitality means extending the privileges of community to people who do not have the standing in the community to expect it; it is treating outsiders like insiders. Another way of saying it is that hospitality is extending privileges across differences. The key word there may well be "privileges." The Big Lies that our people believe center around the idea that not everyone deserves privileges—and that we the insiders get to decide who are given privileges. But the way to counter those lies with the truth of the gospel is to say, "We must offer hospitality to all of 'them' because God offers hospitality to all of us."

What exactly could we do to practice hospitality? There is one answer to this question, and it takes a different form for each person or congregation. The answer is this: "Practice hospitality by extending your privilege to others." This answer is different for each person or congregation because each person or congregation has access to different privileges. If you are talking to high school students, you might talk about the privilege that comes with being a smart person, or an athlete, or a musician, or a gamer. Each identity gives a person access to insider status with a group of people. And each one means that there are stakeholders who will reward them for their status. Smart people, for example, get treated well by teachers, and they get accolades from the school. Likewise, there are other forms of privilege. Society gives advantages to men over women and also to white people over persons of color. Society treats richer people better than poorer people. Society rewards "good" Christians in that people who are moral and upstanding are treated better.[54] So the best way to mobilize our people to practice hospitality is for them to figure out where they have privilege and to share it with others.

That takes us all the way back to the original longings and losses that we described as loneliness. Let us say that we decided to reach out to lonely people. And let us say that we decided to practice hospitality toward them. The easiest (and minimalist) way to do that would be to invite people to a meal. But there is a problem with that: it would be easy to treat the meal as an isolated encounter. After the meal, I could feel good about myself without needing to inconvenience myself in developing an actual relationship—and the lonely person would have temporary relief but remain ultimately unchanged. So that is likely not the best way to do it. This is where Bryant Myers's emphasis on "ministry with" rather than "ministry for" becomes so important.[55] A better way to engage in hospitality may be to invite people who are lonely to work alongside me as we together provide hospitality to others.

For example, my wife (Genie) has been in charge of a "Dorcas" group at our church for a few years. The Dorcas group is a gathering of women who like to sew and knit. The purpose of the gathering was to create quilts and hats for the poor. She would show up the second Saturday of each month prepared to spend her time quilting. But then something happened. She started showing hospitality to the people there. Some of them did not know much about sewing or quilting. So she would teach them. At first, she was a bit annoyed because she spent all her quilting time caring for other people rather than doing the sewing that she thought was her reason for being there. Then she had a realization.

Her Dorcas ministry was not the quilts she produced; it was the care she showed for people. Many of these ladies are older; some are widows and no doubt lonely. Many of them are used to dealing with a world that no longer has patience for them—for what they don't know or can't do. So each time they meet she spends her time going from table to table, fixing a bobbin or rethreading a needle, helping to pick out a fabric or cut out a block. And she engages each person in conversation as she goes. Over time, the group has grown. At no point did she announce to people (or to herself) that the purpose of the Dorcas group was to provide community for potentially lonely people. But she did decide that she bore an obligation to practice Christian hospitality. The key reason it worked is that she invited these women to join her in a common task. She engaged in ministry *with* them. That allowed them to avoid feeling like they were the object of someone's charity. By providing hospitality to these women, she allows them a way to feel useful while feeling less lonely too. Genie practices hospitality.

There are lots of ways to do something like what Genie did. For example, lots of congregations go on mission trips. It is tempting to see that the purpose of the mission trip is to serve people far away.[56] At the same time, lots of youth ministries have come to recognize the power of intergenerational relationships[57] and are hosting gatherings, for example, where older folks meet with younger folks over a meal (i.e., hospitality). I argue that a more effective way to provide hospitality would be to combine the two projects.

A congregation could announce that in preparation for the mission trip, there will be a series of mandatory "training" meetings. I would then extend these to perhaps eight or more weeks of meetings—far more than it would take simply to prepare people to do the work. Then I would use about half of each of the eight meetings to forge intergenerational relationships. I would not announce that the purpose is to build relationships. Instead, I would work each week to get people to need each other. The older person may be an expert on something and able to teach the younger person, thus practicing hospitality. The younger person may teach the older person something and thus carry out hospitality. Working side by side provides a venue for practicing mutual hospitality.

Where does that leave us with hospitality? Earlier in the chapter, we said that we need to reinvent the practice of hospitality. Let me summarize what reinvented hospitality might entail. This will be the first of nine practices that we will reinvent in the next couple of chapters. Each reinvented practice is designed to embody our never-changing beliefs—the beliefs that will make spiritual sense of our people's longings and losses.

Hospitality is a Christian practice that extends all the way back to the book of Genesis. Although in contemporary America people use the term to mean catering a meal or putting on a party, hospitality means far more as a Christian practice. How might we recover the Christian practice of hospitality, especially in a way that brings the wholeness of the biblical practice into contemporary life?

Hospitality is the offer to extend the privileges of community to those who do not have the standing to expect it, especially those who are vulnerable because they are strangers. Hospitality often involves sharing meals, but hospitality is about more than eating. Eating is, for example, one of the privileges of being in my family. My kids have the right to expect to be fed every single night. When I share a meal with them, it is not an act of kindness. I owe it to them. When I share such a meal with an outsider, I invite them into my family for that brief period. Hospitality requires the effort to identify with outsiders and to treat them like insiders. Hospitality is extending privilege across difference.

All of human life begins with God's act of hospitality—with God's making a place for us in the world that God created, a world that we had no claim to inhabit. God knew that this offer was dangerous because we as outsiders might defile God's pristine world. But he welcomed us anyway. "Having been embraced by God," Miroslav Volf says, "we must make space for others and invite them in—even our enemies."[58] *Hospitality is treating outsiders like insiders, just as God treated us.*

Hospitality is integral to the earliest biblical stories. God welcomed Adam into the Garden of Eden. Hospitality is a significant part of Abraham's story in Genesis 12, 14, 18, and 19. Each of these stories turns on the proper (and improper) way to treat a stranger. Later in the Old Testament, Rahab welcomes the Hebrew spies, Elijah receives the hospitality of the widow of Zarephath (1 Kings 17–18), and Elisha is hosted by the Shunammite woman (2 Kings 4). God expands the notion of hospitality to include more than meals. It becomes central to the very identity of what it means to be the people of God. "Treat the foreigner as your native-born," says Leviticus (19:34 alt.). "Love them as yourself, for you were foreigners in Egypt. I am the LORD your God." This commandment is echoed in Deuteronomy 10:19 (alt.): "You shall love the stranger because you were strangers in the land of Egypt." Later in the Old Testament, God's prophets remind Israel and Judah that God will judge them based on how they care for the widow, the orphan, and the stranger (as in Jer. 7:6)—that is, by the degree to which they provide outsiders with the privileges that automatically come to those who are part of the community.

In the New Testament, Jesus practices hospitality and he receives hospitality. He eats with sinners and tax collectors. Accepting their hospitality was not just about sharing a meal; it was a way of identifying with them and making them a part of his community—a point the Pharisees both understood and reviled. Luke 9 is a particularly interesting passage for understanding what Jesus was trying to teach the disciples about hospitality. At the beginning of the chapter, Jesus sends out the Twelve without provisions. He purposely asks them to rely on the hospitality of others. When we Christians (especially those of us with economic power) read the passage, we focus on the message that the disciples carried. But *Jesus intentionally put the powerful message in the hands of powerless people. He made them dependent.* What better way to understand the people entrusted to your care than to live with them on their terms? That is what Jesus did in the incarnation.[59] When we carry the gospel to our neighbors, it is easy to let our own comfort get in the way.

In the same chapter of Luke—right after the disciples return—we see Jesus feeding the five thousand, another act of hospitality. The crowds have overstayed their welcome in a deserted area, and the disciples want to send them away. Jesus tells the disciples to feed these strangers—to treat them as if they are insiders, or part of Jesus's crew. The command to provide hospitality makes no sense to the disciples. So Jesus feeds the outsiders. The disciples are so burdened by their limitations that they do not see the obligation and opportunity they have to extend their privileges to those outside the band. *Jesus wants the disciples to treat the five thousand outsiders like they are insiders* in his chosen band.

We have talked about the Old Testament and the New Testament, but what about the early church? Hospitality in the early church became a basis for evangelism. One of the key reasons why the gospel spread throughout the Roman Empire was that the Christians practiced a different kind of hospitality.[60] Ancient Romans typically practiced hospitality only for important people—that is, only for people who could give them something in return. But the Christians became noted for extending hospitality to all, even the least of these. This was a significant part of how the early church developed a reputation for love.[61] *The early church loved outsiders as if they belonged.*

Why did they do this? Our Christian motivation for extending hospitality to the stranger is our experience of receiving hospitality from God. We were estranged from God, with no claims on God. But God, in his great love for us, offered us hospitality while we were yet sinners. He invited us into his household, not just as guests but as adopted co-heirs with Christ. And God's hospitality came at a cost. His only Son had to suffer and die (and rise again in vindication) so that we might have a place once again in God's family. Hospitality is at the core of the Christian experience.

In the same way, hospitality is often the first experience outsiders have with God's people (and the loving God we represent). Outsiders measure "warmth" by hospitality—by the degree to which insiders treat outsiders like they belong.[62] *That means that hospitality must adapt to the experience of the outsider.* Perhaps I have a friend who is a vegetarian. When my wife and I invite her to dinner, we don't serve steak. That would be rude. Part of being friends with her is our knowing that she is a vegetarian. We have listened to her long enough to know how she sees the world. So we accommodate ourselves to her experiences. Accommodation is different from assimilation.[63] In assimilation, the burden is on you, the outsider, to change if you and I are going to share a culture. In accommodation, the burden is on me, the insider, to change. We in the church know the right way to treat friends: we accommodate ourselves to their needs. Yet somehow, when we deal with those outside the church, we often have the attitude that they should be grateful for whatever we offer and that they should change. But, if hospitality is treating strangers as part of the community, then I owe them the same obligations that I owe my friends.

It is easy to think about hospitality in terms of what food we might offer at a dinner. It is far more difficult (and far more important) to think about what it means to accommodate a stranger when it comes to the things we do as the people of God. We the church insiders have things just the way we like them. We selected a congregation that sings the songs we like, that meets at the time that works for us, and that has sermons on the things we think are important. But if we are going to welcome outsiders, then we bear an obligation to listen to those people who are not like us and then to change our music, our services, and our sermons so that they reflect the tastes of those we intend to welcome. *Hospitality will cost us.*

What about the "bad guest"? Doesn't hospitality leave us open to exploitation? Don't good guests have an obligation to be grateful? Our worries about good hosts and bad guests depend on whether we see ourselves as the hosts or as the guests. We practice hospitality because God practices hospitality. God invited us humans into this earth, which God created. Yet we were (and are) bad guests. We messed up in the Garden of Eden, and we continue to treat each other poorly. We do not show gratitude to God. Yet God keeps offering us hospitality. The only way we can ask about the "bad guest" is if we see ourselves as only being the good host—that is, if we forget that we have all been ungrateful guests at God's table. We must treat other people the same way we want God to treat us.

If hospitality is extending privilege across difference, then it will change the ways we invite people to participate in our community. For example, Reuben and Sonja were a homeless couple in their twenties. They showed up at a church on a Friday, asking for help with food. They were living with their infant in a van. The congregational coordinator, Carol, obtained food vouchers and arranged temporary housing for them. But Carol did something more. In talking with Reuben, she discovered that he played a bass guitar; she saw it in the van. So she invited him to come back in two days to play with the worship band on Sunday. Carol did not ask if he was a good musician and did not even ask if he was a good Christian. She simply welcomed him in Jesus's name. And now, a couple of years later, Reuben and Sonja (and their child) are regular members of the church.

How is that a story about hospitality? Let us say that we had a twenty-five-year-old bass player who was a child of the church. Would the praise band welcome him? Of course. Not only that, they would recruit him. Carol extended to Reuben the privileges that any member of the congregation would have expected. She treated an outsider like an insider. Because of that, he became an insider. That is the Christian practice of hospitality.

5

Reinvented Practices as Shared Stories of Hope

This is the chapter for leaders who feel stuck. We all know what it is like to be stuck. We know what we want to do yet just don't know how to do it. In fact, we are not even sure what first step to take. In that stuck moment, we want some examples; we want some models to copy, something to tickle the imagination, something to give a little momentum. We want a place to start. That's what "shared stories of hope" can do; they help us get unstuck.

We have already encountered some shared stories of hope in the previous chapters. Think back to the IDEO story from chapter 2, where they turned a scary MRI machine into a pirate ship ready for adventure. Think of how you felt when you read that example. Most people smile. When I'm speaking to groups and tell that story, people often interject, "What a great story!" or "That's so cool!" We immediately understand how changing a child's story changes the meaning of the MRI machine for that child. The energy in the room changes when I tell that story. There's a renewed sense of what's possible.

Or think of the story about Jesus in Mark 8. Jesus explains that the Messiah is not a reigning ruler but a ridiculed redeemer. An audience who hears the story will usually react to it. The people can see how the entire story is about the mental models that trapped the disciples, who believed the Big Lie that the Messiah came to conquer the Romans. The people who hear that story can imagine themselves changing someone else's mental model.

We have also encountered shared stories of hope when we discussed the power of inviting people to inhabit a story. We talked about, say, Nathan the prophet inviting King David into a story about a man who killed his neighbor's "little ewe lamb." And we feel the power of the rebuke when Nathan tells David, "You are the man!" (2 Sam. 12:7). That may not have been a hopeful story for the king, but it speaks to those of us who want models for how to help people change. We can be like Nathan. A shared story of hope allows people to step into a story that has hope—that draws them forward, that invites them to be different.

In this chapter, we will start by explaining what shared stories of hope can do to help us get unstuck. Next we will revisit one of the congregations we encountered earlier in the book so that we can picture a specific example of being stuck. Then, for the bulk of the chapter, we will provide examples of how specific reinvented practices might become shared stories of hope for our people in the immediate future.

----------●----------

Reinvented practices work as shared stories of hope in three ways: (1) as positive options, (2) as momentum changers, and (3) as viral content. Let us look at each of these.

Reinvented Practices as Positive Options

My wife and I once had a friend who was a psychologist. He had developed a curriculum for new parents, and he needed some guinea pigs so he could test his material. So he taught a class at our church. This friend had a particular moment in mind. He said that all new parents have a moment when they are uncertain, scared, or confused. And he told us that in that moment, every parent wants what he called "positive options." I love that phrase. Positive options are choices that new parents can make to have a positive effect on a situation. I picture these new parents having a tool bag—or a quiver—of things that might work. And when they don't know what to do, they open their bag and see if they can find something that will work.

When leaders are stuck, they crave positive options. The essence of being stuck is that you don't have anything to try. That's why feeling stuck makes you feel powerless. You worry that you cannot take any action to make things better. Being stuck means you have no positive options. That's why you want models—examples of others taking action to change their situations.

Christian practices can provide those models. No one needs to legitimate or explain why a practice like gratitude is good. But you may not know, when you are stuck, how to reconceive a practice like gratitude so that it helps you make spiritual sense of the longings and losses you hear when you listen to your people. By the end of this chapter, you will have a quiver of up to nine practices to peruse when you feel stuck.

Reinvented Practices as Momentum Changers

I believe in organizational momentum. When things are going well, they tend to get better. And when things are going poorly, they tend to get worse. This is not true, strictly speaking. They don't get better or worse all on their own. But people's perceptions shape what they see. When things are going well, people tend to interpret the next thing that happens in a positive light, as the next step in that direction.

And a single story can create momentum. Over thirty years ago, the organizational scholar Karl Weick wrote about the importance of what he calls "small wins."[1] The idea has remained important because it means more than simply an admonition to break a problem down into parts. A small win is a momentum changer. It is a glimpse of what is possible. It allows people to picture a big change in a small story.

For example, I do a lot of work with the Fuller Youth Institute. One of their key insights about youth ministry is about the power of intergenerational relationships.[2] When we teach youth leaders about creating change in their churches, we encourage them to locate intergenerational relationships that already exist. Then I give them an example from my own life.[3] When my daughter Elizabeth was in middle school, she quit the youth group to join the adult choir. A couple in the choir—Lee and Patricia—volunteered to drive her to choir each week. It started as a carpool. Each week they listened to Elizabeth; for her, they became the ears of the church. When my wife was diagnosed with breast cancer, they were the ones Elizabeth could talk to about her feelings. They meant so much to her that, when Elizabeth was graduating from high school, she sent a Mother's Day card to Patricia. To this day, when Elizabeth returns home, though she often does not have time to see her other friends, she always visits Patricia. That story has become a shared story of hope. I have told it repeatedly inside and outside my church. In fact, when our congregation celebrated its fiftieth anniversary, that story was among those that the video highlighted.

Why does it function as a shared story of gospel hope? It works because people can easily place themselves in the story. They can imagine providing a ride to a young person, and they can understand that it is not hard just to listen. It works because it has such a hopeful ending. Lots of people who hear the story would love to have a young person feel so attached to them. And it works for the purposes of this book because it is ultimately about the transformative power of listening (i.e., "leadership begins with listening").

Practices can be momentum changers. You don't need to get everyone involved in a grand idea for changing the congregation. Instead, you can try recruiting just a few people to experiment with the idea. Then, if it works out well, you can tell their story. It changes the momentum. What once seemed impossible now seems possible. Yet there is one more thing you can do.

Reinvented Practices "Going Viral"

You can find a way to make a story go viral within your congregation. Let's say that you have experimented with a practice like hospitality. And let's say that it has worked, that you have one really good story about the practice. Your next step is to make sure everyone hears it.

The best way to do that is to rehearse the story until you can tell it quickly and poignantly—with a tagline at the end. Jesus would tell parables that began "The kingdom of God is like . . ." and end some parables with the tagline "For the first shall be last, and the last shall be first." When I told the story about Lee and Patricia caring for my daughter, I added the tagline, "All it takes to start an intergenerational relationship is an excuse to listen."

Once you have a story, you need to tell it every chance you get. Do you ever have to attend meetings (he asked in jest)? Do you know that moment before the meeting starts when people chat together? Use that moment to tell the story. When someone half-heartedly asks how you're doing, respond with "Oh, I have to tell you about this thing that happened the other day." Or if you see someone in a hallway, or at a Starbucks, or after a basketball game—anytime you are greeted with a casual "How ya doin'?"—you can respond by saying, "Oh, the coolest thing happened. Let me tell you about it." Then you give the short story with the rehearsed tagline. You want to get to the point where other people are telling you the story. Your congregation is likely small enough that a small but committed group can make a story go viral. Then once it goes viral, you find another story to tell.

Telling these shared stories of hope is a way of planting language (see chap. 4). Once you've told enough anecdotes that people can see a repertoire of stories, then it is easy for them to imagine a hopeful future. This is exactly what Jesus did. He told parable after parable after parable after parable until his people knew what he meant when he said, "The last shall be first."

So when you are feeling stuck, you want positive options, you want momentum changers, and you want stories that can go viral. Shared stories of hope can do just that. Let's look at a few examples.

Revisiting Catherine's Congregation

At the beginning of chapter 3, we encountered Catherine, the single mom who was there the day her church was founded some thirty years ago. Let's look back at her congregation. It has young people like Catherine's two children. It has working folks like Catherine. And it has older people like Catherine's aging and ailing parents. It surely has more varieties of folks than that. But let's start there.

Let us say that her pastor (Morris) and his staff have done just what this book recommends. They have listened to the longings and losses of these groups of people. And let's say Morris wants to make spiritual sense of what he has heard. He stands ready to plant language and to change mental models. But he is not sure where to start. He is, like so many other congregational leaders, stuck. He needs positive options, momentum changers, and stories that he can tell. So he asks us—you and me—for our help. Let us see what Morris heard in his congregation. Then perhaps we can help him get unstuck.

Morris listened to young people like Catherine's children. He heard them talk, for example, about how they are constantly judged by what they can and cannot do. They describe how they are constantly judged by how they perform—whether in class, in sports, in music, and even at church. In his mind, Morris could see that sentiment as a longing; they long to have purpose beyond performance. It led him to realize that they constantly hear the Big Lie that "you are no more than you can do."

At the same time, Morris heard from workers like Catherine and her friends. They talked about how they long for a sense of mission in their work; they want a feeling that how they spend their Tuesday mornings and Thursday afternoons contributes to something that matters. They believe the Big Lie that "only church work is meaningful; what I do for a job only provides a paycheck."

From many older folks, he heard a sense that retirement often brings a loss of identity. "Who am I," they ask, "if I don't have a job [or kids] to define me?" The energy (the longing) of conversations with them involved looking back rather than looking forward. Morris heard a nostalgia about the past, a sadness about the present, and perhaps even a dread about the future from many of the senior citizens in his congregation.

Reinvented Christian Practices

1. **Hospitality:** extending the privileges of community to outsiders (across difference)
   - How might we help people share the privileges that come, for example, with being smart, athletic, musical, or well fed?

2. **Vocation:** loving my neighbor wherever I am planted
   - How might we help people recognize the people entrusted to their care and to serve them?

3. **Gratitude:** the choice to remember God's abundance; gratitude is not complete until it becomes generosity (where *generosity* is extending grace to people)
   - How might we help people recognize an abundance of nonmaterial things like supportive friends, meaningful work, or wise counselors?
   - How might we help people extend grace to people, even and especially when those people don't "deserve" it?

4. **Lament:** crying out to God to say that things are not the way they should be; the message of lament is that God can handle your honesty and even your anger
   - How might we help people express both anger at God and trust of God?

5. **Community** (*koinonia*): engaging mutual accountability and mutual obligation with other Christians
   - How might we help people give up their autonomy?

6. **Prayer:** offering my needs or my people up to God
   - How might we help people hand over a sacrifice of trust and not just make a request?

7. **Sabbath:** a healthy rhythm of labor and rest
   - How might we help people develop a healthy way to labor as well as to rest?

8. **Testimony:** narrating life according to the contours of the gospel
   - How might we help people use Christian categories to describe their everyday experiences?

9. **Discernment:** charting a path along the wide river of options between the banks that define the will of God; the will of God is to love God and love neighbor
   - How might we help people feel the freedom in Christ that comes from knowing the (relatively few) clear parameters for faithful living?

Morris would like to respond to all these longings and losses. But where is he to start? I believe that reinvented practices—that is, a new approach to a traditional practice—can help unstick leaders like Morris. So let me explain the rest of this chapter. In the next section I will describe several Christian practices. This is a continuation of the descriptions we began in the last chapter (with hospitality) and which will continue into the next chapter (with discernment and lament). Each practice will have its own description, with each of the summaries of a reinvented practice like a little sermon or lesson. After we have seen these nine practices, I will describe how the reinvented practices might help Morris get unstuck as he decides how to respond to his people. We will start with longer summaries of two practices: vocation and gratitude/generosity. Then, after that, we will throw in bite-sized summaries of how to reinvent a few more practices.

The Christian Practice of Vocation

Every Christian is called.[4] In fact, every Christian is called twice. Recently there has been much discussion about vocation and calling,[5] with the terms often used interchangeably. The discussion often begins with the Reformers.

Five hundred years ago, Martin Luther argued that we have two responsibilities as Christians—two callings.[6] The first call is the call from God to come and follow Jesus;[7] it is *the call to discipleship*. Until you answer that call, you are not really a Christian. But as soon as you answer God's first call, a second call comes hard on its heels. The second call is *the call to our neighbor*—to love and serve that neighbor. The call to God always involves the call to our neighbor. Luther tied the two calls to the two great commandments: to love God with all your heart, mind, soul, and spirit, and to love your neighbor as yourself. He said that they create the obligations that define us. *To God we owe faith; to our neighbor we owe love.*

This love propels us out into the world as ambassadors, to stand between God and the people God calls us to serve. "The Christian life," Luther said, "sends you to people, to those that need your works."[8] God does not send us out to some generic, impersonal entity that we will collectively call a "neighbor." God sends us out—just as God sent Jesus—to a particular people in a particular time and a particular place (as, for example, Jesus sent the seventy in Luke 10). That is why the Bible calls every one of us ambassadors: we are all sent from God to a people. No matter what your station in life—not just if you are a minister—God invites you to be an ambassador, with people entrusted to your care.

This call from God changes our mental model of "vocation." My vocation is not about me, and your vocation is not about you. Luther suggests that our calling is not defined by our giftedness or our interests or our "passions." Our calling as Christians is defined by "those who need our works." A theology of vocation that begins with my interests (e.g., "Find your passion") or even with my strengths (e.g., Strengths-Finder) can too easily become focused on me. It can too easily become about fulfilling *my* interests.

This is dangerous because it often promises something that the Christian life cannot deliver. Students and young Christians who are told that there is a vocation for them built around their passions and their strengths often hear that statement as a promise that the fulfilling Christian life will not be difficult. They mistakenly think that the Christian life will consist of doing only what they love. I hear students, for example, talk about how disillusioning an internship experience was because of the challenges it posed. The people were difficult, the work was painful, and there were not enough public accolades to justify the labor. I know high school and college-aged Christians who agonize over picking a major or a job because they think that they need to find one that will involve doing only things that they want to do.

In short, they have believed the Big Lie that pursuing their passion means never having to do something that they do not enjoy or find fulfilling. So what started out being a calling to serve others ended up being about serving the comfort of the one being called. Focusing on my passions and my strengths too easily becomes focusing on me.

There is, however, another way to describe vocation. *Your vocation is a calling to a people entrusted to your care.* Christian leaders do not have followers; only Jesus has followers. Christian leaders have people entrusted to their care. Our calling, then, is to serve the people whom God gives to us.

Let me illustrate how this notion of vocation involves having someone entrusted to your care. The first Pixar movie to gain attention was a short called *Tin Toy* (you can find it on YouTube).[9] *Tin Toy* won Pixar's first Academy Award. It is the story of a very alive windup toy that is a one-man band. When the toy walks, its arms bang a drum, its feet clang a cymbal, and its mouth blows a trumpet. The story unfolds as the wary toy encounters a toddling baby. The lumbering child towers over the toy. As the baby approaches, we can see from the look on the toy's face that it is not sure what to do. Because the toy is frightened, it starts to back away—clattering as it walks. But then it notices that the baby enjoys the boisterous sounds. So the toy turns and entertains the child. After all, that is what the toy was created to do. Then the baby, who does not know any better, begins to threaten the toy, grabbing the toy roughly and chewing on it.

Dripping with slobber, the toy flees under a sofa. Huffing with exhaustion and relief, the tin toy turns to find many other toys cowering in fear of the destructive child. There is a moment of peace, but only a moment. In the distance the toys can hear the baby stumble, fall, and begin to cry.

Now comes the turning point in the story. The cartoon won so many awards because with only facial expressions it captures the dilemma the toy faces. The toy can stay under the sofa, where it is safe, or it can face its fears and do what it was created to do—entertain the child. The audience identifies with the toy. We know what it is like when the right thing to do is not the safe thing to do. It is part of what it means to be human. Not everyone is willing to face those fears; that is why so many other toys cower under the couch. But the heroic tin toy sets its shoulders and marches out to entertain the wailing child. It has placed its longings before its losses and embraced its calling. The tin toy has exercised its vocation in spite of the danger and placed the needs of the child entrusted to its care ahead of its own safety. For a moment, the tin toy is a hero.

But that is not how the short story ends. At first the toy is triumphant. The crying baby directs its attention to the toy and coos in delight. The crying child is transformed by the heroic toy. But then the giant baby becomes the danger that the tin toy has feared. The towering toddler grabs the little toy, puts it in its slobbery mouth, then discards the now dented and dripping toy. Next, to add insult to injury, the baby becomes distracted by the box that once wrapped the toy.

The story ends with the mangled toy looking at the camera. The look is an invitation to the audience, an appeal to contemplate with the toy the longings and losses of the encounter. Was it worth it? The vocation of the tin toy is to entertain children; that is why it exists. But, when the toy looks at the camera, it asks us to consider, Is it worth the risk to exercise your vocation—to respond to whatever crying baby you have entrusted to your care—knowing that doing what you are called to do will temporarily help the child and permanently damage yourself? These are questions of the human condition. The animated short is so powerful because it asks a question that resonates for all of us. *Tin Toy* asks how far you will go to exercise your vocation by serving the people entrusted to your care.

Thus, whether you are an individual Christian pursuing your vocation or you are a local congregation pursuing your mission, *you are called not to a task but to a people*. The people may be a large group—in the way that a missionary might be called to the Berber people of North Africa. Or the people might be a parish—in the way that a congregation might be called to the people of the west end of a town or the neighborhood around a particular inner-city park. Or it might be more of an individual call. I might be called to care for the coworkers who share the cubicle space in my department at my company. Or I might be called to parent the children entrusted to my care[10] or to care for a group of elderly people. There are as many kinds of callings as there are groups of people. But either way, the calling is not about my gifts, my passions, or my tasks; it is about the people entrusted to my care. *My purpose derives from my people, not from my plans.*

My calling often begins with my interests, my passions, and my gifts. The most common first step is to ask where my passions and strengths intersect with my people's needs. But here is the key point. The standard (but mistaken) next step for people and organizations is to pursue only those areas of my people's needs where I have gifts.[11] By contrast, I argue that my gifts are only the first step. I need to figure out what my people's needs are and then *cultivate* the strengths to address those needs—whether or not those strengths come naturally to me. I may start with my strengths, but very soon I will discover that *the needs of my people push me beyond what comes naturally to me*.[12]

An example of becoming who your people need you to be comes from the Pixar movie *The Incredibles 2*. At one point in the movie, the superhero father is home with the children and feeling totally out of his element. He is accustomed to duties where he can rely on his super strength. But instead he needs to figure out how to teach his elementary-age son (Dash) how to do new math. At first, the dad is exasperated as together the father and son fail to do the math. But then, after tossing and turning in bed, the dad gets up in the middle of the night, turns on the light, picks up the book off the kitchen table, and wrestles with new math. By morning, he has it figured out and can teach it to his son before Dash heads off to school for the test.

At first, the dad said that he did not have the gifts or the inclination to teach his son. But then he realized that it was his job to become whoever his son needed him to be. That is what it means to have a people entrusted to your care. You figure out what they need, and then you become who they need you to be. When I became a dad, I was passionate about basketball; I did not expect to have to learn why espadrilles are better than pumps for an outdoor wedding. Similarly, Mr. Incredible wants to wrestle villains with his super strength; he did not expect to have to wrestle with new math. *But we are each called to become who our people need us to be—even if that does not fit naturally with our gifts and passions.* It is not about me. It's about the people entrusted to my care.

Gratitude and Generosity (Two Sides of the Same Practice)

Gratitude is about choosing what to remember—and about choosing whom to remember. The Christian practice of gratitude is different from secular gratitude in that it is choosing to remember what God has done. It is choosing to remember the abundance that God provides rather than the scarcity that can seem apparent. Walter Brueggemann points us to the Old Testament story about manna.[13] Every day (except the Sabbath) the people of God received manna to survive in the wilderness, but only enough for that day (and the Sabbath). It was enough to live in a desert that would have brought only starvation, but it was not enough to feel independent from God. So the people grumbled. They experienced God's abundance as scarcity. Brueggemann points out that the people should have felt gratitude; they should have celebrated "liturgies of abundance." But instead, they felt entitled to more and composed a "myth of scarcity."

Gratitude is about what we notice, what we decide deserves the most attention. We make sense of the world by the stories we tell ourselves. And *gratitude is a choice to notice abundance rather than scarcity.* Gratitude is about choosing to remember the gift of God's grace. "For by grace you have been saved, through faith. It is the free gift of God, lest anyone should boast" (cf. Eph. 2:8–9). Gratitude is choosing to remember that God has given me a gift. I did not get what I deserve. If I got what I deserve, I would receive death because of my sin (Rom. 3:23; 6:23). But instead of death, God "lavished" an "inheritance" on me at the cost of his own Son (Eph. 1). Gratitude is not looking at the bright side. It is acknowledging that *God's gift is much brighter than anything I ever deserved.*

There is an easy way to tell when we Christians have become too focused on getting what we deserve and have lost sight of the fact that grace is a gift from God. We tell ourselves, "That's not fair!" Think of it this way. We all want what's fair, especially children. "If you get some, then I get some too." That's fair. "If you get to go, then I get to go." That's fair. First come, first served. That's what's fair. But it's not just children. Fairness is built into American laws. If he gets to vote, she gets to vote. That's only fair. If I can buy a house here, you can too. That's why we have Fair Housing laws. We want things to be fair. What's wrong with that?

Jesus did not always think things should be "fair." He thought the last should be first. In Matthew 20, he tells a story to describe what he means. In this story a farmer owns a vineyard. He hires some workers for his vineyard and agrees to pay them a denarius, a day's wage. After all, that's fair. But then, around 9:00 a.m., the farmer sees some idle workers in the village, so he hires them, saying, "I will pay you what is right." Same scene at noon, at three, and even just before quitting time.

Then at the end of the day, when it is time to settle accounts, he gives everyone a full day's wage. The early morning workers complain, "You made them equal to us. That's not fair." The farmer responds, "I am doing you no wrong." You got what you deserved. The others got more than they deserved. "Are you envious because I am generous?" He was generous, and they did not think it was fair.

What does "fair" mean? It means you get what you deserve. That's when the next question comes. Do you really want God to give you what you deserve? Do you want to set that precedent? What do you and I deserve? If you and I get what we deserve, we get death. *You don't want things to be fair. You want grace.*

What is grace? Youth ministers often define it as "God's Riches At Christ's Expense" (= GRACE). It is much more than that, but let's start there. We receive more than we deserve—and we get it because Christ paid a price we could not pay. It is an undeserved gift. Grace is not fair. But that's the whole point. Jesus's message in the parable is that the last shall be first. That's not fair. You and I are not the first, we're the last—the ones who deserve the wages of sin. You don't want things to be fair; you want grace.

Some tend to spiritualize this parable, saying that anyone who accepts Christ on their deathbed will still get into heaven. And that's true. But that's not the only point Jesus set out to make. Grace is not just something we receive from God. We are supposed to practice grace. "Judge not, lest you be judged," he warned. "Let him who is without sin cast the first stone." Don't just be fair; show grace.

Grace is hard to practice because it scares some people—especially those of us who value law and order. We Christians live between two temptations, which come from our most basic fears. Some people fear the *lack of control*, while others fear being *hemmed in* by rules. Those who fear being out of control—like the Pharisees—tend toward legalism (too many rules). Those who fear being hemmed in tend toward antinomianism (too few rules). In more societal terms, those with power are often tempted to have too many rules, while those without power are often tempted toward not enough rules. Grace scares those who fear a lack of control. They would rather have the fairness of legalism than the antinomianism of grace.

A person does not need to talk like a theologian to say that grace seems unfair, even dangerous. It can feel like grace promotes lawlessness. For example, I was recently talking with a woman named Cathy who wanted to know about the biblical mandate to care for "the widow, the orphan, and the alien in your midst." Cathy could accept that we should care for widows and orphans because they haven't done anything wrong. But caring for aliens, especially illegal aliens? "Doesn't that just reward them for breaking the law?" she asked. "Won't that just encourage others to do wrong?" Shouldn't they get what's coming to them? Wouldn't that be fair? It's a good question, one that the apostle Paul anticipated when he talked about God's grace in Romans 6. "We have grace, so can't we just keep on sinning?" he asked. Or, to put it Cathy's way, should we eliminate grace if it gives some people an excuse to keep on sinning? And then Paul answers himself emphatically: "May it never be!" Grace may be unfair. But you don't want things to be fair; you want grace.

That's when the embarrassed smile comes across my face—the smile that comes when I get caught but don't want to admit it, the smile that used to cause my little sister to shout, "You're busted!" I have to admit that there indeed are times when I want things to be fair, moments when I want God's balance to swing toward righteousness rather than mercy. I know exactly when that happens. The more power I have and the greater my advantage, the more I think I want things to be fair. Yet when I've been wronged or when I am dealing with someone else's sin (especially a sin that does not tempt me), I want judgment. When I'm feeling "righteous indignation," I don't want to hear about grace. I want them to get what they deserve. I want fairness for others, but grace for me.

Yet that is the time when I myself need grace, exactly when I need to practice grace. So I have created a red-flag warning that goes off in my head whenever I feel "righteous indignation" welling up—because it's not really all that righteous, is it? Whenever I get really worked up about someone else's sin (especially someone whose sin does not directly affect me), I have to recognize that I'm probably wrong. I've become the legalist—the one who thinks he can cast the first stone. So I force myself to back off even if I am right (OK, I *try* to make myself back off). I quiet myself because I know that I'm probably asking God to be fair and give them what they deserve. Then I remind myself: I don't want things to be fair; I want grace.

Grace is the connection that unites gratitude and generosity. *Gratitude is not complete until it becomes generosity*. Generosity is not (just) about money. It is about a generous spirit—a willingness to give others the benefit of the doubt. Jesus told many parables about the dangers that come when gratitude does not lead to generosity. For example, in Matthew 18, Peter asks Jesus how often he should forgive a brother or sister. So Jesus tells the story of a man who is forgiven a large debt by the king. The man then chooses not to forgive a much smaller debt from a friend. He wants grace for himself, but he wants to be "fair" with the man who owes something to him. He wants to receive generosity, but he does not want to practice it. That is what Jesus condemns.

Gratitude must become generosity. The New Testament regularly talks about a "generous spirit" and about "denying self" in favor of others. We Christians often mistake "denying self" for a drudging and defeated attitude. But I think it involves instead having a generous spirit. This shows how *gratitude creates generosity*. When I am so overwhelmed by the gifts I have received, it is easy to let others have a little of my good fortune. Sincere gratitude flows into generosity.

Let me give an example. Let's say I have a plate of cookies, and there is only one left. Two of you want that last cookie. Generosity is hard amid scarcity—because it will cost you something. But let's say, instead, that I present you with a plate of forty cookies. Do you mind letting someone else take a cookie? Of course not; you are sharing out of your abundance. Now let's say that, when I give you a gift of forty cookies, someone next to you asks, "May I try one?" It would be insulting to me (the giver) if you did not allow that person to try one. If you and I truly believe that we have enough, then we will be grateful. And if we are truly thankful for that abundance, then we will share it.

The theologian Miroslav Volf points out how our attitudes about gratitude and generosity are bound up in our understanding of God. If gratitude does not lead to generosity, then we have misunderstood who God is. We give because God gave and because God continues to give. We cannot turn God's gift into a transaction—as if God were a dealmaker and we could get the better of him. And we cannot pretend that we owe God nothing—as if God were a cosmic Santa Claus who left us gifts and then disappeared. We owe God gratitude, the kind of gratitude that makes us want to be generous as God is generous.[14]

We have already discussed how every person's longings and losses at some point deal with questions of identity, belonging, and purpose. So how does the practice of gratitude relate to identity, belonging, and purpose?

On identity: *My identity is rooted in God's abundance and not my experience of scarcity*. If gratitude is choosing which story to remember, then we must recognize that choosing gratitude is choosing what my identity will be. Am I defined by abundance or scarcity?

On belonging: True community (and not just a sense of belonging) requires mutual accountability. You make claims on me and I make claims on you. If I lack gratitude, I will find it hard to allow you to make claims on me. *Gratitude keeps me from grasping*. It makes community possible.

About purpose: Generosity (the child of gratitude) is the opposite of selfishness. Any purpose that matters exists on behalf of others. If I lack gratitude, then I lack generosity. And *if I lack generosity, then my purpose will be only about me and my interests*. For purpose to fulfill the basic human longing to matter, it has to be about others. And for purpose to be about others, it must be built on gratitude and generosity.

Samples of Other Christian Practices

My brother and his family love Costco. They even know why. They love the little samples. They wander through the store, looking for people handing out bite-sized cured meats or little cups with some new drink. The samples are their favorite part of shopping.

In that spirit, the next few paragraphs show bite-sized samples of other ways that we might reinvent practices to help us recalibrate the church. (Instead of shared stories of hope, think of these as shared vignettes of gospel hope.) Each one starts with a one-sentence summary of what the practice could mean in the contemporary world, followed by a paragraph-length description.

Sabbath is a healthy rhythm of labor and rest. We tend to think of Sabbath as being about a day of rest. When you are a Hebrew people just escaped from seven-day-a-week slavery, you don't need to learn to work. You only need to learn to rest. But in our world, learning to labor well might be as important as learning to rest well. I think of it this way. We all know that it is important to eat right. And we all know that eating junk food is eating, but it's not healthy. In the same way, I believe that there is such a thing as junk-food labor and junk-food rest. The purpose of rest on the Sabbath is to renew and replenish. Junk-food rest is the kind of leisure activity that will neither renew nor replenish.

For some folks watching television is renewing, but for most it is junk food. In my own life I've discovered that watching basketball on television is as renewing as playing it. I watch like a coach—looking at strategy, evaluating players, looking two steps ahead. It engages a part of my brain in the way that a good novel or healthy conversation might. But watching other television is junk food for me. So it does not count as restorative rest. Likewise, there is productive work and there is junk-food work. We all know what it is like to sit at a desk without being engaged; that's junk-food labor. It involves a lot of procrastinating, avoidance, and distraction. But productive labor captures my whole person. Time slips by without my noticing. I am engaged and alive. In my life I strive to avoid junk-food labor and junk-food rest. Learning to labor well is as important as learning to rest well. Sabbath is a healthy rhythm of labor and rest.

Prayer is entrusting to God the things that I would rather control my-self. In chapter 1, I told the story of learning to pray differently in the face of my wife's cancer. This different kind of prayer extends to how I pray for my kids, for my parents, for my nation, and for the people entrusted to my care. I speak my requests to God. I ask God to bless my children and to heal my nation. But I see that prayer now as planting and watering—knowing that only God gives the increase. I let my requests be made known to God (Phil. 4), but then I turn those concerns over to God—like Abraham offering Isaac.

Community (koinonia) *is mutual obligation*. One driving characteristic of the church of the New Testament was *koinonia* (the Greek term usu-ally translated as "fellowship" or "community," yet sometimes as "part-nership"). We in the contemporary church have reduced "fellowship" to a potluck dinner or a quick conversation over coffee after church. But the *koinonia* of the New Testament involves mutual accountability and mutual obligation. Think of it this way. If I were driving home one day and saw a Chevy in a ditch and the owner on her cell phone, she would likely not expect me to stop (even though I've read about the good Sa-maritan). But what if the owner of the Chevy was my sister? How would she react if I drove right by? I am obligated to stop. The bonds of blood that connect us say that I have a responsibility. Yet in the contemporary church we do not feel mutual responsibility. We believe the Big Lie that says, "Live and let live." But the message of the New Testament is that we are one in Christ, bound together as sisters and brothers in the gospel. *Koinonia* is mutual obligation and mutual accountability.

Testimony is narrating your own life according to the contours of the gospel. It involves using the vocabulary and mental models of the faith to describe your own life. One misconception claims that testimonies are only about good things—that a story must have a happy ending in order to qualify as a testimony. But there are lots of ways to talk about God's presence in my life without necessarily needing to sugarcoat it. I might tell about how I experienced pain and how I cried out to God in anger (see discussion of lament in chap. 6). I might tell of how I trusted God even though I could see no redeeming quality to my suffering. I might describe how I felt betrayed by a fellow Christian or was abandoned in a moment of need—and I might acknowledge that, in this fallen world, we Christians may hurt each other. Or I might tell stories that have happy endings—such as when I was lonely yet felt the Spirit of God with me. So long as I am using Christian categories to narrate my life, I am practicing testimony.

----------●----------

Let us return to our friend Morris—the pastor who felt stuck as he tried to decide how to respond to the longings and losses that he heard in his congregation. You will recall that the young people feel "anxious, busy, and stressed" from being judged by how they perform. Catherine (and other congregants her age) are working so hard that they don't have time for the things that they think are important; they feel fear about the future, and they feel sandwiched between their responsibilities to their growing kids and their responsibilities to their aging parents. And senior adults like Catherine's parents report feeling tired, with their health waning, and they sense that their best days are behind them. What is Morris to do in the face of all of that? The reinvented practices can provide positive options. Morris can look through the nine practices to get ideas for how to respond to what he heard from his people. How might that look?

The practice of hospitality might inspire Morris to tell his congregation to "invite outsiders in." Every one of us is an insider in some ways. Instead of concentrating on where we are left out, hospitality invites us to ask, "Where am I an insider? Who are the outsiders in that setting? What can I as an insider share with those who are outside?"

The practice of vocation might inspire Morris to think about ways to communicate that our identity is not in what we do (whether at school or on the job); our identity is in whom we love (and who loves us). He might tell people to look for "tumbleweeds that blow into your life"—the people whom God invites you to love. Remember, our calling is to love the people around us anywhere that we are planted.

Notice that already we see a theme. It would be tempting for Morris to see his people as objects of a practice. Instead, he sees them doing the practice. Instead of seeing ways that Morris's people can receive hospitality, he can invite them into ways they can provide hospitality.

The practice of gratitude inspires people to see that God gives us gifts well beyond what we deserve. Our people are often tempted to adopt a mind-set of scarcity. Perhaps Morris can invite them to start every conversation by finding a reason to thank someone. Or, from the practice of generosity, they might decide to practice grace by selecting one person each day to receive more than they deserve.

The practice of lament, as we will explain in detail in the next chapter, says that God can handle your honesty. Morris might want to teach middle schoolers like Catherine's children to lament, and perhaps it can inspire the whole congregation, which is exactly what will happen in the detailed example we will visit in the next chapter.

The practice of community teaches us about the biblical concept of *koinonia*. One way to translate *koinonia* is "partnership" (as when the apostle Paul thanks the Philippians [1:5] for their "partnership in the gospel"). Morris can invite his people to look for "partners"—other Christians who can share the journey. He might help them find partners at school, partners at work, partners among senior adults, or even partners across generations.

The reinvented practice of prayer teaches us to turn over to God, with fear and trembling, the things that matter most to us. Morris might invite his people to establish a ritual for the commute. These could happen every morning as you begin your drive, or every morning on your walk, or each day when you open your school locker. Each day, simply pause and say aloud (or under your breath), "God, I don't want to have to trust you. I want things to turn out just the way I want them. But with fear and trembling, I hand _____ over to you. I choose to trust you even when it scares me."

The practice of Sabbath teaches us to establish a healthy rhythm of labor and rest. Morris might invite his people to list what junk-food rest looks like for them. And then they might list what restorative rest looks like. They might look around them at their peers: Who rests well and who labors well? What is one habit you can pick up from someone you admire?

The practice of testimony teaches us to use Christian language to narrate our lives. Morris might ask his people, "In what part of your life does it seem that faith is not allowed? And what would it look like to narrate that part of your life with the language of faith?" For example, say a young person in the church and his grandfather love sports. The grandfather coaches the youth baseball team. How might that child think about sports from a Christian perspective? Perhaps he can pick a teammate to be a person whom God invites him to love. Perhaps he can think about how, as the shortstop on the team and as an all-star player, he has an insider status when compared with the right fielder. Morris could invite that child to share the honor of being shortstop with the right fielder, to bring him into the inner circle of the team.

The practice of discernment (as we will see in chap. 6) teaches us that God's will is wide—not narrow and pinched. Perhaps Morris can invite his people to embrace the idea (from Gal. 5:1) that "for freedom . . . Christ has set you free." Ask them where they feel constrained and then work with them to imagine what freedom—including from fear—might look like.

Each of these practices provides a positive option and a shared story of hope. When Morris feels stuck, he can run to the list and see what sparks his imagination. He might, for example, find half of the practices irrelevant to any given situation. But that does not matter. So long as one or two reinvented practices seem germane, then he can feel inspired. That is often all it takes to get unstuck.

6

A Process for Innovation

There is a giant redwood tree in my grandmother's tiny backyard. Towering sixty feet tall, it has no business growing in a suburban neighborhood. There is, of course, a story. In the 1920s, when a man named Lester owned the place, he went to visit the redwoods. While there, he discovered a redwood seedling. He carried it home in a coffee can and transplanted it in his yard. For many years he watered it while it struggled to put down roots. Then, when those roots hit the water table, the tree shot up until it became the tallest tree in the valley. Lester's redwood is a metaphor for innovation, at least that is what the stereotype would tell you. But the stereotype is wrong. The standard story is that a lone genius—like Lester—discovers one big idea. It starts as a tiny seed. He nurtures it through hard times until it becomes a towering achievement. But all the research says that Lester's brand of innovation is a myth.

The Redwood Myth of innovation is a myth made up of many myths. There is the *myth of the lone genius*, epitomized by Thomas Edison working in his attic. But Walter Isaacson has shown that most of these "lone geniuses" are really embedded in communities of laborers. Edison, for example, formed a team of engineers working side by side. As one scholar put it, the team created the innovations, and Edison created the team.[1] He created a community of people all working together to turn out innovations. Innovation happens in community.

Then there is the *myth of the visionary leader*, the person who rallies a people around an idea just as Lester picked up that little seedling. But, as

Linda Hill and her team found, "leading innovation cannot be about creating and selling a vision."[2] Visionaries often tell people what to do without telling them how to do it. Innovation must include a plan of action.

Finally, there is the *myth of the Eureka moment*.[3] The patron saint of the Eureka moment might be Albert Einstein, working with just his intuition, isolated in his lonely Swiss patent office. But Einstein himself debunked the myth. "Intuition," he said, "is nothing but the outcome of earlier intellectual experience" that comes from interaction with the ideas of others.[4] Walter Isaacson summarizes it this way: "An invention," he says, "usually comes not from an individual brainstorm but from a collaboratively woven tapestry of creativity." For "only in storybooks do inventions come like a thunderbolt, or a light bulb popping out of the head of a lone individual in a basement or garret or garage."[5] Ideas are not like a lone redwood tree. We will need a process for generating many ideas rather than risking everything on a single idea.

But there is something important about that Redwood Myth. It emphasizes that ideas grow. They are the product of the planting and watering that we have said are the essence of a leader's work. They start small and vulnerable. They need care—and the right environment. The problem comes in thinking that one tree stands alone.[6] I would like to offer an alternative to the Redwood Myth.

Ideas are like saplings; you never invest in just one. If you are a farmer who wants to raise trees for sale, you do not grow one tree and hope it gets to be big. You plant rows of saplings. Some of the trees will die—as the parable goes. But from those rows you know you will get some excellent adults.[7]

Ideas are like saplings; you grow them in numbers. The currency of innovation is new ideas, not great ones. Contrary to conventional wisdom, nineteen little ideas will yield more fruit than one big idea. And here is why. No idea is great at the beginning. It may be the seed of a great idea (a seedling, as it were). But rarely does a great idea come out fully formed. Great ideas are grown from small seeds; they do not hatch fully formed. So the hallmark of an innovative organization is the ability to regularly generate lots of new ideas.

Ideas are like saplings; you cannot know which one will grow into being a great idea. The innovation literature regularly repeats this, usually quoting Thomas Edison, who said, "To have a good idea, have a lot of them."[8] Edison built his lab around this idea of saplings—or what Edison called "the rapid and cheap development of an invention"—by creating "a minor invention every ten days and a big thing every six months or so."[9] Or, as another scholar put it, innovation only comes from "a portfolio of ideas."[10]

Ideas are like saplings; you measure them in quantity, not quality. Because we cannot know which saplings will grow into great redwoods and we cannot postpone evaluating our work until the ideas have grown, we measure innovation in numbers, not size—just as Edison did. He measured innovation in ideas generated per week—or in saplings planted. He trusted that the right nurture would turn those saplings into trees and that some of those trees would become towering inventions.[11] We need a process that generates lots of ideas—all of them focused on the people entrusted to our care.

But that prompts the obvious question of how to "nurture" ideas so that they take root.[12] Google, for example, draws on the work of Jim Collins and Jerry Porras, who described the need for a systematic process of "branching and pruning"—the companion to a Christian leader's work of planting and watering. What Google means by that phrase is "trying a lot of stuff and keeping what works."[13] You do not put all your energy into one seed but instead nurture many ideas until you see which ones will bear fruit. Ideas are like saplings.

Christian organizations tend to do the opposite: we tend to try one big (expensive and loud) plan. We announce it before it is fully formed—often with a logo and theme music. We put enormous pressure on the sapling to bear the weight of a mature tree. And when it does not take immediate root, our churches complain and abandon the project—having learned the lesson that such innovations do not work.

Lester had one tree and hoped it would grow. Lester got lucky, but we cannot bank on luck. Ideas are like saplings. If you want to have a great idea, then have lots of ideas. You never know which one will erupt into a giant idea. Innovative leaders value quantity over quality.

---------●----------

We know many things about the church and innovation: The church as we know it is calibrated for a world that no longer exists. We will need to recalibrate—to innovate. The kind of innovation that Christianity needs is the innovation of meaning—the kind of innovation that changes our mental models and thus allows us to see the world differently. Innovation will require us to recalibrate to match a dual standard; we need to calibrate for the ever-changing culture and for the never-changing gospel. We will meet the needs of the ever-changing culture by paying attention to the longings and losses of the people entrusted to our care. We will make spiritual sense of those longings and losses by anchoring ourselves to historic Christian practices—even if we need to reinvent those practices. Any pastor would sign on to all these commitments. But any pastor still needs a process. That is the purpose of this chapter. The goal of this chapter is to explain *a process that Christian leaders can use to create innovation.*

The process that we use in the church needs to be different from the process that a business might use. We can learn much from secular ideas, but we cannot be devoted solely to secular ideas. As with everything in this book, we need to preserve the never-changing parts of the Christian tradition.

There are at least three requirements for what a process for Christian innovation should do. Let me name the requirements here and summarize the process. Later in the chapter, we will walk through an extended example to show how the process might work out.

What are the requirements for a process of Christian innovation? We want a process that, first, embodies the Christian practice of discernment. Given the last chapter's emphasis on Christian practices, our process should certainly also embody discernment. We want a process that, second, follows the contours of *practical theology* (PT). Christian theologians have, over the centuries, come to some consensus on how we Christians can reason together in making sense of a situation.[14] That process has come to be called practical theology. So our process will need to follow PT's method. We want a process that, third, leads to innovative thinking. Secular innovators, especially in the tech world, have over the last two decades developed something called human-centered design (HCD), which enables companies to design an innovative response to a situation. So we want a process that takes the best from secular ideas and brings them in companionship with the Christian tradition. Thus, our process will have to embody discernment, follow the contours of PT, and lead to HCD's innovative thinking.

It turns out that the scholars who work in these various areas have independently come to similar conclusions. Practical theologians and design scholars, for example, each emphasize that the process is a cycle and cannot be seen as a simple, straight line. The processes of discernment, practical theology, and human-centered design each begin at the same place. It is a place that anyone who has read earlier chapters will find familiar. It begins with listening. Furthermore, each of the processes has within its cycle a divergent move (where participants explore lots of ideas) and a convergent move (where participants eventually narrow those ideas down to a tight goal). And each of the processes has a place to experiment with how to implement key ideas. Because there is such overlap between the three processes, it is possible to create one overarching innovation process that incorporates the ideas of each of the three areas. But, before we get to that overarching process, let me give individual explanations of discernment, practical theology, and human-centered design. Then we can describe how they fit together.

The Practice of Discernment

Let us begin with discernment. Discernment is a Christian practice, similar to the Christian practices we discussed in the preceding chapter. The purpose of discernment is to seek and discover the will of God.[15] Discovering the will of God is easier than you might think. Let me explain.

Most people have a distorted mental model of discernment because they have a distorted mental model of the will of God. They believe the Big Lie that the will of God is some narrow, specific thing that is devilishly hard to discern. Yet the will of God is rarely a specific thing. *The will of God is a way of life.* I understand how we get this distorted view of discernment. There are places in Scripture, indeed, where leaders asked God for a specific answer to a specific question and received a clear and specific response. Gideon, for example, put out a fleece, asking God to make Gideon's next step clear. Samuel was directed to anoint a specific person as king. The prophets sometimes spoke direct orders to the Hebrew kings. And the surviving eleven disciples cast lots to determine who would replace Judas the Betrayer. But these isolated situations are relatively rare in Scripture. The prophets usually told the king how to act (e.g., protect widows) rather than what specifically to do. Likewise, the disciples spent far more time learning how to be disciples than dickering over who got the title. These isolated situations of direct instructions stand out because they are extraordinary.

The majority of Scripture makes clear what is the will of God. The will of God is to "love the Lord your God with all your heart" and to "love your neighbor as yourself." The will of God is to "worship no other gods," to "honor father and mother," and to "remember the Sabbath day." The will of God is to "care for the widow, the orphan, and the alien in your midst." The will of God is to be generous with your money, especially toward the needy. The will of God is to "be poor in spirit," meek, and merciful—to be salt and light, and to turn the other cheek. That is what it means to "present your bodies as a living and holy sacrifice." That is what it means to "prove what is the will of God, what is good and acceptable, and perfect."

This is why the apostle Paul says in Galatians 5:1 that *"for freedom . . . Christ has set us free."* We are free to love God; free to love neighbor; free to care for the widow, the orphan, and the alien; free to be generous; free to be poor in spirit, meek, and merciful; free to turn the other cheek; and free to be holy. That is how we prove the good, acceptable, and perfect will of God. When Paul writes about freedom at the beginning of Galatians 5, he adds, "Do not submit again to a yoke of slavery" (NRSV). He is specifically talking about the Judaizers, who believed that good Christians had to first become good Jews—complete with circumcision and a Pharisaic devotion to a narrow reading of the law.

The Pharisees got so caught up in finding just the right way to honor God in obedience that they actually stopped honoring God. They narrowed the law into a series of prohibitions. Don't be unclean. Don't work on the Sabbath. Don't get caught in adultery (especially if you are a woman). But the will of God is not like that. For freedom Christ has set you free.

The will of God is more about what to do than what not to do. Love God. Love neighbor. Be generous. In short, practice grace as your Savior practiced grace. But the Pharisees did not want to do what they were called to do, so they emphasized the things that they were not supposed to do. Jesus, on the other hand, spent more time on what to do than on what not to do—and incurred the Pharisees' wrath for it. Jesus saw a vulnerable woman rather than just a sinner caught in adultery. Jesus constantly took the side of the vulnerable people. "He eats with sinners and tax collectors," they said. The Pharisees saw it as a violation of the law, but Jesus saw it as the fulfillment of the will of God to love the outcasts. For freedom Christ has set us free. We are free to love God and love our neighbor in myriad ways.

The will of God is not some narrow, pinched, agonizing thing. The will of God is open and wide. Think of it this way. I regularly hear young people talk about earnestly praying to find just the right person to marry or just the right college to attend. But the way we teach them to pray distorts God's power by making God seem weak. Think of a high school student. We will call him Tran. What if Tran prays earnestly to select the right college? And what if Tran selects the wrong one? What happens then? Is God so weak that God's will can be thwarted by one seventeen-year-old's wrong choice? Of course not. When I was growing up, I often heard the phrase "being out of God's will." If Tran loves God and loves his neighbor; if Tran cares for the vulnerable widows, orphans, and aliens; if Tran is poor in spirit, meek, and merciful; if Tran does those decidedly Christian things at one college as opposed to another—can any of us say that Tran is "out of God's will"? Surely, Tran should pray for God to lead him to the right school, the right spouse, and the right job. But God seems far more interested in what Tran does when he attends college than in which college he attends. I constantly need to remind myself, "I am not that powerful. I cannot thwart God's will by an honest mistake—or even by a willful act of disobedience." For freedom Christ has set you free.

I don't think of God's will as a narrow path through the forest, where I must pick my way through the brambles, duck under branches, and cautiously avoid wasps. There is, of course, a narrow gate. Enter by the narrow gate. The narrow gate is Jesus. Once inside, God's will is wide. When I think of God's will, I think of being on a sprawling river in a small boat. The goal is to head downstream. And the parameters of the river (i.e., the riverbanks) are quite clear. But I can sail along anywhere I like on that river. I can be near the riverbank or in the middle of the wide river, anywhere I'd like, so long as I am headed downriver. I have lots of freedom.

It is in the context of that freedom that we can revisit the practice of discernment. At its most basic level, discernment is, according to Ruth Haley Barton, the "capacity to recognize and respond to the activity of God."[16] That is why we began our discussion of recalibrating the church with the statement from 2 Corinthians 5:19–20 about God's activity. God is in the world, "reconciling the world to himself in Christ," and therefore we are "Christ's ambassadors." All that we do begins with what God has already done—and is doing—in Christ. Discernment, then, involves knowing how to participate with God in the work that an ambassador is called to do.[17] The New Testament scholar Luke Timothy Johnson summarizes it this way: discernment is "that habit of faith by which we are properly disposed to hear God's Word, and properly disposed to respond to the Word in the practical circumstances of our lives."[18] To become "properly disposed" to hear and to act is the work of discernment.

Discernment begins with listening. Indeed, it involves four kinds of listening. It involves listening to God, listening to Scripture, listening in community, and listening to the people entrusted to our care. And when we do that, we have the freedom to act in any way that conforms to God's reconciling acts—that is, in any way so that we love God, love neighbor, care for the marginalized, and enact the Sermon on the Mount.

We have the first requirement for a Christian innovation process. It must begin with listening: listening to God, listening to Scripture, listening in community, and listening to the people entrusted to our care.[19] We will call that kind of listening *systematic listening*. (For a summary of ideas on systematic listening, see the appendix.)

Practical Theology

Anyone who reads Scripture knows that the Bible was not constructed as a book of rules and guidelines. It is filled with stories about God's people, with prophecy to specific Hebrew kings, and with letters to early Christian congregations. From that treasure trove of material, we Christians discern how to live faithful lives. In fact, there is a branch of theology devoted to determining how to integrate the many voices in Scripture so that we know how to live in the world. It is called practical theology (PT).

There is not room here to go into detail on the depth and breadth of practical theology.[20] But I will use a summary shorthand that I created a decade ago.[21] Think of the process of practical theology as a cycle[22] that has four[23] movements or nodes—four activities we pursue. I will describe each of the four briefly, using four questions I have taken from Richard Osmer, but I could just as easily use any number of similar summaries.[24] Then, later in the chapter, we will revisit each node in more detail.[25]

The four movements of practical theology are description, reflection, construction, and strategy (see figure 6.1). *Description* is a listening task. It involves determining what is happening in all its detail.[26] Osmer summarizes it with the question "What is going on?"[27] The second step in the PT cycle is *reflection*. In it, we gather as many interpretative voices as we can find. We bring Scripture and theology to bear on the situation(s) we have described. We bring scholarly voices from sociology and anthropology. And we gather perspectives from people we trust. Osmer summarizes the reflection stage with the question "Why is it going on?"

The third PT move is *construction*. Out of all these disparate voices and perspectives, at some point, we need to decide on what we want to accomplish. We need a goal—something to aim for. Osmer calls this the normative move because it answers the question "What ought to be going on?" Finally, we need to pursue a *strategy* for accomplishing the goal(s) we just set. Too often Christians meet to talk about an issue and, after hours of debate, decide what they want to do—only to neglect the question of *how* to do it. The strategy move asks, "How might we respond?"

Figure 6.1
Practical Theology Cycle

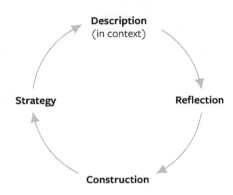

Thus, we have a cyclical process that summarizes the method for practical theological reasoning. Any innovation process we create must take this four-part framework as its structure. But there is one more discipline we need to visit before we can finalize our innovation process.

Human-Centered Design (HCD)

There has been, in the last decade or so, an enormous emphasis on innovation. Most of the attention has been on creating devices like the iPhone or apps like Google Earth. But behind these innovations is a process—a process that is surprisingly focused on meaning making.

In an earlier chapter, we told the story of IDEO, a design company focused on innovation. They were the ones who figured out how to get kids to sit through an MRI by telling them a new story. The people behind IDEO have come up with a process for pursuing innovation. They call it human-centered design (HCD).

Human-centered design has been explained in a number of ways, each with a slight variation. The two most common ways come from IDEO[28] and from Google.[29] Google modified the process to create something it calls a sprint process—where a sprint is a way to condense the HCD process into a single week's work. Human-centered design is also a cycle (see figure 6.2).[30]

The process begins with *empathy*, specifically with an empathetic description of the situation from the perspective of the people who will be using the innovation. So, with the MRI example, the process began with understanding

Figure 6.2
Human-Centered Design

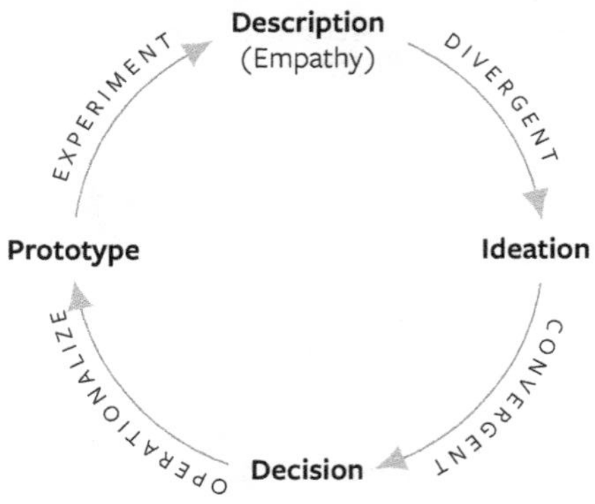

the MRI experience from the perspective of the child—and not from the perspective of the manufacturer or the medical technician. Seeing the process through the eyes of a child transforms the experience. The next step is a divergent move to what they call *ideation*. That's a fancy word for thinking up as many ideas from as many perspectives as possible. A team might approach the MRI problem from a meaning-making perspective, but it could also approach the problem from a technological perspective. But once the team has settled on a meaning-making perspective, they would list as many ways to make meaning as possible. This emphasis on multiple perspectives and multiple ideas is why they call this a "divergent" move. But, after diverging for a while, it becomes necessary to converge to make a *decision* about a clear goal. Ultimately, the team has to narrow all the options down to the best way to convince a child to tolerate an MRI. They eventually decided to tell a story that would allow a kid to see the MRI as an adventure. That leads to the next move, which is to create a *prototype* or a simple version of the envisioned project. In this case, the MRI team mocked up a scenario (like a pirate story) that would invite the child into playing pretend. The final move, of course, is to test the prototype and then begin the process all over again.

A Process for Christian Innovation

So now we have three perspectives that we want to merge in order to create one innovation process: the practice of discernment, practical theology, and human-centered design. Figure 6.3 shows how they converge. We start with

Figure 6.3
Christian Innovation Process

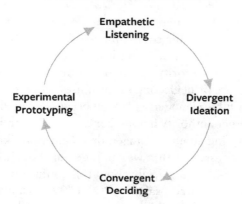

empathetic listening, make the move to divergent ideation, followed by convergent deciding, and then trying an experimental prototype.

To illustrate how all this works together, the rest of the chapter will be an extended example. The example begins with one insight that comes from years of listening to longings and losses. The insight is this: the appropriate biblical response to loss is *lament*. Let me explain what lament means, then use the innovation process to explain how I came to understand lament, and finally show how Erica, our pastor from Florida, took this process for innovation and built her own innovation around lament.

Lament is the appropriate biblical response to loss. A lament allows the people of God (or an individual) to cry out to God in protest—to say directly to God that things are not how they should be—and to call on God to change whatever is amiss. Laments are often raw with emotion and untidy in that they come from the heart and not the head. We Christians can lament both for ourselves and for others, both for individual complaints and for societal concerns. Our model for lament comes from Scripture, especially the psalms of lament and the book of Lamentations.

About half of the psalms are psalms of lament.[31] How do you know which ones are laments? They are the psalms that are not generally read in our churches, the ones that cry out to God in pain and protest. They perhaps are the most honest and raw statements in Scripture. But that is the point. *The message of the psalms of lament is that God can handle your honesty, even and especially if you are angry at God.*[32]

We need models for lament because it would be easy to draw the wrong conclusion about our complaints by thinking that God is like other authority figures we have in our lives. It often is not safe to speak honestly to a human authority figure—especially if we want to accuse that authority figure of neglecting his promises. But God invites that. We need so many biblical models of lament because we easily forget that God is not like other authority figures. For example, we think that if we refrain from speaking about our anger, then God won't know that we are angry. But that assumes that we can hide our thoughts from God. Indeed, there is a psalm specifically about this confusion.

One of the most beloved psalms is Psalm 139 (it is, in fact, my favorite). We do not normally think of it as a psalm of lament. That is because of how it is used in most of our congregations. We selectively edit the psalm so that it loses its ferocity. But if we read the whole psalm, we will see a raw sense of honesty before God.

The first eighteen verses of the psalm are all about how well God knows us. The psalm revels in the "fearful and wonderful" fact that we cannot hide from God. It is wonderful because God will never leave us. But it is fearful because God "knows my thoughts from afar"—even if I have been thinking something that I might otherwise want to hide from God.

Then, after this eighteen-verse description of how well God knows us, there are four verses that we Christians typically skip in our reading of the psalm. If your church reads the psalm aloud, watch how naturally we Christians skip right over these four verses. But these four verses are, in fact, the point of the psalm. "O, that you would slay the wicked," the psalmist pleads in verse 19, and I can give you their names. The psalmist wants God to kill some people for him. He is not hiding the desire from God.

Indeed, the whole point of the first eighteen verses is to say, "Since I cannot hide anything from you, I might as well be honest. I want these people dead." And then the psalm concludes with the famous "Search me, O God, and know my heart" (v. 23). "See if there be any hurtful way in me, and lead me in your everlasting way" (v. 24 alt.). The message of the psalm is clear: you know me so well that I might as well be honest; I want you to kill people for me; and if that is not right, fix me. This is not a polite message. It is raw with emotion. As such, it is not fit for many of our well-mannered worship services. So we edit the psalm; we strip it of its emotion because we cannot handle its honesty. Yet we cannot hide our thoughts from God. God can handle our honesty.

That means we cannot hide our anger from God. What are we to do when we think that God is not doing what God promised to do, when we think that things are not the way God said they should be? We are invited (called? commanded?) to take those thoughts directly to God. There are so many models of psalms of lament because we need a biblical example to legitimate our emotional outbursts.

The psalms of lament exist because God knows that we humans do not trust authority figures to handle our anger well. In those days, it was totally expected that a king might kill anyone who displeased him (e.g., Saul throws a spear at David) or told him what he did not want to hear (ask the prophet Nathan about that). The psalms of lament provide a language—a script—that allows us to say things to God that we might never say on our own.[33] The psalms of lament provide a model for how to complain rightly to God.

The psalms of lament follow a form—a structure—and that structure contains the elements that separate healthy lament from sinful whining. We are all familiar with how the structure of a statement communicates more than just the words. Think of a business letter. Suppose I get a letter from my bank. It starts out "Dear Scott" and ends "Sincerely." Think of how foolish it would sound if I took those words literally. "Oh, look," I'd say, "my bank calls me 'dear.' They must really love me. Only my family calls me 'dear.' My bank must love me as much as my mother does." That would be ridiculous. "Oh, and look at this," I might say, "my bank ends the letter with 'sincerely.' Now I know they are being sincere when they call me a dear." It would be comically naive to take the opening and closing of the letter at face value. The structure communicates as much as (or more than) the words. It is the same with psalms. The structure is a message, just as the words are. These psalms follow a format. Traditionally, a psalm of lament has these parts: (1) the opening address, (2) the complaint, (3) the statement of trust, (4) the petition for help, and (5) the vow of praise.

The most famous use of a psalm of lament comes when Jesus is hanging on the cross. He cries out, "My God, my God, why have you forsaken me?" In so doing, Jesus is not asking a philosophical question or wondering about what God has in mind with the crucifixion. He is quoting the first line (the opening address) of Psalm 22—a psalm of lament. Just as you or I might invoke a song by quoting the first line ("Amazing grace, how sweet the sound" or "O say, can you see?"), Jesus invokes the entire psalm by its opening line at a moment when he does not have time to say the whole thing.

Psalm 22 is a powerful example of lament. The complaint in verse 1— "Why are you so far from saving me, so far from my cries of anguish?"—is followed by a statement of trust: "Yet you are enthroned as the Holy One, . . . the one Israel praises." There are requests for help, "Do not be far from me. . . . Rescue me"; and promises of praise, "I will declare your name to my people." The psalm is particularly appropriate for Jesus's experience on the cross: "I am poured out like water, and all my bones are out of joint. . . . All my bones are on display; people stare and gloat over me. They divide my clothes among them and cast lots for my garments." And it ends with a note of hope: "They will proclaim his righteousness, declaring to a people yet unborn: He has done it!" The lament of Psalm 22 is just the right message for Jesus as he suffers. He just does not have the energy to quote the whole thing as he suffers. So he simply uses the first line. Even Jesus—especially Jesus—uses a psalm of lament to cry out to God in the midst of loss.

I understand that many congregations are not used to giving God their honest complaints. But the psalms include both rejoicing and lament. When we gather in worship, it seems to me we should talk to God the way the psalms talk to God. Some portions of the service should allow us to rejoice with those who rejoice, and some portions should allow us to weep with those who weep. The appropriate biblical response to loss is lament.

As I spent time listening to the losses of the people entrusted to my care— and as I came to see the importance of Christian practices—I began to wonder how we might rediscover the Christian practice of lament in order to help our people make spiritual sense of their losses.

----------●----------

For the rest of the chapter, we will work through this example of lament, using the innovation process. The goal will be to illustrate the process and to give one more example—one more shared story of hope—for how we might make spiritual sense of our people's losses.

Hanging over every innovation process is one question or another. Answering this question is the reason for doing the innovation in the first place. Earlier we looked at other examples: IDEO asking how to create an MRI for children,[34] and Ralph Winter asking if the age of missions was ending.

When working through innovation, we call that opening question "How might we?" (HMW).[35] "How might we create an MRI that children can tolerate?" asked the design firm IDEO in an earlier chapter. "How might we understand the role of missions now that there are Christians in almost every country in the world?" Ralph Winter asked in the same chapter. In this chapter we ask, "How might we use the biblical practice of lament to help young people make spiritual sense of their losses?"

Each of the three words are important: *How. Might. We.* The word "how" is important because the result of the innovation process must be more than a goal. It has to be a plan for *how* to accomplish that goal. Too often in Christian circles we talk about a problem without making (or executing) a plan to do anything about it; the talking makes us feel better, and we move on. The innovation process is interested in talking only insofar as it leads to action. The word "might" is important because it emphasizes the many options available. We *might* do it this way, or perhaps we *might* do it that way. A significant part of the process involves listing many, many reflections on the problem. The word "we" is important because it emphasizes that this is a communal process. As you will see, the kind of reflection that innovation requires works much better in community. Of course, this fits with the Christian practice of discernment, which is almost always a communal process.[36] How might we _____? The HMW that will occupy us in this chapter is this: How might we use the biblical practice of lament to help young people make spiritual sense of their losses? As we pursue this HMW, we will work our way around the innovation cycle.

You will recall that we built a four-part cycle for working our way through the innovation process. This example will follow those four steps. Perhaps as you see the steps in action, they will make more sense to you. The steps are (1) empathetic listening, (2) divergent ideation, (3) convergent deciding, and (4) experimental prototyping. To make the example more specific, let me talk through an experience I had a couple of years ago. I have been working closely with the Fuller Youth Institute (FYI) on two parallel projects. One is called Youth Ministry Innovation (YMI), and the other is called Ministry Innovation with Young Adults (MIYA). The projects use the process we have outlined here to help cohorts of youth ministers innovate new ways to minister to youth and young adults. As a way to concretize our example, I will walk through the process, highlighting my own thinking as I brought the practice of lament to our work with teenagers. In other words, we will recast the HMW to be even more specific: How might we use the biblical practice of lament to help young people make spiritual sense of their losses?

The purpose of this chapter is to provide a process that you can repeat again and again in your context in order to recalibrate the church. The first time someone goes through the process, a question often comes up. People working through the procedure notice that the whole process depends on listening. That often causes people to ask, "How do I learn to listen well?" Before we go any further in describing the process of innovation, we will take time to describe how to learn to listen so as to be transformed. If leadership really does begin with listening, it is the necessary place to start.

Preparation: Learn to Listen Well

This section will offer an analogy for how to learn to listen so as to be transformed. Then it will offer some steps to help you and your congregation learn to listen well. The steps are these: (1) establish rules to live by; (2) practice living out those rules every chance you get; (3) measure what matters; (4) establish accountability; and (5) start where you have jurisdiction. But before we get to the steps, consider the following analogy.

When I went off to do my PhD at Yale, I was a poor writer. This was not just a suspicion on my part: I had the documentation to prove it. When I was in seminary, I did a research project that became part of a national study. The national study group wanted to publish my research. The project was what got me into Yale. I was terribly proud—at least until I read the letter offering to publish my study. It said that the research was good but that the writing was so abysmal that they would pay for an editor to help me rewrite it. Ouch! So I arrived at Yale thoroughly intimidated and a bit embarrassed. Then it got worse. I discovered that each of my advisers had recently been nominated for the Pulitzer Prize. I was in so much trouble.

Then I realized I could use their work to my advantage. I made copies of everything that each of them had written and began to take their writing apart. I talked to each of them about what made for good writing. Eventually I came up with four rules. I knew that if I could master those four rules, I would be a clear writer.[37] But knowing the rules was not enough. I had to learn to practice them. So every time I wrote something—an email, a memo, a sermon, or a note to my wife—I tried to practice the four rules.[38] Over the course of months, I got to the point where I felt good about my writing. In short, I discovered some rules and then assiduously tried to make them instinctive.

That takes us back to the question of how to learn to listen well. You can learn to listen well this way. Find some rules to live by, and then practice them every chance you get. Notice how this is a way of planting language in your own life. You water it regularly and ask God to make it bear fruit.

Establish Rules to Live By

Here are seven rules for listening well to the longings and losses of the people entrusted to your care. The rules for listening build on our long discussion in chapter 3. The rules are as follows: (1) listen to the people entrusted to your care, (2) listen for longings and losses, (3) listen without wanting control, (4) listen across difference, (5) listen with empathy, (6) listen for Big Lies, and (7) listen in order to be transformed.

Practice Every Chance You Get

For almost everyone, any week is full of opportunities to listen. You encounter people all the time. Perhaps you go to a meeting early and sit around with people before the meeting; use the time to start a conversation about longings and losses. When you sit with your spouse or kids at the dinner table, practice listening without wanting control. Perhaps you run into acquaintances in line at Starbucks and can think of them as people entrusted to your care, tumbleweeds that have blown into your life. If you end up next to another dad while waiting for your daughter's soccer game to start, practice listening long enough that you can hear a Big Lie. Or perhaps you run into someone near the copy machine at work; practice seeing if you can listen to them long enough to hear something that transforms you. Use every opportunity to practice listening.

Instead of talking about the weather with those you meet, ask them about something that you think might matter to them: their kids, their parents, their vacation, their hobbies—anything that gets them telling stories about things that make a difference to them. Then make a point to remember what you hear; that makes the next conversation easier. For example, if someone shares about a medical concern or speaks about ailing parents, take the time to remember so that you can ask them about it the next time you see them. If you make this a priority in every encounter, it will eventually become a habit—a way of seeing the world, a way of seeing each person you encounter as a person potentially entrusted to your care.

We can summarize the last few paragraphs in three steps: (1) start where it is safe, (2) look for ways to listen, and (3) keep what you hear (write it down, type it into your phone).

Measure What Matters

There is a saying, "What gets measured gets done." If you are serious about learning to develop a cultivated instinct like listening, you need to quantify the work you want to do in order to get better. For example, if you want to get stronger, you might say, "I will add ten pushups a week until I can do one hundred of them," or "I will do yoga twice a week." Do not accept good intentions (as if talking about listening will make you a good listener).[39] And do not accept a substitute for the practice of listening.[40] You want to measure how often you have tried to implement the rules you created for yourself. For listening, these are some metrics you might consider: the number of people you listened to and the number of stories you collected.

Establish Accountability

The best way to establish accountability is to make a commitment to someone you trust, preferably someone who has some kind of authority with you. It could be a friend or a coworker. It could be someone who works for you—that is, someone you do not want to disappoint. But it works best if you do it with your boss. Here's how you might go about it.

Start by writing out how listening to the people entrusted to your care is crucial to the work you need to do (write it out so that you can show it to someone). You may need to be explicit about which people are entrusted to your care. Once you have a clear sense of how listening is crucial, make an appointment with your boss. At that appointment, explain that you want to become a better listener because listening is crucial to your job. Then propose two metrics for measuring your progress as you practice listening: people and stories. Commit to meeting with at least two people a week for the specific purpose of listening in order to be transformed (although you may not tell them that is why you are meeting). Commit to gathering at least two stories of longing and loss from each person. And commit to writing the stories down so that you don't forget them. Then ask your boss to hold your feet to the fire. The next time you meet your boss, come with a sample report: how many people, how many stories (only count the ones you write down), and a write-up of the best story you heard about longing and loss. Then repeat that process until such listening becomes second nature.

A common retort at this point is "But I don't have time to do that." That is like saying that you don't have time to treat your people as anything but a stereotype, that you don't have time to listen to the most important things in the lives of the people whom God calls you to serve, and that you don't have time to do something that you just established is crucial to your job. You may need to negotiate what you will leave undone in order to become good at listening. But you cannot neglect listening to the people entrusted to your care.

Start Where You Have Jurisdiction

If you are a boss, go over this material with your team. Commit to doing it together. Hold each other accountable. Inspire each other by sharing what you have learned (respecting, of course, any confidentialities).

If the idea of approaching others intimidates you, then start where you can. Start with family or friends. Ask people if they would be willing to help you out on a project you are doing. Then slowly expand to include more and more people in an ever-broadening circle.

One more thing. Sometimes people ask how they can do this if they do not have authority in their congregation or if their congregation as a whole does not listen well. Then build what Jim Collins calls a "pocket of greatness."[41] If you are a missions pastor, make sure you and your team listen well. If you are a small-group leader, start by listening to your small group, then mobilize them to listen to the people entrusted to their care. If you are a computer programmer sitting in a cubicle, then listen well to the people who share your office. Every grouping can build a pocket of greatness.

So there you have it: five steps you can take to learn to listen well.

1. Establish rules to live by.
   - Listen to the people entrusted to your care.
   - Listen for longings and losses.
   - Listen without wanting control.
   - Listen across difference.
   - Listen with empathy.
   - Listen for Big Lies.
   - Listen in order to be transformed.
2. Practice every chance you get.
3. Measure what matters.
4. Establish accountability. Make a commitment to someone you trust.
5. Start where you can.

Figure 6.4
Alternative Expression of the Innovation Process

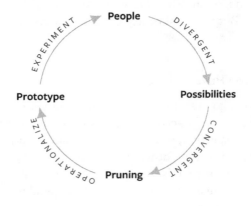

Moving through the Innovation Process

Now that we have prepared to listen well, we can take a closer look at the four steps that make up the innovation process. Figure 6.4 provides an alternative way to express the steps in the innovative process. The first step in the innovation process is empathetic listening, which involves the following: listening to God, listening to Scripture, listening in community, and listening to the people entrusted to our care.

By beginning with a commitment to *listening to God*, we honor the commitments of the Christian practice of discernment. When I begin an innovation process, I start by reflecting on the following as a way to listen to God. I reflect on who God is, what God desires, and how God responds to the human condition. In this case, God is the one who created all people in God's own image, who is grieved by our sin (especially by the way the effects of sin destroy our lives), who sent his Son as an example of what God intends for humanity (even arranging for that Son to be raised in a human family just like any teenager), who allowed his Son to suffer a shameful death on the cross, who then vindicated that Son by raising him from the dead, and who sent the Holy Spirit so that we might have a comforter and a counselor. This God spared nothing in order to provide for the people entrusted to his care. God is the one who desires to mold our people (even and especially teenagers) into the image that they were created to be, who desires for them to experience hope, and who desires for them to be in community with other Christians. God responds to the human condition with sacrificial love, with grace, and with the

Holy Spirit. So, as I began my ruminations on this HMW (*How might we?*), I started by reflecting on God and especially how who God is and what God desires are not what young people hear from the church. I was particularly struck by the need for a gospel of grace at a time when young people hear an almost-Pharisaical emphasis on rules that they should follow.

Listening to God, of course, leads directly to *listening to Scripture*. This is where the emphasis on lament becomes important. About half of the psalms are psalms of lament. They are psalms that cry out to God. As the renowned Old Testament scholar John Goldingay puts it, the psalms of lament allow God's people to shake their fists at God and say, "This is not right."[42] I am particularly taken by two particular psalms. Psalm 139 emphasizes the freedom for honesty with God—and the foolishness of thinking that we can hide anything from God. And Psalm 22 provides the language of lament, especially when paired with Jesus's use of the psalm to lament while dying on the cross. The second part of empathetic listening is listening to Scripture.

We are also called to *listen in community*. The New Testament scholar Luke Timothy Johnson, in his study of discernment in the New Testament, emphasizes that discernment happens in community and that discernment is for the purpose of building up the community.[43] As I was working on the HMW around lament for teenagers, I spent a lot of time listening to the people who know a lot more than I do about young people. I met regularly with the scholars at the Fuller Youth Institute, and I sat with the youth ministers who come through FYI. More importantly, I tested my ideas with them before I solidified the ideas. That kept me from some foolish errors. For example, I recall that Kara Powell (the head of FYI) suggested that I was becoming trapped by my own narrow experience with youth ministry. I knew the youth ministry that shaped me as a teenager and the ones that shaped my children. But I did not have a lot of experience with ministries that were different from the ones I knew. That's what inspired me to spend time listening to youth ministers from diverse contexts. It also pushed me to take advantage of gatherings at Fuller where I could listen to persons of color and those from social circumstances that were not like mine. Listening needs to take place in community.

Empathetic Listening to People

All this listening, then, sets up *listening to the people entrusted to our care*, which is the most important listening we do in preparing for innovation. The purpose of starting with empathetic listening is to ensure that every innovation responds to the lived experience—the longings and losses—of the people entrusted to our care, people who live in a very specific context and with deeply contextualized experiences. Grounding our work in the context of our people (and not in the context of our congregations, which can be out of touch with the life situations of the people entrusted to our care) ensures that we do not impose our own agendas. We need to hear our people when they are not at church. Each person has a church persona and also a real-life persona. If I am going to reach the things that keep people awake at night, then I need to get beyond the parts of themselves that they present at church. I must listen so that I can be transformed by what I hear.

So, since our sample HMW focuses on lament for young people, I spent some time listening to high school seniors from two graduating classes. Both groups were composed of high school girls bound for college. Each group was at a middle-class high school, although five of the six girls had working-class parents. I was especially interested in what they were thinking about college and noted that for them this was a time of great longing and of surprising angst and loss.

The phrase I took away from these observations was "anxious, busy, and stressed." The groups had some overachievers and some more average students. The overachievers felt burdens with schoolwork and with planning out the rest of their lives just so they could pick a college. "In order to pick a college," one reasoned, "I have to pick a major. And in order to pick a major, I have to pick a career." It felt like the only way to take one step was to plan out all the steps. The more average students also felt stressed. They knew they wanted to go to college (if for no other reason than to get out of the house) but did not really feel qualified to decide which one.

I was particularly taken by the ways they experienced loss. I could easily have focused on longing. After all, these groups of young women regularly talked about the future and expected good things in the future. Yet I was struck by the energy (and angst) in their voices when they talked about their fears, their worries, and their sense of feeling overwhelmed. In short, *the losses carried more weight for them than the longings.* That is what I mean by "anxious, busy, and stressed."

Our *empathetic listening must be systematic listening.* In the appendix, there is a short process that your team can follow to ensure that your listening is systematic.

The "empathy" part of empathetic listening is particularly important here. You will recall that Brené Brown (following Theresa Wiseman) describes the characteristics of empathy, one of which is particularly important when listening to teenagers. "Staying out of judgment" is crucial but often difficult for adults listening to teens.[44] The problem is that we want to judge them. We want to control them. ("Empathy cannot want control.") We want to point out ways they contribute to their own pain and loss. All of that is absolutely true. And it is irrelevant.

If we are going to follow the model of Jesus, we will not have any examples of his pronouncing judgment on people in pain—especially those who are on the margins of society. He has no qualms about speaking judgment to Pharisees, to government leaders, and even to his disciples. But to people in pain, he responds with compassion and grace. Since the message of the psalms of lament is that "God can handle your honesty," we have to ask ourselves if we in the church can handle honest teenagers.

This is why it is so important to begin our discernment with a focus on God. In lament, we (the people entrusted to God's care) are invited to indict God—even though God has done nothing wrong. God can handle our honesty. God does not need to correct us. We cry out to God as if God is to blame for human sin. Rather than correcting us, God provides the language for us to cry out all the more. God meets our pain with compassion, even when our pain becomes misplaced anger. We then, those who follow the God of compassion, must do the same when we hear teenagers talk about pain and loss. We need to recognize that, at some level, some of the complaints are misplaced. But that is beside the point. The point is the pain, the anger, the angst, and the loss. We begin our innovation process with empathetic listening.

Divergent Ideation to Discern Possibilities

If innovation is measured in quantity rather than quality, then the process of generating lots of ideas in a short time is called "divergent ideation." It is divergent because the ideas take us in many different directions and not along a single path; indeed, ideas at this stage often contradict each other. That is perfectly all right. Our goal is to have many choices along many paths. We stole the word "ideation" from IDEO because they use it to mean the act of coming up with lots of ideas. "Ideation" means generating many ideas. Simply put, "divergent ideation" is the *process of quickly listing lots of disparate ideas that fly in many directions.*

This is where we embody the idea that quantity leads to quality—that having many decent ideas is better than having one great idea. To further convince you about how quantity creates quality, let me tell you a story from a book called *Creative Confidence,* written by the founders of IDEO. They describe an enterprising ceramics teacher who conducted an experiment. He divided the pottery class into two parts. To one group, he said that they would be graded on the quality of the one best piece they created in the semester. So that group toiled meticulously on their one item, seeking quality. To the other group, he said that they would be graded on the total amount of clay that they used in the semester. So that group burned through many projects, making a new one from scratch every time the class met. Which group produced the highest quality work? The one that aimed for quality, or the one that aimed for quantity? It was the group that aimed for quantity.[45] Every iteration—every attempt—taught the student a little more. In the end, *quantity creates quality*.

The current example is to think of as many uses of lament for young people as we can generate. To do that, we will use a process that the innovators at both IDEO and Google have created to encourage the rapid creation of diverse ideas, to encourage quantity over quality.[46] It is called the "eight-minute exercise" (Google refers to it as the "crazy eights exercise"). The concept is simple. Pick a topic for which you want to think up lots of ideas. For our first round of brainstorming (there will be more), we want to list everything we know about lament. Fold a piece of paper so that it has eight boxes. (Usually that means taking a piece of 8.5 × 11 paper and folding it once hot-dog style and twice hamburger style). Then set a timer for one minute. Take that minute to fill a box on the paper with an idea and all the ways that the idea can help you. When the timer buzzes, hit it again and repeat the process by filling in the next box with a different idea. In that way, you develop eight ideas in eight minutes. (For reasons that will become clear in a moment, we usually don't have people write directly on the paper. Instead, we have them write their ideas on sticky notes and then put each note in one of the eight boxes.) The ideas are usually different approaches to the same situation. You write out the idea and then use the rest of the minute to list all the ways you think that the idea might help you. It is not a problem if this brainstorming process takes us in competing directions (i.e., if the ideation process is divergent) because later in the innovation process, we will narrow the options down to one goal.

There is something powerful about the momentum of moving from one idea to the next after only a minute. We have worked this process with over a hundred groups of Christian leaders. One of the common themes is that at some point a leader becomes stuck. They just don't think that they have eight good ideas. That is fine. Just write whatever you think up, even if you think it is a bad idea. Again and again we have heard that leaders thought they were tapped out of ideas after, say, the fourth minute, but the leaders who stick to the process often report that their best ideas often come in the sixth or seventh minute. In other words, the momentum of the process carries them to their best ideas after they think they have run out of ideas. The goal is to keep writing. Put down as much information as you can in the one minute. At the end of the exercise, you will have eight divergent ideas.

Let me illustrate with lament. I'll begin with what the eight boxes might say if I did an eight-minute exercise listing what I know about lament. Then I'll explain them. (Remember that they don't have to be good ideas or related to each other in any way; you just want to keep generating ideas.)

Psalm 139 • skip past lament part • God knows me; might as well be honest	John Goldingay • wife (Ann) had MS (personal) • now laments for Darfur (far off)	Leslie Allen (sick people) • commentary on Lamentations • OT scholar • chaplain at hospital	Soong-Chan Rah (the oppressed) • also commentary on Lamentations • justice
"God can handle your honesty, even and especially when angry at God"	Form Criticism • combines complaint with trust	Psalm 22 (Jesus: "My God . . .") • like "Amazing grace how sweet the sound . . ."	Lament versus grumbling • Psalms versus book of Numbers • difference is "trust"

Let me explain what I wrote in the boxes because they each reflect part of the listening that comes early in the innovation process.

I listed two psalms (Ps. 139 and Ps. 22). This is an extension of the listening to Scripture that I did in the first part of the innovation process. Not only did I read these psalms, but I also read some scholars who write about the psalms. Specifically, I learned from these scholars that the psalms follow a format (like a business letter). And that form has five parts. I am particularly intrigued by Patrick Miller[47] and John Goldingay,[48] Old Testament scholars who describe the form of the lament psalm.

I listed the work of three scholars—one who laments about personal pain (his wife's multiple sclerosis) and about injustice far away (Darfur), one who laments about the pain of the patients he visits in the hospital, and one who laments the injustice that his immigrant and African American neighbors experience. Let me explain a little about each one.

John Goldingay is one of the world's leading Old Testament scholars. But his encounter with the psalms of lament is intensely personal. He describes how his wife, Ann, had a debilitating case of multiple sclerosis and, after many years of deteriorating, became noncommunicative.[49] John used to push her everywhere in her wheelchair—to class, to faculty meetings, to church—even as she became a shell of herself. John describes how in the evenings he would pray lament on her behalf. He says that he would shake his fist at God and cry out, "This is not how things should be." And he would hold God to

God's promises for a better world. Eventually, after Ann passed away, John married a woman named Kathleen. Now, in the evenings, John and Kathleen pray lament for the people suffering in Darfur, where Kathleen's daughter ministers. Goldingay prayed lament about an intensely personal situation and now prays about more public concerns. He uses lament to speak honestly and directly to God, even in anger.

The scholar Soong-Chan Rah wrote a commentary on the book of Lamentations that uses each chapter to describe the situation in urban America.[50] Dr. Rah, who grew up in urban Baltimore, has ministered in multiracial settings in Boston and Chicago. He uses the language of Lamentations to express the pain of poverty and racism in urban America.

Meanwhile, the Old Testament scholar Leslie Allen wrote a similar Lamentations commentary about his experience volunteering as a hospital chaplain after he retired from teaching Old Testament at Fuller Seminary.[51] Each chapter begins and ends with a discussion of a specific hospital situation where someone is suffering. It uses the language of Lamentations to express a Christian response to the pain of deteriorating health and the loss that comes with death.

Whether it involves intensely personal pain (like MS) or very public suffering (like the experience of African Americans in urban America), whether it involves pain experienced across the ocean in Darfur or the plight of the sick in a local hospital, the practice of lament allows people to cry out to God—to say to God that this suffering is not what God intends, and to call on God to do what God has promised: to end suffering and make things right.

In my crazy-eight exercise on lament, I also took time to distinguish between the complaint that the book of Psalms calls lament and the complaint that the book of Numbers calls grumbling. There is an enormous difference. We know from the Psalms that God invites lament, yet from Numbers we know that the penalty for grumbling is forty years of wandering in the wilderness. So it is important to know which is which. The difference, it turns out, is embedded in the form or structure of the lament. The difference is trust. Psalm 139 says, essentially, I trust you so much that I will be completely honest with you; the complaint in verse 1 of Psalm 22 is followed immediately by a statement of trust in verse 2. Complaining to God out of trust is welcome; it is the honesty that comes as part of true relationship. The grumbling of Numbers is the opposite. The children of Israel have lost trust in God. They complain about the manna that God provides for them; later in Numbers, they say that it was better back in Egypt. They have lost trust and complain. Both the Psalms and the book of Numbers use the word "complaint." Yet it is clear that God welcomes the trusting complaint of lament and that the untrusting complaint of grumbling will get you forty years. My crazy-eight note is a reminder that any use I might make of lament must include the proper form so that it automatically includes a statement of trust.

As part of my crazy eights exercise, I also listed some of my own ideas, such as this: "The message of the psalms of lament is that God can handle your honesty." This comes from teaching lament to first-year ministry students. As I have them write their own laments, it is common for students to have a fear about being honest. They project their mental models about human authority figures onto God. They think that perhaps God will like them better if they never say aloud what they are feeling internally. But the power of Psalm 139 is to remind us that God already knows and does not condemn us. Rather, God invites us to bring even our darkest secrets to God in faith.

Those are eight ideas about lament. The way I have written them up, it would be easy to think that this kind of divergent ideation can take place isolated from community. But the crazy eights exercise is only the beginning. When I work this process, I have groups do the eight-minute exercise individually, but then I have them process it in community. Usually, people are in groups of three or four. As they do the eight-minute exercise, I don't have them write directly on their papers. Instead, I have them write their ideas on sticky notes and then put the notes into the eight boxes on the paper.[52] The reason I do this is that it helps the groups to process the eight-minute ideas. The group of perhaps four gathers in front of a blank poster board or whiteboard. One by one, they explain their own idea briefly, then stick the note on the board. The next person who comes along either adds ideas to the clusters of ideas that already exist or creates a new group. After all four people take their turns, the group decides if they need to combine any of the clusters. Now we have thirty-two ideas (four people and eight ideas each) arrayed into clusters of ideas about lament.

But none of the ideas are necessarily about young people. The HMW we are working on for this chapter is this: How might we use the biblical practice of lament to help young people make spiritual sense of loss? So the next step is to work a second eight-minute exercise that focuses, this time, on how lament might show up in the lives of young people. The goal here is that, once I have heard the ideas I have generated about lament and ideas that have come from my compatriots, I will be ready to think about how to bring lament into the lives of young people.

Here is a replica of the eight ideas that I generated. They may need a little explanation.

Lenten prayer calendar • like One Great Hour of Sharing calendar	Bookmark for the Bible • "God can handle honesty" • list psalms of lament	Poster in youth room "The message of the psalms of lament is that God can handle your honesty . . ."	Write song
Special service of lament • like All Souls' Day	Use corporate prayer to memorize lament	Wailing Wall (like Nate Stratman)	Write a lament

Some of the ideas are quite simple, such as a bookmark or a poster in the youth room that would capture key ideas. These ideas are designed to build new mental models that can replace the old ones that a teenager might have. Some of the ideas provide a special event or setting for specific lament. There is, for example, a tradition in some branches of Christianity to take All Souls' Day as a way to remember loved ones who have died in the previous year. It would be a short step to turn some portion of that service into lament for the pain felt by the loved ones left behind. Some ideas involve a form for modeling lament. This illustrates how speculative these crazy-eight ideas can be. I think it would be tremendously powerful to write a lament song that would be part of a youth group's regular time of singing. But I really don't have any of the skills to write such a song. I put the idea down, and I hope that someone else in my community has the ability to run with it.

One idea on my crazy-eight sheet requires a little more explanation. I wrote "Wailing Wall." This comes from a conversation with Rev. Nate Stratman, who was then at First Presbyterian Church of Colorado Springs. He heard me talk about the power of lament and the need for young people to express their losses. So he went back to his congregation and used painted Styrofoam to create a Wailing Wall for their youth room. Then he provided his people with little slips of paper and small pencils. They could write anonymous messages and slip them between the cracks in the wall. They were told that adult volunteers would read the papers and lift their statements up to God. Sometimes the teens wrote requests out of their pain. Other times they wrote complaints. Some just emoted without stating any specific situation. But they knew that the adults who read it (and the God whom those adults served) could understand and express that pain. It dramatically increased the honesty in the youth group. Something else happened as well. Eventually the adults in the congregation heard about it and asked to participate. As a result, a Wailing Wall was incorporated into a Sunday morning service in the sanctuary. This example was really powerful to me because it illustrated how important it is for people to use their whole bodies in lament.

Before we leave this part of the innovation cycle about ideation, I need to say one more thing about the process of generating many diverse ideas. *Fear makes ideas small.* When working this process with groups, leaders might self-edit. They can sometimes think that there is no way their congregation (or their bosses) would allow a particular idea. So they don't go there. We often need to invite leaders to go through a third round of the eight-minute exercise. We ask them to take their fears and think through them. We don't tell them that their fears are unfounded; leaders often have good reasons for their fears. But we ask that for the next eight minutes, they put those fears aside and imagine ideas that go beyond their fears. This habit is important because fear makes ideas small.

Those are eight ideas about ways to bring lament into youth ministry. We can combine the ideas with the previous table of ideas in any number of ways. So the two tables together account for more than sixteen ideas. Once they have been processed in a group of, say, four people, we might have sixty-four ideas about how to connect lament to youth ministry.

Those sixty-four ideas are a gift, but they are also a burden. At some point, we who lead God's people need to narrow all these ideas down into a goal to pursue. To do that, we move from diverging to converging.

Convergent Deciding via Pruning

If the purpose of divergent ideation is to list as many separate ideas as possible, the purpose of convergent deciding is to weave the best of those ideas into a single goal. That goal will then be the outcome we hope to test when (in the next phase) we engage in experimental prototyping. In short, we can describe the final two steps of innovation as deciding *what* we want to do and then prototyping *how* we might do it. This section will describe the deciding-what part, and the next section will explain how to prepare a prototype.

The first convergent step is to decide which ideas to pursue. There are too many ideas to try to enact them all. The best way to proceed is to pick one promising idea and then try to use it as the spine to hold other ideas together. Then perhaps begin again by selecting another idea as the spine and seeing if it might work to connect with other ideas.

This is a process that usually takes place in community. The group of perhaps four who are working on the problem go over the clusters of ideas that they generated as they clumped sticky notes together in the divergent phase. I have done this with groups many times. What happens in most cases is that one or two ideas naturally bubble to the top. They become the spine around which the group then builds everything else.

I recall one situation, however, when a group could not decide. They felt very strongly about two ideas, but the ideas were incompatible. So they negotiated and debated for quite some time. That is when they asked for help. I suggested they simply try out both ideas. At first they were reluctant. They really believed that to do the process "correctly," they had to pick the best idea. I finally convinced them to take a bit of time to run with the first one and then take time to develop the other idea. The momentum is part of the process. I told them to just keep moving forward. As expected, after they developed each idea, the momentum led them to pursue one idea instead of the other. There was just more energy about it.

It would be wise, then, to use the lament illustration in order to demonstrate how one might narrow down divergent ideas into one goal. Usually this would happen in community. But for the sake of demonstration, I will continue the example here.

I needed to narrow down the number of ideas. In my opinion, the best ideas from the lament chart (i.e., the ones that I wanted to weave together) are as follows:

- Laments can be personal (as for Goldingay's wife's MS), far off (as for Darfur), about sickness (like Allen), or about justice (like Rah). I would expect that the more personal they are, the more difficult those laments are to share with other people.

- Laments have a form (carrying both complaint and trust), and that form prevents good lament (like the psalms) from being bad grumbling (like the children of Israel).

- Learning/using lament in the youth group setting will likely precede learning it in small groups or individual prayer.

- I really like the phrase "God can handle your honesty" because young people are surrounded by so many people who cannot handle honesty.

Then I experimented with different ways of arranging the ideas. While not as formal as an eight-minute exercise, I tried to walk rapidly through a number of ideas for arranging the disparate ideas into a coherent whole. I happened to do it by taking a single sheet of paper and using different colored pens to write up different ideas. I like the way the varied colors let me see at a glance that there are different possibilities on the same sheet of paper. But using different colors is not required. The point is to try your hand at arranging the pieces into a single idea.

When I experimented with different ways to assemble the ideas, I noticed that one idea kept coming up. The fact that it kept coming up taught me that it was probably more important to me than I had realized. Every time I took out a piece of scratch paper to experiment with how I might arrange the ideas, I always pictured the same location. Our church has a designated room where the high school group meets on Wednesday nights and where the middle school group meets on Sunday nights. All my ideas seemed to take place there (rather than in a small group or with teenagers doing something at home) because I want to be with them when they first experience lament. I don't want them to be in a small group or other setting where I cannot observe their response. Indeed, I want to introduce them to lament and have them experience communal lament for an extended period of time before I send them off on their own. That insight allowed me to put together the following goal.

I want to use the praise and worship portion of our youth gatherings to encourage teenagers to memorize a lament. I think a young person would find it intimidating to pray for their own deepest losses, at least at first. So I aim to introduce the lament by repeating the exercise weekly over time so that our youth become accustomed to praying the lament about other people before I expect them to be comfortable praying for their own losses. Eventually I will teach them to write their own laments about personal things, including anger at God. That is the goal I hope to pursue.

I picture building a time of lament into each youth group meeting. To do that, I have to plant some vocabulary. Before singing each week, I might say that God invites us to celebrate with those who are feeling joy and to lament with those who are feeling pain or loss. I would tell the group, "We are going to learn to talk to God the way the psalms talk to God." Part of being in community, I would say, is celebrating with grateful people even when we feel sad and lamenting with another's pain even when we are feeling joy.[53] For the first few weeks, we would pray over things that are far away (and thus not particularly personal), things like floods in Asia or fires in California. Then, as they get used to the language of lament, we might pray for something closer to home—things like injustices that they can list or people whom they know. And, after a time, we can make it even more personal. Perhaps they have a family member who is sick or in a situation that galls them. We will pray lament for that—all the while using the same words. Finally, we might ask them if they have anything in their own lives for which they might like to lament. At first that can be a silent prayer. But eventually I'd want to invite them to pray their lament out loud if they so choose.

Only after weeks and months of praying while using the same lament would I give them a chance to write their own lament. I would introduce them to the five-part structure and then, perhaps, give them some samples. Here I am inspired by Mad Libs, the fill-in-the-blank party game. I would give them the first half of a sentence and then let them fill in the rest. It might say, "God, I look around and I am angry because _____, but I want you to know that I still trust you because I can remember when _____." The convergence process, thus, led me to come up with a way to bring together the disparate ideas I generated in the divergence phase.

Experimental Prototyping

The purpose of the final phase is to come up with a prototype. A prototype is a sample that can be tested.[54] For example, if I wanted a prototype for a song, I might come up with a bit of the melody and a few of the words. If I wanted a prototype for a website, I might use PowerPoint to create what the first part of the website would look like, and then use the next PowerPoint slide to simulate what would happen when someone clicked on the first page. If I developed a prototype of a mission trip, I might create a PowerPoint with a series of scenes showing what would happen during the preparation stage and what would happen once the group left town. The goal of the prototyping phase is to be able to map out what would happen when someone does the thing for which I created a prototype.

There are three parts to the prototyping phase. In the first, we storyboard the process of what we picture happening. In the second, we build what we need so we are ready to engage in a first-step experiment. In the third stage, we make a list of things we will need to do in order to advance the experiment.

To create a storyboard, draw a series of empty boxes on a piece of plain paper (or array a series of sticky notes in rows). In the first box, write out where you are today. In the last box, write out where you want to be at the end. Then fill in the boxes in between. Figure 6.5 shows a representation of my storyboard for the lament project.

I want to create a short, well-written lament that our youth group can use every week. Each week we spend some time singing praises to God. I imagine a short prayer time between some of the songs. I picture using that lament word-for-word every time we pray. I think that their young brains eventually will memorize the lament just because they encounter it again and again. At first, I picture them repeating words that were written for them. Then we will teach them to write their own laments about situations in the world that do not get too close to home. Finally, they will get to the point where they can write their own laments about personal pain and even about their own anger at God.

Figure 6.5
Storyboard on Lament

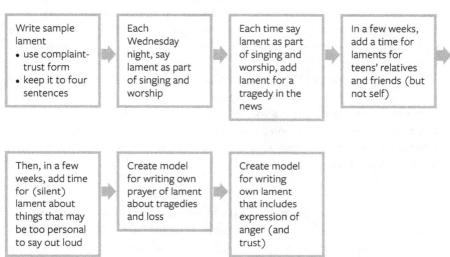

Once we create the storyboard, the next step is to write up the prototype lament. It does not need to be perfect (it's not). It just needs to be something that I can try out in order to get feedback. Here is what I have:

God, there are things in the world that make me sad and even angry.

Right now, I am especially thinking about _____.

Why, God, do you allow this to happen?

It is not right. Please make it stop.

I bring you this honest prayer because I trust you.

After we have the sample lament, we can plan the experimentation phase. In this case, I go back to my team and discuss with them the ideas about lament—specifically asking them to evaluate the ideas by using the criteria we established. Then I invite them to act as wordsmiths with me to produce the sample lament. After a few rounds of revision, I ask them to alpha-test the process. We will not test it yet with young people. I will incorporate the lament into our regular meeting of adult volunteers, and I will invite the youth ministry volunteers to make the lament a part of their own devotions at home. We will provide time to discuss what we have learned by using the lament. Then we will rework the wording of the lament (e.g., we may decide that five sentences are too many or too few). Then, after beta-testing the revised version, we will finally be ready to try it on a Wednesday night. By the way, I think the weakest part of the whole process is also the easiest to fix. I really dislike my first attempt at a sample lament. But that is why it is so important to work in community. I am confident that a group of us can make it much better.

We started with an HMW (i.e., "*How might we* use the biblical practice of lament to help teenagers make spiritual sense of their losses?"), and we proceeded to walk through a four-part innovation cycle—from *empathetic listening* to *divergent ideation* to *convergent deciding* to *experimental prototyping*. So now that we have seen a generic version of the innovation cycle, let us see how it has worked out in someone's life.

----------●----------

Erica is a youth pastor at an Anglican church in Florida. An abbreviated version of her story was presented in chapter 1. In 2017 she visited Pasadena as part of a cohort of pastors who wanted to learn about youth ministry innovation. The project was sponsored by the Fuller Youth Institute. She and her cohort did an online course before they came to California. In it, they learned about meaning-making innovation (chap. 2 above). They learned about the importance of listening to the longings and losses of the people entrusted to their care (chap. 3). They learned about reinventing practices (chap. 5) in order to make spiritual sense of those longings and losses (chap. 4). And they learned about the Christian innovation process that combines practical theology with human-centered design (chap. 6). She also read through this chapter's example of how to use lament with young people.

When she came to California to spend three days working an intensive version of the innovation process, Erica decided that she wanted to focus on lament; specifically, she wanted to engage middle school students in lament.

Before coming to California, she and her team spent hours engaged in empathetic listening. They met regularly with young people over frozen yogurt and at ball games. She listened to them talk about the things that kept them awake at night—things like "homework, fitting in, school stress, sports performance, family dysfunction, and conditional acceptance." Erica summarized all those anxieties around one question: "Am I valuable?" She decided that she wanted her teens to experience "grace-based identity." As she put it, it is about "being known and loved anyway" because that kind of authenticity is "liberating, increases boldness, and provides honest connection."[55] Erica wanted her students to be able to be completely honest with God.

While in California, she worked through the innovation process. Erica and her ministry partner filled out many, many sticky notes with divergent ideas. They went all over the place. She thought about how she might use the Book of Common Prayer because she is at an Anglican church. She thought about how she might use songs—including secular, contemporary songs—to express the angst and anxiety that teenagers feel. And she realized that, if possible, she "wanted to create something physical to symbolize and assist the movement through lament."[56] Erica wanted it all to happen in community. These ideas were the product of her divergent ideation.

Then she had to narrow these options down. This is what we have called convergent deciding. She and her ministry partner decided that they would do two things. They would, over the course of ten weeks, teach these middle schoolers to lament. And second, on the church grounds she would try to build a labyrinth so that the teenagers had a place to walk—a place to contain their lamenting.

She then created a prototype. In this case, she did three things. First, she wrote a simple lament, using almost a Mad Libs style for each of the components of a lament:

- God, I don't understand _____.
- God, please fix _____.
- God, I trust you with my future even if _____.
- God, I will praise you even when _____.

Second, she mapped out a labyrinth on a piece of paper. Third, she roughed out what ten weeks of lessons and practicing lament might look like. She knew she wanted an older adult from the congregation to come and tell stories. And she knew that she wanted to teach about Psalm 22, Psalm 42, and Lamentations. Erica brainstormed song lyrics. She laid out how the teens would start by lamenting for things outside themselves and then, as the weeks progressed, lament about things that were more personal. She decided that it would be important to have a parents' night halfway through in order to assess what was happening.

When she was back in Florida, she decided it was time to test her ideas. She got together with a couple of middle school girls. She talked them through Psalm 22 in order for them to learn about lament. Next she walked them through the Mad Libs version of their laments. Then she asked the young women what they thought. "I used to think we had to be nice to God," one of them said, "but now I know I can be really honest with God." Another said, "It's hard to see how love and anger can go together." But she eventually got it. "I see it better now," she concluded; "I see how trusting someone even in anger makes a deeper relationship." This beta-test of Erica's lament project told her the time was almost right to pursue the full project. She did, however, add one preliminary step.

Before initiating the lament project, Erica engaged in what she called "empathy training" for church leaders, then parents, and eventually the whole congregation. She started by training the adult volunteers who worked with her small youth group. The volunteers gathered for a one-day retreat designed to cultivate their capacity for empathy. They began the day by focusing on lament. She asked each person to think back to their personal experience of middle school. Each person named their middle school longings and especially their losses. Then they engaged in group lament, expressing their own adolescent pain.

The volunteers at the retreat focused on learning to "walk alongside" a young person. They used this image of "alongside" as a way to describe "listening with," and they did it because the metaphor fit so well with the movement that happens when walking a labyrinth. She showed the group the Brené Brown video on empathy that had been part of the training we gave her.[57] The group processed it together. Then they talked about how to create a holding environment for young people.[58] And they emphasized the idea that we discussed earlier: "Empathy cannot want control." Finally, they discussed eminently practical ideas, such as "Every time you want to speak as you listen, take a sip of water to stop yourself from saying, 'Yeah, but . . .'" Once they had completed the empathy training, Erica was ready to pursue the full project.

The project itself began with the middle schoolers meeting on a Sunday night. The first week Erica asked them to name lyrics from songs they know that expressed loss, or anger, or whatever else they might be feeling. The young people pointed to Christian songs and to secular songs. That first week Erica also brought in a storyteller from the community so the teens could hear about the power of stories—including their own stories. The storyteller told them about Psalm 22, Psalm 42, Job, and Lamentations.

Then, in the second week, the group cooperated to list issues that they thought were lamentable, and they replaced lines from the song lyrics they discussed the previous week in order to express their own pain. During the third week, they wrote and recited together a group lament on the topic of their choosing, using the Mad Libs format.

The fifth week's meeting was parents' night. The parents came to learn about lament and participated as each teen used the lament structure to write about something that was happening with a friend. During the teaching portion of the evening, Erica reminded the parents and teens that sometimes they might want to lament about something for which they themselves were partially responsible. In other words, they might make confession part of lament.

In the sixth week, Erica did a group assessment (more listening) to see how the young people were experiencing the process. Then for the seventh, eighth, and ninth weeks, she allowed each young person to write and pray their own lament. Finally, in the tenth week, they wrapped up the experiment. After ten weeks, the middle schoolers had a habit of lamenting.

After Erica took up the project, something surprising happened. The adults in the congregation heard about what was going on and asked to be a part of it. She made plans to preach about lament and to prepare them to walk the lamenting labyrinth as part of a Lenten reflection.

The church as we know it is calibrated for a world that no longer exists. If we are to recalibrate, we need a process for innovation. This chapter outlined a process that combines the emphasis on listening, which is part of the Christian practice of discernment, with the structure of practical theology and human-centered design. The next issue is seeking how to prepare, as leaders and as organizations, for innovation to thrive.

7

Organizing for Innovation

We have said that the work of a Christian leader is planting and watering. And we have said that ideas are like saplings in that quantity is more important than quality. There is another way that this agricultural metaphor helps us. Just as in farming, innovation requires the right environment to thrive. The soil is as important as the seed.[1] Yet most Christian organizations, as we have seen, are calibrated to nourish what already exists. They are not calibrated to be rich soil for fragile seeds—or to be a friend of the new. That highlights the importance of having leaders who tend the soil. "A leader of innovation creates a place—a context, an environment—where people . . . do the hard work that innovative problem solving requires."[2] They tend the soil as they plant and water. Leaders create an environment for innovation, and the environment they create is called the organizational culture.

Culture is crucial. Culture forms the informal rules by which people navigate working together. The beliefs and values about how things should be (the mental models that comprise the organization) join to create what we call organizational culture.

It is easy to discount the power of organizational culture. Most leaders who want to make changes focus on structural changes. They change a job description, or they hire a new person to fill an old job description. But, as the management giant Peter Drucker liked to say, "Culture eats structure for breakfast."[3] I think of it while using a slightly different metaphor. Culture is like the tide in the sea or the current in a river. We humans might concentrate on the boats that we make to steer us where we want to go, but the current in

151

a river is far more important. Any captain who ignores the current will end up stuck on the rocks. *If we are going to organize for Christian innovation, we will need to address congregational culture.*

Recently there has been a lot of good scholarship focused on how to create an organization where innovation blooms. The rest of the chapter will describe the characteristics of such an organization. There are any number of ways to present the themes that appear in these studies. This chapter will follow the contours that Harvard's Linda Hill and her team use to describe organizations that create what she calls "collective genius."[4] She identifies five characteristics of innovative organizations. We will look at each of these five in turn:

1. Identity-creating purpose
2. Communally shared values
3. Diversity-rich collaboration
4. Experiment-driven learning
5. Integrative decision-making[5]

Identity-Creating Purpose

An innovative organization cannot perform innovation as one of its tasks, as if it were one of many things on a checklist. It must *exist for a purpose that demands innovating.* Innovating is itself not enough of a purpose. There must be a final goal for its innovation. For Google, that final goal is the user. The goal is not innovating for the sake of innovating; it is innovating for the sake of the user. This idea of purpose must be so strong that it becomes the organization's identity. As Hill's team put it, *"Purpose is not what a group does but who it is and why it exists."*[6]

This need for an identity-creating purpose is why congregations need to clearly understand the people entrusted to their care. The calling of any Christian or any Christian organization is to make spiritual sense of the human condition as experienced by the people entrusted to their care. The people entrusted to our care define us. We exist to serve them and to demonstrate for them how God in Christ responds to their longings and losses. Innovation is necessary because in recent years the church has not been able to respond to the human condition of the people entrusted to its care.

Whenever we as Christians get lost or confused, whenever we want to evaluate the merits of new ideas, whenever we need to set priorities, we can go back to listening to the people entrusted to our care. Whenever those people do not hear the gospel as God's response to their longings and losses, we must innovate. And since we cannot innovate a new gospel, we must innovate a better way to communicate that gospel message. We do not exist for ourselves. We serve God by serving them.[7]

In an earlier chapter, we discussed the absolutely crucial work of Robert Wuthnow, who explained what he called the crisis in the churches.[8] The root of the spiritual and financial crisis in the churches is that we Christian leaders have not focused on responding to the daily experiences of our parishioners. Wuthnow is the one who pushed us to think about the things that keep people awake at night. An innovative congregation must exist for the purpose of innovating new ways to respond to the human condition of the people entrusted to its care.[9]

But churches regularly get distracted by the weekly activities of being church: creating a worship service, paying the bills, and running the programs. The programs become more important than the people whom the programs were intended to serve. The congregation tends to adopt the dangerous attitude that says, "If we are doing our programs, we must be serving our people." But the programs were established long ago. And people have certainly changed since then. So that's how we end up with a church calibrated for a world that no longer exists.

If we do not exist to keep innovating—to regularly remain connected to the needs of our people—then we will fall into exactly the state that Wuthnow describes. Innovating is not merely a task that we do. Finding new ways to present the never-changing gospel to an ever-changing people must be why we exist.

Communally Shared Values

Another part of the environment where innovation thrives involves values. These values come out in the way that the organization constructs its incentives and disincentives.[10] Because most organizations are calibrated to extend the world that already exists, they build their reward structure around the standards of the current configuration. Thus, they inadvertently create barriers to innovation.

For example, Carl is an executive with a mission agency. He determined that the organization's ongoing work in an important region of Africa was never going to accomplish the goals the organization had set, because the society had changed too much. He pioneered and tested a set of new ideas. Then his organization gave him permission to devote half his work time to creating experiments, thereby to see if the mission agency would be able to implement the ideas at scale. It was going very well. Unfortunately, the evaluation process of the organization did not have room for such innovative work.

At his year-end review, the categories for assessment all reflected the part of his job that had nothing to do with the innovation; the evaluation did not ask about the work he was doing in innovation because it was not formally a part of his job description. Because he was only supposed to be working on that portion of his job half the time, it looked on paper as though he were doing only half a job. Only through the intervention of an executive-level champion was he able to continue the work. The values of the system were aligned with the work that the organization was already doing, but the organization's assessment process did not have the flexibility to take innovative work into account.[11]

Let me give one more example to show how the reward systems of organizations tend to retard innovation—whether they intend to or not. An old, wise colleague told me this story when I first became a professor. Irma Martin was a bright young ethics professor at a theological school in the eastern United States. One year the dean of her school, Harold Pointer, approached her about participating in a pedagogical experiment. "The school has decided to devote more resources to integrative work, especially in the field education program," he said. "We would like you to lead one of the 'Reflection on Ministry' seminars that students take each week during their internships. You seem ideally suited to this because you care so deeply about the connections between ministry and ethics." At first, Irma demurred, saying that an untenured professor needs to write in order to get promoted. But the dean persisted. He pointed out that her next book was already at the publisher and that her tenure review would stand or fall on its merit. Since the field education task was not part of her course load, Irma then asked about the effect this assignment might have on her salary. Annual merit raises were tied to scholarly output. Harold assured her that he considered the application of her discipline to the work of the school an appropriate scholarly output. Irma agreed to take on the seminar. She found the experience to be invigorating to her work and rewarding for the students. The experiment seemed like a success.

But that, unfortunately, was the last year that Irma participated in the "Reflection on Ministry" seminars. Her merit salary increase that summer was far lower than in any other year before or since. When she gingerly inquired of the dean about her meager raise, his answer was not reassuring. "This has been a particularly tough year to decide on increases," he said. "So many of your colleagues have done exemplary academic work that we had to be quite rigorous in applying our standards for scholarly output to quantifiable projects." Harold either forgot about his previous statements to Irma or chose not to mention them. And Irma never brought it up directly. Instead, she learned her lesson. In the years since, she made sure to write several short but duly quantifiable book reviews and at least one major article. So each year she got her share of the merit increases. But she never participated in the reflection seminars again. The culture's commitment to evaluating for the present swallowed even the dean's plan to innovate for the future.

Churches tend to do the same thing. Leaders are judged by how well they put on the programs that the church has always been doing. They are judged by the people the church has always served. There is rarely a concerted effort to do the hard work of listening that keeps a congregation tied to its people's needs.

Most organizations are constructed to reward the people who put their heads down and work each day to fulfill their job description. Look, for example, at "responsibility to community"—one of the values that Hill and her team found in innovative organizations. A pastoral leader can preach and teach without any real interaction with the congregation. The assumption is that if congregations hear their pastors preach, those pastors must be connecting with their congregations. If they keep their heads down and just keep preaching, they will be rewarded for doing the job. That will not work in an innovative congregation. Innovation requires shared values, especially values aligned with the collaborative pursuit of the bold but amorphous problem of keeping in sync with the church people's needs.[12]

The same is true for a youth minister, or a children's director, or the lay leader who runs the mission trips. As long as they do what they have always been doing, people will assume they are doing their job. But if the congregation has a commitment to listening, and if that congregation regularly hears about the changing needs of its people, then the congregation will never be satisfied with doing what it has always done.

I recognize that such a commitment can be disruptive. But that is the point, even if it is too much for some congregations. As I was coaching a congregation through an innovation process as part of Fuller's Youth Ministry Innovation project, I met with the pastor of a traditional Lutheran congregation. After a couple of meetings, he confessed that he did not really expect to "do any of that listening," as he put it. "I don't have time," he said. "My job is to preach, and any extra time goes into running the church. I really don't have the time or the energy to be listening." Hence, I ask readers, Where do you think that congregation will be in ten years? Keeping up with the ever-changing needs of your people requires an identity-creating commitment to innovating and a communally shared commitment to listening. Without those commitments, innovation will not happen.

Diversity-Rich Collaboration

"Innovation usually emerges when a diverse people collaborate to generate a wide-ranging portfolio of ideas."[13] Diversity is necessary because it takes many and varied nutrients to feed innovation. For example, the Kelley brothers of IDEO and the Stanford d.school (design school) talk about how a person who wants to become creative needs to "get outside what you know" in order to see the world from a different point of view.[14] They regularly put their students into diverse groups and then take those groups to visit well-known settings, to see those sites from unexpected perspectives. Likewise, Julian Birkinshaw talks about how it is important not just to hire people like yourself but to "bring in outsiders" who see the world differently from you.[15]

The respected Stanford scholar Kathleen Eisenhardt explains why diversity is so important to innovation. She has learned that innovation rarely happens by following the logical next step in a line of thinking. "Innovation is the result of synthesizing, or bridging, ideas from different domains." She calls it "the result of *simultaneously thinking in multiple boxes*."[16] If we see innovation as being about one person doing all the work, then it becomes very difficult for that person to master many different domains of experience. But if we see innovation as residing in the group or organization, then it is easy to see how a diverse group has access to more domains of experience. *Diversity enables innovation.*

That means that fragmentation (or an organizational structure that has silos, isolated units) is the enemy of innovation. Many of our Christian organizations have silo structures. In a religious nonprofit, perhaps the soup kitchen is separate from the outreach ministry. Or in a congregation, the youth group may be isolated from the other ministries. Or in a seminary, the departments operate independently.[17] There is a perspective claiming that the best way to honor diversity is to give each group its own silo. But scholars have shown that, in the long run, this cannot work.[18] Diversity is good for an organization, but only when the diverse peoples collaborate. *Silos inhibit innovation.*

Let me give you an example of how diversity works to a congregation's advantage. Last week I was talking about evangelism with a pastor (John) in a well-known congregation. We were talking about Mark Granovetter's insight about the "strength of weak ties."[19] This idea says that organizations like churches rarely grow from the efforts of their most committed members. The most committed church members often know few people who are not Christians. They know the faith well, but they don't have anyone to tell about the faith.

By contrast, the best evangelists are usually congregants who are only loosely tied to the congregation. They have friends in many social settings. They have lots of contact with people who don't go to church. Because of that, they are "boundary-spanners," people who live in more than one social world. That describes ambassadors—citizens of one country who go to live in another country with the expressed purpose of creating goodwill between the two. And that discussion of the "strength of weak ties" led John and me to discuss diversity. He realized that congregations need approximately the same skill set to pursue evangelism as they do to pursue diversity.

Diversity increases the gene pool for ideas. When we have people from multiple settings with multiple perspectives, we have more raw material for the kind of mixing and matching of ideas that makes innovation thrive. Think of a healthy diet. A diet that has only one kind of food (no matter how good the food is) is not healthy. Diversity drives innovation.

Experiment-Driven Learning

For the first three characteristics of an innovative culture (purpose, values, and diversity), we have talked about many kinds of organizations. But for the final characteristics, we will focus on specific organizations and on what they can teach us about creating innovative congregational cultures. We will also use them to provide examples of how one organization (Google) ensures that its innovations resonate with its people and how another organization (Pixar) uses stories to make meaning. In each organization, we will see that they do it by emphasizing experiment-driven learning. Let's start with Google.

Google did not start out as an innovative environment. It started out as Lester's redwood, a single big idea—in this case, a radically different way to search the internet. But soon thereafter, the founders realized that their future depended on expanding around multiple ideas. They could not long survive with just one tree. So they started planting many saplings—small ideas that they hoped would someday grow into big initiatives.

Google has its own way of implementing the three characteristics we have seen so far (purpose, values, and diversity). For purpose, Google has a simple goal. "Our prime directive when it comes to product strategy," Google says, "is to focus on the user." The goal is not necessarily to make money. "We will always focus on the user, and we trust that our smart creatives [employees] will figure out how to make money from it." Notice how this is another way of saying that leadership begins with listening to the people entrusted to your care. The company exists to serve its user.

For an example of their commitment to focus on the user, Google executives Eric Schmidt and Jonathan Rosenberg describe their purchase of a company called Keyhole. They bought Keyhole because Keyhole had figured out how to visualize maps in a way that Google thought users might like. They did not have a plan. They simply purchased a sapling and turned it over to their employees to figure out how their users might find it helpful. Eight months later, Google used that technology to launch Google Earth, an innovation that made the company millions of dollars. Google focuses on the user.[20]

Google is also very clear on its values. It looks for specific traits in its employees—and refers to those employees either as Googlers or "smart creatives." The values that Google puts in place are designed to maximize the innovative capacity of these smart creatives. The values include "trust," a "culture of Yes," "humor and fun," and the famous phrase "Don't be evil." This commitment to "Don't be evil" was how the organization planted a vocabulary that allowed Googlers to argue over what is right and what is wrong.[21] The executives at Google describe the phrase as being like the "Emergency Stop" cord on a Toyota assembly line. When an engineer protests that a new feature would be evil, he is "pulling the cord to stop production, forcing everyone to assess the proposed feature and determine if it is consistent with the company's values."[22] Those values make for a better user experience.

The same goes for diversity. "A multiplicity of viewpoints—aka diversity—is your best defense against myopia," the Google managers say. "People from different backgrounds see the world differently," and "these differences of perspective generate insights that can't be taught." The goal remains: innovating the best user experience. A diversity of perspectives working collaboratively is, Google believes, the best means to that end. So we can see how Google illustrates the first three characteristics we have discussed about innovative organizations. Let us move on to the fourth one: experiment-driven learning.

Google has *constructed its management practices around experimentation.* "To innovate, you must learn to fail well," say Google executives Schmidt and Rosenberg. "Learn from your mistakes. . . . Morph ideas; don't kill them. . . . Don't stigmatize the team that failed." To "fail well," you must "fail quickly, but with a very long time horizon" (i.e., take the time to go through many cycles of experimental learning). All this rapid failing is necessary because innovation is an iterative process. "The key" to innovation, they say, "is to iterate quickly and to establish metrics that help you judge" how to take your next steps.[23] They emphasize that innovation is a cycle; it's not a linear process. Each experiment leads to a new experiment. And each idea builds on what you have learned from your last experiment. This calls to mind a favorite phrase from my dissertation advisers: "There is no such thing as good writing, only good rewriting." There is no such thing as good innovation, only good re-innovation. Innovation requires cycles of experimentation.[24]

There are several characteristics about experimentation that we can observe from Google's experience.

Experimentation Involves Failure

When we think of "learning by discovery" in the sciences, we picture physicists running experiments to discover, say, the secrets of the atom. We recognize that they follow a "scientific method" that involves incremental learning. But, more importantly, we recognize that "successful" experiments are usually the final result of many cycles of "failed" experiments, or experiments that move step by painful step toward "success." In the sciences, we do not judge a project after the first experiment. We see the initial experiment as the first foray into uncharted territory. Thomas Edison connected this idea to innovation. He reportedly said that before he invented the light bulb, he found many different ways not to make a light bulb.[25] His point was that experimentation creates innovation. Without experimenting, there can be no breakthrough innovations.

This is important because, as we shall see, we who lead Christian organizations have a very low tolerance for "failure." We too quickly label things that do not work the first time as failures, and we become inoculated to their ideas. *It would be like judging each step of a journey to be a failure except the one that finally took us through the door.*

Innovation requires experimentation, experimentation requires a tolerance for failure, and a tolerance for failure requires a safe environment. The one "established idea" about innovation, Julian Birkinshaw of the London Business School has said, is that innovation happens only when organizations create "an environment where it is safe to experiment," by which he means an environment "where it is possible to 'pilot' and 'test' ideas . . . before they are subjected to [management's] stringent performance metrics."[26] Experiments are crucial because, as scholars have known since the 1990s, the biggest competitive advantage is the capacity to learn.[27] "The key to success" is not being first to market or having the best idea; it "is learning quickly," according to Vijay Govindarajan and Chris Trimble. "The competitor that learns first generally wins."[28] Experiments are crucial, then, because *we learn more from failure than from success.*[29]

Of course, experimentation in Christian contexts will likewise involve failure. Think about something as simple as telling a good story—one that can become a shared story of hope. The first few times I tell a story, I likely mess up the cadences or get the facts in the wrong order. I likely don't say anything untrue. But I probably don't tell the story well. However, the more I practice (the more iterations I go through), the more likely I am to find a version that flows. That is when I am ready to make the story go viral. I need to get the wording right—to fail on my way to getting it right—before I can have a strong enough story to proclaim to all the people I know.

Experimentation That Leads to Innovation Is Cyclical, Not Linear

One experiment generates learning that leads to another set of experiments and more learning. This cyclical nature of experimentation leads scholars of innovation to use a different metric for talking about experience. The Kelley brothers (of IDEO and Stanford) say that experience is measured in cycles of experiments, not in years on the job. So a twenty-two-year-old who has run one prototype a week for six months would have accumulated more experience than an executive who has been in the same job for twenty years. The Kelleys quote the innovation scholar Diego Rodriguez, who uses the term "informed intuition," which they take to mean that "relentless practice creates a database of experience that you can draw upon to make more enlightened choices." This is particularly important in situations of significant ambiguity[30] because "rapid innovation cycles" result in "reduced anxiety in the face of ambiguity."[31]

This cycle of experimentation and learning means that *success is often a matter of failing at an increasing level of competency.* My wife and I learned this as we watched our toddlers grow. They were constantly failing at some new skill—tying their shoes, making their bed, learning the alphabet. But whatever they struggled to learn on one day, they had mastered by the next day. But late on that next day they would take on a new and more difficult skill. Learning the alphabet gave way to reading picture books, which in turn became reading chapter books—and so on. Mastering one skill only led to struggling with a new one. It is an important metaphor.

Every organization has things that it does poorly. But a successful organization has a trajectory of learning over time. In an innovative organization, the things we could not do last year are what we take for granted this year. That buys us the time to take on a new struggle this year. And so on. Every day Thomas Edison's lab struggled with some experiment that was failing.

And every day they kept working so that each of those failures eventually brought new knowledge. The best way to measure an innovative organization is to measure (1) ideas generated per week, and (2) how long it takes to learn from our cyclical attempts. *We fail our way forward.*

That gives us a new metric for our work in the church. There is a saying, "Measure what matters" (or, in another wording, "What gets measured, gets done"). And let's say that we want to collect stories of longing and loss as we listen to the people entrusted to our care. Then we ask our team to listen to two people a week for three months. Each week when we get together for a staff meeting, we ask people to report. "How many stories did you collect this week?" If we measure how many stories, then people will focus on collecting stories. We believe that if we collect enough stories of longing and loss, then that will change how we understand our people.

This is also important as we figure out how to respond to those longings and losses. The innovation scholars teach us that you can expect "your initial expectations are wrong"[32] and use experiments to "test your beliefs"[33] about the people entrusted to your care. Google's work with "user experience"[34] shows that people rarely receive a message in just the way you intended to send it. So even the most enlightened innovation will still require cycles of experimentation to ensure that the audience hears what the speaker intends.

This is particularly important when we are making spiritual sense of our people's longings and losses. If I don't listen well, I will treat people as stereotypes. And if I don't test my ideas (the ways that I am making spiritual sense), then I will assume that people hear whatever it is I meant to say. We need cycles of experimentation.

Run Experiments on the Margins

If we make too many mistakes in public, people will start to wonder about us. The solution is to run experiments on the margins. This is, of course, the opposite of what we tend to do as Christian organizations. Usually we announce our intentions as big plans.

For example, I have worked closely with the Fuller Youth Institute in training churches that want to implement Sticky Faith,[35] an innovative way of doing youth ministry. We teach the congregations to try experiments on the margins without fanfare. But many ministries pursue the opposite strategy. They announce a new program, give it a name, and perhaps design a logo. They publicize it as if it were a finished product. Then they lose credibility when the first experiment is a successful first step but not a finished product. They invite people to watch them make their rookie mistakes.

Let me offer an analogy to show why this is a bad strategy. I taught my daughter to drive by taking her to the church parking lot on a quiet afternoon to practice simple maneuvers. But let's say that my daughter was really nervous about learning to drive. So I decided to get her some support. Perhaps I built a grandstand in the church parking lot and invited all her friends and family, her youth group, and her grandparents. They all sat in the grandstand cheering her on while she fumbled through her first attempts to drive. They held up banners with her name. They chanted encouraging messages. They even waved giant cutouts of her head like it was a college basketball game. Would she experience that attention as support or as pressure? It surely would just make it harder to learn. Every mistake would be magnified by the attention. It would no longer be a safe place to experiment: the cost of failing forward in public is too high.

Yet that's what congregations do when they announce big plans and make big promises about innovative programs before they have worked out the kinks. Experiments need to be done in the quiet shadows so that people have room to fail their way to building success.

Instead of a grand announcement with a logo and theme music, youth ministries could try experiments that incorporate new ideas into what looks like the ongoing work of the youth ministry. Use a portion of the singing time to do something a little different; try a new way of teaching; incorporate a new idea into a weekly small group; or take a portion of the annual mission trip to do something new. All these experiments come under the cover of what looks like ongoing programs. No one outside the leadership team needs to know that they are experiments. Stealth experiments reduce the cost of failing our way forward.[36] Every rookie makes mistakes.[37] It takes time to learn. *Don't sign up to make your rookie mistakes in public.*

Experiment with Ways to Follow Your People

We need to be careful not to think that, once we develop a new idea, we are done learning. Lots of experimentation goes into creating a new prototype. But there is also a lot of learning that happens once we start to test that prototype. Because the measure of success for our endeavors is the degree to which they resonate with the people entrusted to our care, we cannot know how successful they will be until we have seen how our people receive them.

This is how innovative organizations like Google operate. Google intentionally releases new products to their users before the products have all the small details set. (They do lots of beta-testing before shipping but know that the product cannot be completed until the customers have worked with it.) Google does this in the name of the user. They know that they will never be able to anticipate fully how a user will want to use a product. So they release the product before the concrete has hardened, as it were, so that they can easily adapt the product to the feedback that Google assiduously collects. They call the process "ship and iterate."[38]

The important idea here is that Google cannot follow the artist's process of prototyping because Google measures its purpose according to its audience's reception. In the humanities, we know that the audience will make its own interpretation. But that is not the artist's problem. Artists create what they want to express: their process is not really connected to how the audience receives it. Google cannot do that—and neither can we in the church. Google's entire goal is to connect to its audience. So a product that excites Google will be discontinued if it does not connect with the audience. At Google, innovation is an iterative conversation with its users. In the same way, *Christian innovation must create an ongoing conversation with the people entrusted to our care*: our goal is to create the kind of spiritual meaning that helps people see their daily lives in a new light.

There is another example of how to follow the people entrusted to our care. Think of a school district that builds a new high school. I would have thought that the district is not ready to open the school until, say, the sidewalks of the school have been paved. But in the last decades, I am told that architects and builders have followed a different course. They put up the buildings. Then they open the school without paving all the sidewalks that connect the buildings. They see where the students walk. And that is where they eventually lay the sidewalks. You see, the builders got tired of guessing wrong. They would make a plan for where the students should walk and lay the new sidewalks according to the plans. Then in the first year, they would watch in dismay as the students walked on the grass between buildings. Now the builders wait to see where the students will walk, and that is where they put the sidewalks.

It is a wonderful metaphor. As Christian leaders, we cannot change the buildings we construct. Every high school needs a chemistry lab and a history classroom. And every Christian program needs to talk about the resurrection of Jesus and the call to daily discipleship. Those are set in concrete. But how we connect them—the pathways between them—are not yet paved. We need to work with our people as we decide where the sidewalks should go.

There are many more ideas that we can learn about experimentation. But perhaps the best way to encounter them is as a list.

1. *Learn from mistakes.* Most leaders hide from their mistakes. We bear a tremendous responsibility to learn from our mistakes because our experiments involve real, live human beings.[39]

2. *Morph new ideas; don't kill them.* We give up on new ideas too soon. The next time something goes poorly, ask yourself how it can change. Then try again.

3. *Retire projects that have run their course.* Just as we give up on new ideas too soon, we tend to keep old ministry projects too long. Is there something that you are doing solely because you have always done it?

4. *Celebrate the team that fails.* We tend to stigmatize the group that fails because they did not accomplish the goal. But what if we stigmatized NASA because Apollo 1 did not make it to the moon? Celebrate the process and the courage that it took to try.

5. *Train good people.* Train them and trust them. In the business world, companies choose their employees. But in the church world, we deal with volunteers. Training is far more important than recruitment. Good people are trained rather than found.

6. *Try soft openings.* Restaurants invite friends before they open to the public. Then when they open to the public, they practice for a few weeks before having a grand opening.

7. *Avoid experiments in the worship service.* A worship service is the most public part of a church's life. Experimenting in the worship service is signing up to make your rookie mistakes in public.

We need to take up one last characteristic of innovative organizations. Recall that the outline of this chapter is built around the characteristics that Hill and her colleagues named when they studied innovative organizations. We have covered purpose, values, collaboration, and experimentation. The final characteristic is integrative decision-making.

Integrative Decision-Making

While most discussions of innovation focus on producing devices, recent scholarly studies have also singled out an organization that produces stories, the movie studio Pixar. We will examine Pixar's process in some detail because they make meaning by telling stories, which is quite similar to our stated goal of creating shared stories of Christian hope in response to the longings and losses of the people entrusted to our care. Indeed, we might say that the movie-going audience comprises the people entrusted to Pixar's care. And Pixar is quite careful to invite the audience into stories where they can identify with the longings and losses of the main character. They want the audience to take on the main character's condition as its own. *Every Pixar story is about the human condition.* Let me show you what that means.

Look at the central questions at the heart of Pixar movies. In *Toy Story*, Woody the cowboy has to choose between his friends (the toys) and the boy who has been entrusted to his care. It asks which is more important, friendship or duty? In *A Bug's Life*, the main character finds a purpose and a calling. Meanwhile, *Toy Story 2* asks, according to its director, "Would you choose to live forever if it meant a life without love?"[40] And *Toy Story 3* is about letting go. How do you continue to love someone, it asks, even if you no longer have responsibility for their care? Likewise, Mindy Kaling summarized the movie *Inside Out* by saying it is "a story that tells kids that it's difficult to grow up and it's OK to be sad about it."[41] Elsewhere this book has described the longings and losses in the opening scene of the movie *Up*. Each Pixar movie turns on a deeply human question. It is no accident that Pixar's movies have this resonance.

So let us start with seeing how Pixar embodies the lessons we have seen so far about building an innovative organizational culture and then see if perhaps their organizational process is something we can emulate.

We started this chapter by talking about an *identity-creating purpose*. At Pixar they are clear on their purpose—and they know what they are not. Most people would say that Pixar is first and foremost a computer-generated animation studio. Pixar would not say that. They would not dispute that they use computers to animate, but that is not why they exist. Computer animation is simply a means for them. It is not their end. They exist to tell stories, especially stories that resonate, that draw in the audience. From the very start, "the first principle was 'Story is King'"; it continues to be their "defining goal."[42] They just happen to use computer-generated animation to pursue that goal.

Likewise, they are quite clear on their *shared values*. Ed Catmull (the long-time head of Pixar) writes about how "candor" is a crucial value for Pixar.[43] They refer to it as a "virtue," a very Christian word. For Pixar, "the word [candor] communicates not just truth-telling but a lack of reserve." The key storytellers do not mince words when they talk to each other. "A hallmark of a healthy creative culture," Catmull says, "is that people feel free to share ideas, opinions, and criticisms. Lack of candor, if unchecked, leads to dysfunctional environments."[44]

This is an example of how healthy organizations manage competing commitments. Most organizations value candor, but they value politeness more.[45] In most organizations, it would be impolite for me to tell a colleague that I think there is a flaw in her screenplay. At Pixar, it would be rude to think that there was a problem and not to say anything.

This candor has an added benefit. It allows me to hold loosely to my opinion. I may think there is a problem with your screenplay. If I never talk about it, I will never change my mind. But if I tell you about it, and then you speak with the same candor back, I may well learn that I missed something crucial and that I was wrong all along. Or you and I may start a conversation in which we both learn something. But without candor, I may send a mixed message, that I approve of what you are doing even though I secretly think it is wrong. And, as Chris Argyris has shown, organizations that lack candor live trapped within the chaos caused by mixed messages.[46] Candor encourages a diversity of opinions.

A misunderstanding or improper use of candor can, however, create as many problems as it solves, especially if the candor becomes mean or is used to put people in their place. In a few paragraphs we will say much more about how Pixar creates space for healthy interactions. Meanwhile, it is important to note that the overriding goal of creating good movies that resonate with people is such a strong value that it tends to police bad behavior. Bad behavior makes bad movies. And bad movies are unacceptable, which makes dysfunctional candor unacceptable.[47]

For our churches, lack of candor creates outdated ministry. Not long ago I met with a pastoral staff that was asking, "How do we tell our beloved pastor that he is out of touch with everyone under sixty?" The congregational culture said that polite people never criticize anyone. At Pixar, everyone encourages criticism. At Pixar, bad movies are unacceptable. In the church, outdated ministry should be unacceptable. So let's see what we can learn from Pixar's experience with bad movies.

Catmull is quite clear about one point. All Pixar movies start bad—even the award winners. That is why experimentation is so important. Catmull puts it this way: at the beginning, all "our films are 'ugly babies.' They are not beautiful, miniature versions of the adults they will grow up to be. They are truly ugly: awkward and unformed, vulnerable and incomplete. They need nurturing—in the form of time and patience—in order to grow." That is where administrators come in. "Our job is to protect our babies from being judged too quickly. Our job is to protect the new."[48]

I find this idea of "ugly babies" quite reassuring. In an earlier section, we learned that it is important to "morph new ideas" rather than to abandon them. Pixar understands that every new idea is going to appear malformed at first. It takes many cycles—many iterations—with the Braintrust (see below) before the baby grows into something that the studio can celebrate. In the meantime, the job of a leader is to keep the cycle going—to keep iterating until they have something beautiful.

So what did I say to that group of leaders with the out-of-touch preacher? I said to start where you have jurisdiction: start with each other. Talk at staff meetings about the importance of candor. Practice candor with each other (but not with your boss). Allow the pastor to see how candor helps you. Then invite him into the conversation. Plant the vocabulary. Use the word "candor." And invite the pastor to be candid with you. Once you have established the vocabulary, then you can slowly introduce it into the preacher's life. Don't start by criticizing his preaching; that's too close to home. Find safer topics on which to practice candor—things that would cost him little to change. And then, and only then, you can slowly broach the most sensitive topics. *The way to promote candor is to invite candor.*

Catmull believes that the people who lead innovative organizations have a particular role that no one else shares. The senior leaders need to "protect the new" because the momentum of the organization—what Catmull calls the "hungry beast"—will instinctively devour anything that is vulnerable. Now, Catmull recognizes that not all things can or should survive. Some saplings don't make it. He acknowledges that. But he understands something about the nature of innovation that places a burden on senior leaders. "When someone hatches an original idea, it may be ungainly and poorly defined," Catmull says, "but it is also the opposite of established and entrenched—*and that is precisely what is exciting about it.*"[49]

The hungry beast of daily duties does not have the categories to decide if the ugly baby is worth more resources. *The organization is calibrated to dismiss innovative ideas—specifically because they are innovative.*[50] Thus, "part of our job" as senior leaders "is to protect the new from people who don't understand."[51] Catmull illustrates this by telling the story of Andrew Stanton's initial pitch for the idea that became the Oscar-winning *Finding Nemo*. The plot he pitched was a tangled mess of complicated subplots and distracting flashbacks. As a story, it was an ugly baby. But when Catmull and John Lasseter first heard the pitch, they only needed to hear two things to sign and approve the project. They heard that it was a story about fish and that "the tale Andrew wanted to tell got to the heart of the struggle for independence that often shapes a father-son relationship."[52] In other words, it was a story about the human condition. So Catmull knew that it was an ugly baby that he needed to protect. He trusted that Pixar's process—especially the value of candor—would iron out the problems that made the baby so ugly. The virtues of candor and protection go hand in hand.[53]

I should say one more thing about the hungry beast of daily duties. As we have taken dozens of congregations through the innovation process, the chief reason why congregations have given up—the central reason that they did not innovate—is that the project got swallowed by the hungry beast of daily duties. That is why it is so important to set up a separate group meeting at a separate time. When youth ministers, for example, tried to incorporate innovation into a regular meeting with the youth team, the project got eaten up by the needs of running a youth program. When congregational leaders tried to make innovation part of the regular staff meeting—or the monthly board meeting—the hungry beast ate them as well. Pixar teaches us that the role of a leader is to protect innovation from the hungry beast of daily duties.

Now we have seen how Pixar illustrates what Linda Hill and her colleagues call purpose, values, and collaboration.[54] Pixar is a particularly resonant innovation example for Christian organizations because they create stories, not devices. Like Christians, Pixar tells stories that make meaning, even meaning that challenges our mental models.[55] We will continue to use Pixar as an example as we look at the next characteristic of innovative organizations: *experimental learning by discovery*.

Learning by discovery happens because each movie evolves as a series of experiments. After *Finding Nemo*'s initial pitch, Lasseter and Catmull sent Andrew Stanton off to work on the next iteration of the story. Then it went through more cycles of trying prototypes for each character. They used storyboards to picture the flow of the movie. When the flow did not work, they created another cycle. They rapidly went through many cycles. This gave them the experience that comes from repeated experimentation. At no point did a clunky plot point feel like a failure; it was a step in the right direction. But they did not make the mistake of showing their ideas to the public too soon. We Christians like to announce new programs and then invite the public to watch us make our rookie mistakes. That would be like Pixar hosting a red-carpet event to premiere its ugly baby. Pixar is committed to rapid and repeated experimentation.

Hill and her colleagues outline one final characteristic in the innovation model: *integrative decision-making*. Its purpose is to create a forum where it is appropriate to speak productively with candor, to create a space where candor is constructive, not destructive. The goal, according to Catmull, is to "put smart, passionate people in a room together, charge them with identifying and solving problems, and encourage them to be candid with each other." He believes that "without the crucial ingredient that is candor, there can be no trust. And without trust, creative collaboration is not possible." Thus, his "primary role" as a senior leader is "making sure that the compact upon which the meetings are based is protected and upheld."[56] This word "compact" is important. It is supposed to call to mind the social compact (or social contract) that holds groups together, the contract that turns a group into a community. To understand this compact, we need to understand the venue where Pixar expresses this candor. They call it the Braintrust.

The Braintrust, "which meets every few months or so to assess each movie [Pixar is] making, is [Pixar's] primary delivery system for straight talk." The Braintrust began as the meeting of the creative heads of Pixar. These are the folks who would be the writers and directors of Pixar's movies. Over time, they have included other diverse people, "whose only requirement is that they display a knack for storytelling" (because at Pixar "Story is King" in that it drives the purpose of the organization). This emphasis on storytelling is crucial. The purpose of the meeting is to hone the story that will become a Pixar movie. So the credibility of each person in the room depends on their ability to contribute to that goal. (For example, Catmull attends for management purposes but is largely silent because his strength is not in storytelling.) No one is allowed in the room who is "motivated by the kinds of things—getting credit for an idea, pleasing their supervisors, winning a point just to say you did—that too often lurk beneath the surface."[57] All that matters is getting a good story.

Nevertheless, there is a problem when you put that many creative people in the same room. There are too many ideas to fit into one story, and the details that matter to me may not be the details that matter to you, because we are telling slightly different versions of the story. The Braintrust handles this by designating that every movie has only one director. The director, the one whose vision is the final arbiter, decides which pieces of advice to remove and which feedback to incorporate. This clear sense of whose vision matters yields an important rule. "The Braintrust has no authority. This is crucial: The director does not have to follow any of the specific suggestions given." *The Braintrust generates ideas; it does not issue commands.* By removing the power dynamic, Pixar creates "an environment where people want to hear each other's notes."[58]

Catmull says that "we give our filmmakers both *freedom and responsibility.*" In this way, the Braintrust is a holding environment, the ideal setting to do adaptive work (see chap. 8). A holding environment must be uncomfortable enough that people cannot stand still yet safe enough that they can experiment with a new way of being. Ronald Heifetz describes how a leader needs to "turn up the heat" in order to make it uncomfortable enough and "turn down the heat" to make it safe enough.[59] The responsibility (in the form of feedback) turns up the heat, while the freedom (in the form of autonomy) turns down the heat. This makes a Braintrust meeting like a holding environment.

We should say one more thing about this idea of heat. Heifetz uses the term "heat" to mean a level of discomfort that comes from having to face a problem that a person would rather avoid. But there is another way that we talk about heat. Sometimes it means the discord that comes with conflict—we sometimes talk, for example, about more heat than light.

If candor dominates a meeting, will people get offended, will they shout at one another, will passionate people throw so much passion into the argument that someone's feelings get hurt? In an interview with the celebrated consulting firm McKinsey and Company, Brad Bird, one of Pixar's directors, was asked about how passion plays out. Indeed, McKinsey phrased it by asking if innovators need to be angry. Bird answered, "I would say that *involved* people make for better innovation. Passionate involvement can make you happy, sometimes, and miserable other times. You want people to be involved and engaged. Involved people can be quiet, loud, or anything [in between]— what they have in common is a restless, probing nature: 'I want to get to the problem. There's something I want to *do*.' If you had thermal glasses, you could see heat coming off them."[60]

This then is a third way we can talk about heat: as passion radiating off of engaged people. Hence, we must recognize that engaged people will sometimes be loud and argue with each other. We need to teach our people how to engage in an argument, even loudly, without taking permanent offense. I must let you say something with candor—even if I think it is mean, even if you say it loudly—because I know that you have listened with empathy and because I trust that you are not just defending your turf. You are trying to reach our common goal. And you must let me answer back with just as much vigor. In the end, we need to remain partners. In premarital counseling, we regularly tell young people that every married couple needs to learn how to fight—how to argue so that, as one of my friends says it, "It is not you versus me; it is you and me against the problem."[61] We need to teach our passionate, innovative Christians to do the same thing.

So how does the Braintrust work? At each meeting, the team looks at the progress of a script, at the development of the experiment in telling this story. They identify what is working and where there are problems. Let's look at an example from a Braintrust meeting about the movie *Toy Story 3*, where the screenwriter Michael Arndt was told about a problem with his plot that he had not seen before. An important turning point in the screenplay is when, as Catmull tells it, "Lotso—the pink teddy bear and mean-spirited leader of the day-care center toys—is overthrown after the toys' mutiny. But the problem was that the mutiny wasn't believable." Andrew Stanton commented that Lotso was like Stalin and the giant toy called Big Baby was like Stalin's army. There needed to be a reason for the army to rebel. Stanton did not explain how to fix the problem. But he gave Arndt the feedback he needed to construct a backstory that, when revealed, caused Big Baby to flip in allegiance.[62] The point is that Arndt would never have solved the problem—nor known about it—without Stanton's candor.[63]

How might this idea of the Braintrust play out in a Christian organization? Let's look at a case study.[64] The Ebenezer Partnership is an inner-city social service project with a day care and tutoring program, a food bank, a counseling center, and a job training and placement service. The new executive director (called the exec, specifically not the president) is Bert Martin. Judy is the head of the day care, and Maggie is in charge of the jobs program. There are also heads of the counseling center and the food bank, but they do not play into this case. Most presidents (or in this case, the exec) convene a regular staff meeting for the purpose of streamlining administrative tasks like the budget. It makes sense for Bert to continue that. But Bert could also treat each of the divisions as Pixar would treat a movie; Bert could treat Judy and Maggie like Pixar would treat a director. It would mean that every month Bert would convene the four heads of the divisions, and they would work like the Braintrust. They would present the projects that they were pursuing and ask for feedback. They would speak to each other with candor but not arrogance, and Bert would ask each one to execute a vision.

All this works in theory, but it is hard to practice. In an article debunking the idea of employee empowerment, Chris Argyris explains why it is so hard to practice. The key to the Braintrust is the director accepting both freedom *and* responsibility, just as empowerment means that managers give up power and employees accept responsibility. Argyris shows that most employees and managers engage in a subtle game that thwarts empowerment. Managers, he says, will pretend to give up power and allow employees to pretend to take responsibility. Yet managers don't want to lose control, and employees don't want to be held accountable. So the two sides collude and pretend. The Braintrust model can work only if both sides follow through on their commitments.

That takes us back to the Ebenezer Partnership. When Bert was the new executive director, he discovered that Judy comes in late, leaves early, and rarely supervises her employees. Bert also found that Maggie is distracted from her task of job placement because she has a secondary role as a fundraiser. How do these facts apply to the Braintrust?

It would not work to have Judy be a part of the Braintrust because she would likely not be willing to accept the responsibility that being in the Braintrust entails. In other words, the Braintrust only works when you have the right people in place. It is a way to free up the right people to do innovative work. But it cannot make up for the wrong people in the wrong roles. Pixar found good storytellers and gave them an environment to thrive. But wrong seeds will never produce good saplings. Maggie, on the other hand, would be a good member of the Braintrust because she has both passion and talent. But Bert would need to free her from the fundraising duties if he expected her to be truly innovative in her work with job placement and vocational training. A Braintrust can work in a Christian organization if we have the right people and free them to do innovative work.

In the last few pages we have described the kind of organization that can be an environment for innovation to thrive. If we accept that "ideas are like saplings," then we want an environment that nurtures innovation. That congregational culture has (1) an identity-creating purpose and (2) communally shared values, as well as the ability to innovate built around (3) diversity-rich collaboration, (4) experiment-driven learning, and (5) integrative decision-making.

8

Innovation and Change

nnovation requires change. But congregations often don't know how to change. And Christian leaders often don't know how to lead change. It takes agile leaders to know what kind of change they face and how to lead their people through it. As I have worked with hundreds of congregations over the last few years, I have heard a common theme. Learning what to do, the leaders report, is much easier than knowing how to make it happen.

The purpose of this chapter is to guide you through the steps that lead to change. Specifically, we will focus on one question: *How do you help people change who desperately need to change but desperately do not want to change?* This question is especially important to the work of innovation because it describes so many of our churches. We know we must be different because our people's needs have changed, but the very thought of making the attempt is terrifying. And so we resist the change. The chapter's insights build on the research of Ronald Heifetz of the Kennedy School of Government at Harvard.

He shows how to walk with your people as together you face the change needed. The chapter will begin with two stories—stories of groups of people who absolutely, positively needed to change but absolutely, positively could not change. I invite you to picture yourself in these stories. What would you do, and how would you react? And then, once we have told the two stories, we will lay out eight steps that you can follow—positive options you can try—when you find yourself facing a similar kind of change. The first story takes place in the state of Washington.

Heifetz tells the story of a community outside Tacoma.[1] We'll call his story the Tacoma case. A copper smelting plant was spewing arsenic into the atmosphere. For decades the people near the plant pretended that there was no problem. They could not see the arsenic. They could point to generations of children who seemed no less healthy than other children. But the Environmental Protection Agency (EPA) had the data saying that the plant was poisoning their community (and the community of Vashon Island across the water).

The first thing the EPA did was shock the community out of its denial. They threatened to close the plant. How did people respond? Very few people appeared grateful that the government was protecting its citizens. Instead, one former mayor (and third-generation plant worker) said, "The government [is] trying to take our children's livelihood away."[2] He was angry and blamed the government for the problem. Notice how he framed his anger: he was still avoiding the problem. In his mind, the problem was not that the plant was spitting poison into the sky. No, the problem was that the government was taking away jobs. In retrospect, everyone agrees that the government did exactly the right thing—and they were blamed for it. Yet how the EPA guided the community makes this a story of hope.

The EPA started by gathering people for community meetings. They educated the people about the process and about the issues. People in town quickly divided themselves into two groups. One group came to town meetings wearing buttons that said "JOBS," and the other group came wearing buttons that said "HEALTH." After a while, people blamed the EPA for not "fixing" the problem that, they said, the EPA created. The issue received national attention. Newspapers, including the *New York Times*, castigated the EPA, and an environmental group claimed that the EPA was "copping out." They said that leaders are supposed to make tough choices, and they expected the EPA to decide how the community needed to change. "We elected people to run our government," one local citizen said. "We don't expect them to turn around and us to run it for them."[3]

But the EPA said that only the people themselves could decide how they were going to change. So they kept hosting meetings and kept educating people on the problems and possible next steps. Eventually things turned. Some people started showing up with a new button—one that said "BOTH" instead of just "JOBS" or "HEALTH." Soon the people were demanding that the EPA provide them with exactly the kinds of alternatives that the EPA wanted to provide all along. But now, instead of resisting it, the people embraced it. In the end, the EPA did not have to close the plant. The parent company did that.[4] But the community was, by the time the plant closed, ready to embrace job retraining and other alternatives. Indeed, when a paper mill in the area had a problem with water pollution a few years later, they followed the Tacoma example because the community was now, in the words of a local official, "used to looking at an issue together without taking a litigative approach."[5]

The Tacoma case is important because it is the story of a people who desperately needed to change and desperately did not want to change. Yet it is also a story of hope because people eventually found a way to change. But the Tacoma case is not about a church. What would that look like in a church setting? Let us look at a second example.

There was a church near Seoul, South Korea, that absolutely had to move and absolutely could not move. The church had outgrown its building and its parking lots.[6] The mission of this congregation involved evangelism. Hence, the pastor wanted to move the congregation a few miles away so they would have room to welcome more people who wanted to hear the gospel. But there was a problem.

When the pastor broached the issue of the move with the elders, many opposed it. The building had enormous symbolic importance to the elders and to the people of the congregation. During the Japanese occupation, Koreans were not allowed to worship God. The church protested and put up this building. When the soldiers came and boarded up the building, the congregation worshiped just outside its doors. Some people were killed for doing so. This building became the place where the community stood up for Jesus against the Japanese invaders. One elder summarized the sentiment of the people when he said, "My fathers died here, and my brothers built it block by block." Your congregation probably does not have martyrs, but this one did. The church was not leaving its building.

This created something of an impasse. The pastor knew that the congregation absolutely, positively needed to move in order to honor its mission of evangelism, but he also knew that the church absolutely, positively could not move because the people could not imagine how they could claim to honor their forebears if they did move. This was a classic example of competing commitments. There seemed to be no way to honor the church's mission and to honor the church's martyrs. What was the pastor to do?

Korean pastors carry enormous authority within a congregation and a community. Therefore, one option available to the pastor was to make the decision for the congregation despite the opposition. There is, after all, a tradition of Korean pastors following their own counsel. But Korean elders also have great authority, especially those who are both advanced in years (i.e., aged elders) and duly designated for congregational leadership (i.e., elected elders). And there was the implicit authority of the martyrs who died for the right of the people to worship in that building.

Often in such situations, Korean pastors will choose to exert their authority even if some elders choose to leave the congregation. But the pastor did
not want to split the church. Other pastors might shelve the idea of moving
because it might open too many old wounds. But the pastor knew that the
congregation had outgrown the facility. Pretending that the problem would
go away did not seem to be much of a solution either.

So the pastor informed the elders that he had decided what they should do.
He had decided that they would not move unless the elders were unanimously
in favor of the move. Of course, those who were opposed to the move joy-
fully said that they had won because they knew that they would never vote
to move. Having the pastor announce a consensus process turned down the
heat, but it also made them want to ignore the problem. Surely there were
elders who wanted the pastor to stop talking about a potential move now
that they had won.

The pastor's next move was to get them to feel what Heifetz calls the "pinch
of reality." They needed to understand that staying in the old building was
creating deep and significant problems. So the pastor conducted a survey that
gathered the complaints about classrooms and parking in writing for the elders
to see. He documented that some people had to circle for fifteen minutes, looking for a parking spot. By planting the complaints of the people in the minds
of the elders, he made it difficult for them to deny that the problem existed.
In other words, he made avoidance difficult by inviting them into the story.

Yet when the results of the survey came back, he did not push his agenda.
He had turned up the heat with the complaints, so he turned down the heat
by letting the elders discuss the survey at their own pace. He did not want
them to feel trapped any more than he wanted them to deny that the problem
existed. The pastor kept the elders focused on the question but did not assert
his own prerogatives. "I will wait," he announced, "until everyone agrees
with this project." Then he gave his reason: "If it is God's will, we all will
agree with each other and do it happily." But he did not let them ignore the
problem. Each month when the elders met, they discussed the people who
were circling the parking lots—people who came to meet Jesus and gave up
because the church could not solve the parking problem.

Over time, some of the elders began to understand the need to move. Now
more elders argued in favor of the project. But the pastor did not let them
advance their cause. No one had yet come up with a way to deal with the
fact that the building itself carried deep symbolic meaning. By continuing
to say that the church would wait for consensus, he kept those who opposed
the project from flying off of the handle. But he kept the elders focused on
the problem out of a trust that eventually a new option would emerge from

them. He made them keep looking until they found a way to honor both the mission and the martyrs.

After many months, an elder spoke who had not been particularly vocal. He was an architect who had used the months of extended discussion to research the church's problem. "I can design the new church right now," he began, but it would be far more expensive. He proposed that they take the current church apart block by block. "And we can use the blocks from the current church building to construct the new one." It seemed that the new option the pastor hoped for had emerged.

Still, the pastor did not push the dissenters. "We respect you as aged elders and as elders of the faith," the pastor said. "We need more time to think and pray." He wanted to protect those who still did not agree with him so that there was time for the new ideas to take root. The pastor wanted to let this solution that the elders had cultivated grow in the dissenters until it became their own. The elders met many more times. Finally the elders all agreed. They would build a new church from the blocks of the old one. They raised the extra money and built a larger version of their church a few miles away.

---------●----------

Two situations, an ocean apart. Each community faced an intractable choice: jobs versus health, mission versus martyrs. In each case, the leaders helped the community through a process that led them to surprisingly hopeful results. *Our work in innovation often begins when our churches realize that they have terrible choices. They must change, but they cannot change.* Innovation can eventually emerge as the surprisingly hopeful way that no one at first expected. So, let us go through Heifetz's process and see how we might use it to enable our churches to change, even when they are afraid of change.

Get on the Balcony

Heifetz begins with the image of a dance floor.[7] Picture yourself on that dance floor. People are swirling all around you. There is no way to get the big picture of what is going on. If you want to see the pattern, you need to climb up to the balcony where you are above the action.[8]

Heifetz uses this balcony image as a metaphor for the need to pull yourself away to a place where you can reflect. You may not be able to leave the physical space, but you can take your mind out of the action long enough to see the big picture. So long as you are trapped within the swirl and chaos of the moment, you will have a hard time seeing the big picture.

This image of the balcony has a particularly helpful connotation for church leaders. Think of the balcony in a traditional church. It is often the place where the atypical members sit (e.g., the youth, the latecomers, those who want to sneak out early). What would the story of the worship service look like from the balcony? What would communion look like? Or the sermon? In Isaiah 40:9, God commands (through the prophet), "Get you up to a high mountain." In that passage, the high mountain is important because for thirty-nine chapters the people have felt abandoned by God. They have endured his punishment and his absence. They have begun to wonder if God has abandoned them. Then, in Isaiah 40:1, the whole tenor of the book changes. A new prophecy begins. It is a story of hope. What does the prophet do (and see) when he gets up to the high mountain? He sees the most glorious thing, the thing he and his people have longed for. "Say to the people, 'Look, here is your God!'" The prophet says that God has not abandoned us after all. Look, I can see him there. When you climb up to the high place, you see things differently. It becomes easier, indeed, to see God's story of hope for our oncoming future.

What Kind of Change Are You Facing?

Let's look at a different example of difficult change. Imagine that you go to see a cardiologist. The doctor tells you that you have a problem. You need to lose weight, quit smoking, and have heart surgery. Which of those things can the doctor do for you? Well, certainly the heart surgery. No one should try operating on their own body. But can the doctor lose weight for you? Can the doctor quit smoking for you? Of course not. There are some problems that no expert can solve for someone else—no matter how gifted or caring the expert is. You can't quit smoking for someone else.

Let's not leave that statement too quickly. Suppose you have a friend who loves you very much. In fact, you have the best friend anyone has ever had. Can that friend quit smoking for you? No, your friend cannot. But I just told you that your friend loves you very much. Surely if you love someone, you should be able to quit smoking for them. But you cannot. If you are a leader, you must be absolutely convinced of that if you are going to lead God's people through change—because time and again you will be tempted to believe (and your people will tell you in many and varied ways) that if you really love someone, you should be able to solve their problems for them.

We are called to help people to grow, to change—indeed, to be transformed. But our most important goals often lie just beyond our control. How do you help someone change who desperately needs to change but desperately does not want to change—and how do you do it when you know there are some problems that no outsider can fix? You can't quit smoking for someone else. So what do you do?

We are going to distinguish between two kinds of problems—those you can fix for someone else and those you can't. And we are going to separate these kinds of problems because the methods we use to address these problems need to be radically different. Heifetz calls the fixable issues "technical problems," and he calls the other kind "adaptive challenges."[9]

Technical problems have a solution, and by a solution he means that things will go back to the way they once were. For example, once I had a student who was the executive pastor of a very large church in West Los Angeles. They had just built a large wing onto the building. One Saturday night a pipe burst, and my student showed up on Sunday morning to discover that the entire new wing was flooded with six inches of water. This was an enormous problem. It took them weeks to assess the damage and clean up the mess. Then there were months and months of reconstruction. But a year and a half later, they had fixed the problem. Everything was back to normal. That was a technical problem. It was solvable. *With a technical problem, some combination of money, time, and expertise can make the problem go away.*

Let me give a quick way to distinguish technical problems from adaptive challenges. Learning to change the tire on a bike is a technical problem. I can give you step-by-step instructions. You can look up an answer on YouTube. An expert can do it for you. And when you are done, the problem goes away; things go back to the way they were. Learning to ride a bike is an adaptive challenge. You have to experience it. I cannot give you foolproof instructions. No expert can learn to ride for you. Then, once you learn, you will never go back to a time when you don't know how to ride.

We are accustomed to thinking that all problems are technical—that if we work a little harder and try a little more, we can fix whatever is wrong. Indeed, that is how we usually judge our leaders. We think of successful leaders as people who make things happen; they fix problems. But some problems cannot be fixed; they cannot go away. Think about smoking. Say you heed your doctor's advice and you quit smoking. And then, after a few months, you go back to the way things once were—that is, you start smoking again. Is the problem "fixed"? Of course not. Things will never be the same again. You can't quit smoking and then take it up again and act as if that has "solved" a problem. This is why Heifetz created the term "adaptive challenge." *With an adaptive challenge, things will never be the same again.*

Adaptive challenges occur, according to Heifetz, "when our deeply held beliefs are challenged, when the values that made us successful become less relevant, and when legitimate yet competing perspectives emerge."[10] Look back at that definition. Adaptive challenges happen when we ask people to adopt new beliefs, when we hope people will pursue better values, or when we help people see that the ways they have been doing things in the past will not work for them. Well, that's the exact moment when innovation is necessary. There is no meaning-making innovation without new beliefs, values, and actions. Heifetz did not have Christianity in mind when he wrote about adaptive change. Indeed, he was more interested in large social problems. But his work is crucial for those of us who lead in God's name because of a key insight Heifetz makes about adaptive challenges. *You cannot use technical means to reach adaptive ends.* In other words, the techniques that we all learned for solving technical problems will not work if we want to change people's beliefs, their values, or the ways that they always do things.

Let me illustrate *how* it won't work, and then we will talk about *why* it won't work. Let's start with an easy example. Suppose I have a friend who needs to quit smoking. What's the first thing we all do? Well, we treat it like the problem is solely about the transfer of information. I would try to explain to my friend why smoking is bad for him. Exactly what do I expect to happen when I do that? Do I really think that my friend will turn to me and admit my wise counsel? "Thank you for explaining that. I did not see these giant warning labels on the side of a cigarette packet. I guess I'd better quit now." Of course not!

But we try the explain-it-to-him plan because that's what we know. If my friend needed to learn how to change a bicycle tire (or change a diaper), then I could help him by explaining the process of change. Transfer of knowledge would work then. So, what would you guess I might do when I discover that my smoker friend was not bowled over by my knowledge? When explaining does not work, I will try the next thing. I'll say the same thing, only louder—or with more emotion. But we all know that's not going to work. I can't tell him to quit. He has to *discover* for himself that he needs to quit and that he wants to go through the pain that quitting will entail.

But I don't want to give the impression that there is no role for explaining things. For example, once my friend decides to quit, there is a lot I can do to explain to him about how hard it will be. I might explain, say, about the addictive qualities of nicotine so that he does not try to quit cold turkey. Perhaps I introduce him to nicotine gum so that he can taper off the addiction. If he did not know that nicotine is addictive, he might try to quit and find the cravings so overpowering that he gives up before he has even started. So there is a crucial role for explaining. But explaining will not make someone change. Why?

Who Needs to Change? What Will It Cost Them to Change?

Adaptive change is painful. It costs someone something to respond to an adaptive challenge. It requires a lifestyle change. Think of my friend the smoker. One reason smokers don't quit is that it is really hard to kick the habit. When someone tries to quit smoking, physiological symptoms appear (mostly about chemical addiction). There are social reasons too. It became a habit, a way of occupying the hands or something to do to fill the silences and relieve the stress. Even if we replace the physical need, the social need remains. That is true of lots of adaptive challenges. Changing a belief or a way of doing things is hard for me because I have built a lot of ideas around that belief and my routines around that way of doing things. It will be painful to change; it requires a lifestyle change.

Up to this point, I have avoided giving biblical examples because they are too easy to misunderstand until you have a mental picture of adaptive change. But now you have it. Adaptive change is like quitting smoking. It is painful. You can't quit for someone else. It is like learning to ride a bike. You cannot just tell them: they need to experience it. So what does that look like in Scripture?

Think back to Mark 8, when Jesus explains what it means to be the Messiah. No one had more authority—more credibility—than Jesus. The disciples have seen Jesus do miracles. They have seen him calm the sea, walk on water, and feed the five thousand. They have no doubt heard that at Jesus's baptism, God himself testified, "You are my Son." None of us in our ministries is going to get a real voice from heaven. But Jesus did. After Peter has pronounced him Messiah, Jesus turns to the disciples and explains that their concept of the Messiah is mistaken. He explains that the Son of Man must suffer and die and rise in three days. According to the Gospel of Mark (8:32), "He spoke plainly about this." And how did the disciples react? They told him he was wrong. This was an adaptive challenge in that Jesus asked them to give up a cherished belief.

How hard adaptive change is! Jesus himself, in all his authority, tried to explain something to them, and they told him he was wrong. Why? Because it would have been painful to recognize that he was right. What did the disciples sign up for? They expected a Messiah who would conquer the Romans. They expected a big throne for Jesus and little thrones for themselves—that's why James and John were so interested in where they would sit. Why was this adaptive change hard? Because it meant giving up the thrones. If ever there was a moment when technical means would work toward adaptive ends, it was in Mark 8. Jesus had walked on water and had God himself testify on his behalf. None of us will ever have that kind of authority. But what happened? Adaptive change was so hard for the disciples—it would cost them so much—that Jesus himself could not convince them by using technical means. And if it did not work for Jesus, how is it going to work for you and for me?

Our next step builds on another key insight from Ronald Heifetz. "People don't resist change," he has said. "They resist loss."[11] People are not afraid of change. They are only afraid of changes that will cost them something. Let's say someone shows up at my door and says, "Hello. I am from the IRS. We apologize, but there has been a terrible mistake. We owe you a million dollars. So here is a check." What am I going to do? I'm going to cash the check. I would not resist that change. But, now let's say that same person knocks on my door and says, "Hello. I am from the IRS. We apologize, but there has been a terrible mistake. You owe us a million dollars." Do you think I'd resist that change? You bet I would.

This is a fundamental insight about change. Adaptive change is painful because people lose something; it costs them something. When we discussed Mark 8, we recognized that it cost the disciples something to recognize Jesus's way of defining the Messiah. James and John pictured Jesus as coming into his kingdom and hoped to be seated at his right hand and his left. They really thought there would be thrones. When Jesus said he would suffer and die and rise, they had to recognize that they had it all wrong. It was going to cost them something to adopt Jesus's mental model.

People don't resist change; they resist loss. And all loss requires a grief process. When a loved one dies, we can easily picture that a person will need to grieve. It will take some time to come to grips with the loss. But I believe that *any significant loss requires a grief process.* And that is true for people going through adaptive change as well. Adaptive change requires grief.

Anyone who has spent time counseling people in grief is probably familiar with the work of Elizabeth Kübler-Ross. She has written about the five stages of grief.[12] We teach seminary students the stages of grief so that they know what to expect as they counsel people and so they have at their fingertips some strategies for helping people at each stage. People facing adaptive change often need to go through these stages of grief. Furthermore, I think that understanding these stages will help Christian leaders know what to expect and how to help people who face the loss that comes from adaptive change.

I encourage leaders to memorize the stages of grief[13] so that they don't need to look them up in the midst of leading. The stages of grief are denial, anger and blame, bargaining, depression, acceptance.

Denial

When people feel the pressure to change, many respond with denial. They pretend that there is no need to change. They do this either by saying that there is no cause to change (e.g., cigarettes don't cause cancer) or by saying that the pressure to change does not apply to them (e.g., I don't smoke enough to get cancer). Of all the things I teach, I have the least trouble convincing people of the power of denial. You probably don't need to look long and hard for examples of denial. It is likely you can just look back on your own life. Think of times when you desperately tried to pretend that you did not have to deal with some issue—even though everyone around you was trying to get you to pay attention. Or you can look at your favorite congregation. You can probably list places where the church is avoiding hard questions. Denial is *the immediate and reflexive reaction to pain*. We pull away and avoid the thing that hurts us. We all know how powerful denial is.

There are many ways to rouse someone from their denial (we will talk specifically about some of those ways in a few paragraphs). But, before we do that, let us look at the rest of the grief process. Let us suppose that you have been successful in rousing someone from their denial so that they now know they must deal with the problem. If this were a technical problem, then just transferring the knowledge might be enough. Now that they know they need to change, they will change. But in adaptive change, rousing someone past denial is just the beginning. Let's say you did it. You got someone to recognize that they cannot pretend the problem does not exist. What is your reward?

Anger and Blame

Your reward for successfully waking a person from their denial is anger and blame—often directed right at you. We all need to understand that, if we do our job and help people past their denial, then we can expect that some of them will move to anger and blame. This is why it is so important to understand the stages of grief. It can keep you from taking it personally when someone is angry at you while you are trying to help them. Let me give a quick example.

I have a student who is a chaplain. The other day she was sent to see a patient. The woman had come in pregnant but had just experienced a miscarriage.

When the chaplain arrived, the woman was getting dressed; she had come to the hospital alone. She introduced herself as the chaplain and asked if she could talk to the woman. The woman said, "I don't need you." So my student said, "I understand. I'm just going to sit down here with you. I won't say anything if you don't want me to." Then she sat down. Well, rather soon the woman was talking. And she was angry. She was angry at God, at the hospital, at everything. So here is my question for you: Did the chaplain take her anger personally? Of course not. "That's just the grief talking," she said as she told me the story.

We need that expression: "That's just the grief talking." There will be moments when people are really not themselves. This is normal. When a leader makes it so that people must face their problems, the common response is to blame the leader. In fact, doctors report that patients often become angry at the doctor when the doctor finds a medical problem like cancer. The doctor did not cause the cancer. But it is normal for people to want to *shoot the messenger* because if the messenger disappeared, then the people could go back to denying the problem.

This presents an interesting and difficult moment for the leader. A leader cannot take it personally when someone blames them for something they did not do. Let me repeat that because it is crucial. If you want to guarantee that your people never grow into adaptive change, all you have to do is take it personally when they become angry at you. What is more, your life experience bears this out.

Think of a thirteen-year-old asked by his father to sweep the garage when the teen would rather be watching basketball (not that I was ever that teenager, mind you; this is a purely hypothetical example). The first thing the teen does is to try to stall, to ignore, to do anything he can to pretend that he really does not have to do it. Then, when that does not work, he knows that the best defense is a good offense. So he starts an argument. He makes it inconvenient for his father to make him do something he does not want to do. And he hopes that the father gets sidetracked by arguing about who is in charge—with the argument taking place in the TV room while the game keeps playing in the background. We have all tried that.

Now think back to that chaplain with the mother who just lost her child. Somehow the mother starts to think that it all would have been better if the chaplain had come earlier to pray for her. Perhaps she gets angrier and angrier. Now imagine you are the chaplain. *In your mind, you know that her anger is not about you. You don't take it personally.* You don't meet her anger with your own anger by saying, "How dare you blame me for your child's death?" You would not do it because you know that she is using you as a scapegoat—*a repository, a place to put her anger until she can deal with it in a healthier way*. In fact, you know her anger is not really anger. It is fear and loss masquerading as anger. It's the grief talking.

The key point here is that you don't take that personally. You understand that it is not about you. You understand that your job is to hang in there with her no matter how angry she needs to be. Why? You do that because you know that it is the best way to help her through to the other side. And you know that her getting to the other side is far more important than any wounding your pride might temporarily feel. You remember that *it is not about you. It's about the one who is grieving*.

In the same way, when you are helping people through adaptive change, you need to remember that it is not about you. Your job is to help them through their pain to the other side. Heifetz put it this way: Leaders become "repositories for our worries and aspirations, holding them, if they can, in exchange for the powers we give them."[14] The role of the leader is to hold people's fears and parcel them back to the people at a rate they can stand. Think of a repository as a vessel, a bowl, or a cup. We accept people's anger, their blame, their worries, and their fears. We hold them and save them. Then we take them out when the people are ready to work on them.

In our example from earlier in the chapter, the EPA accepted the blame and the anger directed at them by the community. They did not become defensive. That would have sidetracked them. Instead, they stayed focused on the task at hand, which was to help the community deal with the life-threatening problem looming in their skies. In the same way, *I need to remember that I am helping people deal with big and difficult issues. I don't have time to get sidetracked by personal slights.* When I do feel personally slighted, I remember something. They are usually mad at me because it is too scary to be mad at God. I am God's representative. There are lots of times when God does something wonderful in someone's life, and I get the accolades, even though I did nothing to deserve them. In the same way, I remind myself, I sometimes take the heat because people are angry at God. So, I do what God does. I hang in there with them and keep inviting them to deeper relationship. Remember the psalms of lament. God can handle people's anger. He gives us the language to express it in those psalms. And if God can handle their anger, so can I.

Bargaining

Blame and anger are, however, only a stage. If I hang in there with people, they often move to the next stage—which is bargaining. This is, perhaps, the part of Kübler-Ross's work that has gained the most attention. You know how bargaining goes. We spend our time imagining deals we would make. "If I promise to be good, will you get me out of this?" But it is more than that.

Bargaining statements can often be phrased, "If only . . ." If only I promise to cut down to half a pack a day, can I keep smoking? If only we cut arsenic emissions, can we keep the plant open? If only Jesus had arrived sooner, Lazarus would not have died. We enter a temporary magical world where we pretend that there is a way to make things better, to make things go back to the way they once were. (Remember, the heart of an adaptive challenge is that things will never be the same again; things cannot go back to normal. I can't quit smoking and then start up again and pretend I've dealt with the problem.)

Bargaining behavior is extremely common; it often happens when we don't expect it. Think of the congregation that has a generational divide between older members and younger members. They are fighting over music, and the music minister gets caught in the middle. Now the church is on its third music minister in five years. They are engaging in bargaining behavior. If only we find a new music minister, perhaps that person can bridge the generational divide. It is too painful to deal with the divide directly, so we look for technical solutions (like finding a new music minister), and we pretend that solving that easier problem will suffice.

I see it all the time. And I have come to welcome bargaining behavior (it is a lot more pleasant than anger and blame) because it is a next step on the way to acceptance. I know how to work with someone engaged in bargaining behavior. *I just take the bargain seriously and name it for what it is.* "So you think that if we hire a new music minister," I say to them, "we will no longer have a generational divide?" I try to get the people to *discover for themselves* that the music question is a symptom, but it is not the problem. It takes a while. But I find that it is easy to hang in with someone doing bargaining because I know that *bargaining won't ever really satisfy them.*

Depression

The reason I keep hanging in with them is that I know what is coming. I have compassion for them. I know that ultimately bargaining won't work and that eventually they will move on to the next stage, what Kübler-Ross calls depression. This is not usually clinical depression in a psychological sense. But they are depressed by this one issue. And for good reason.

Remember why they are going through these stages of grief. They are grieving because they need to face some change, and they know that the change is going to cost them something. *These grieving behaviors are designed to fend off the pain that will inevitably come when they acknowledge that change is necessary.*

They experience depression when they finally realize that the loss is permanent—when they acknowledge that they cannot ignore the problem, they cannot make someone else the scapegoat, and they cannot bargain the problem away. In such a moment my job is, once again, to hang in there with them (don't worry; in a few pages we will describe exactly what you are doing when you are hanging in there with them). I keep supporting them because they are almost ready for the next step.

Acceptance

The final stage is acceptance. Eventually, if we are successful, a person or a people recognizes that they must deal with the problem. But this whole process can be tricky. We have presented these stages in such a way that they appear linear—as if once you have passed through denial of a situation, you never revert to that point again. It's not so easy. *When something happens that causes someone to feel the depth of a problem in a new way, they often jump back to denial or blame.* It is a defense mechanism. Just like a boy overwhelmed by his mother's death might revert back to denial or anger around his mother's birthday, so people are often overwhelmed by the magnitude of a change they have to make and revert back to an earlier stage. All you can do in that moment is to hang in there with them and help them build up the emotional courage to face the problem again.

So we have five stages of grief. When I present Heifetz's ideas to people who are interested in change, they often tell me that they seem too complicated or too difficult. They say that there must be an easier way. But I recognize that for what it is. It's bargaining behavior. If only there were an easier way to help people change, then I would not have to learn this new and painfully difficult way to lead. It's true. If there were another way, you would not have to learn this one. If there were a way to treat adaptive challenges as technical problems, then you would not have to accept people's anger and sit with them in their pain. But there is no other way.

The first steps to pursuing adaptive change are clear: Get up on the balcony in order to give yourself perspective. Ask yourself: What is the adaptive challenge? Who needs to change? And what is it going to cost them? The next step will tell you where you have leverage to act.

Get Authorized

What are you authorized to do? The word "authorized" means what you have the authority to do. Sometimes your authority comes from a job description. But there are other ways to gain the authority you need to act. Let's think back to my friend the smoker. If I want to help him change, I will need to have the authority to speak into his life. That authority is not going to come from a job description.

It may, for example, be relational authority that allows me to speak. But the authority in that case depends on the nature of the relationship. If I am a casual acquaintance, I don't have the same authority that I might have as a family member or a trusted friend.

Likewise, there is what is called cultural authority. For example, in the Korean church there are two kinds of elders: elected elders and aged elders. Elected elders have formal authority. There is a document that describes their authority as members of the church board. But then there are aged elders. They have authority because it is deeply important in the culture to "respect your elders." There are relatively few elected elders, but anyone can be an aged elder if they wait long enough. You need to recognize that you can only do what you have the authority to do.

Then that brings up the question of what you should use your authority to do. Both the head of the EPA and the leader of the Korean congregation were wise in how they used their authority. Everyone expected them to use their authority to make a decision. But neither one did that. Instead, they used their authority to create a process. The EPA decided that only the people would decide the final step and that the process would be a series of public meetings. The Korean pastor decided that they would wait for consensus and that each month they would take time at the board meeting to consider the people circling the parking lots.

I am often asked, "How much authority do I need to engage an adaptive challenge?" The answer is simple. *You only need enough authority to create and maintain a holding environment.*

Create a Holding Environment

A holding environment is a psychological space that is both safe and uncomfortable. Picture the stereotypical dad running alongside the kid learning to ride a bike. The kid is safe in that the dad is there to catch her if she falls. But the kid is uncomfortable because she is the one doing the work—the balancing, the pedaling, the steering. She is the one learning the new behavior. So long as dad is holding on to the bike, it is not a holding environment because he's doing the work. But if he is only there with his outstretched arms not quite touching her, then it's a holding environment.[15]

Let's define the concept more clearly because everything we do in adaptive change depends on our abilities to create and maintain a holding environment. Specifically, a holding environment is a psychological space uncomfortable enough that a person cannot avoid the problem but safe enough that the person can experiment with a new way of being. We earlier said that you cannot pursue technical means to adaptive ends. Now we know what you should do. *Every approach to adaptive change must include creating a holding environment.*

Heifetz talks about two reasons why people avoid doing adaptive work. They don't do adaptive work when they don't feel the problem strongly enough. And they don't do adaptive work when they feel the problem too acutely—that is, when they feel crushed by the weight of the problem.

Think about the kid on the bike. As long as daddy is holding on, the kid does not need to learn to balance and steer. She can avoid the hard work and just enjoy pedaling. While daddy is holding on, it may feel like she's riding a bicycle, but she's not. Only when he lets go and she must do the balancing is she learning to ride. And what happens when daddy first lets go? She gets scared and yells for him to grab on again. Think of kids you have known in that moment (perhaps even yourself). Some kids embrace the moment and learn quickly. That's great! But remember the question that really animates: "How do you help someone change who desperately needs to change but desperately does not want to change?" The kid that embraces the challenge is not the one who desperately does not want to change.

There are two other ways kids react. Some kids shout for dad and keep pedaling. Then as dad runs alongside encouraging them, the kids are learning to ride—whether they want to or not. Those kids are in the holding environment. Dad's presence makes it safe enough that they can try a new way of being, and because dad is not holding on, it's uncomfortable enough that they have to keep trying.

Yet there is another way that a kid might react. One of my children had a hard time learning to ride a bicycle. When I let go, she would stop pedaling. That kid felt the need to change so much that she panicked. I had to keep hanging in there with her. I would hold on for a long time, let go for a moment, and then I'd grab hold again. Next I'd let go a little longer and then grab on again. Then I'd let go even longer. And so on. I had to keep it safe enough that she would keep pedaling, even if her first attempts lasted just a second or two.

The holding environment is uncomfortable enough that the person cannot ignore the need to change, but it is safe enough to try a new way of being.

Notice the temptation for the father in this example. He has to be willing to make his child face her fears. In that moment it's tempting to grab on to the bike and never let the kid feel uncomfortable. But if you do, you guarantee that she never learns to ride a bike. The same thing happens for leaders. People will say to the leader, "We will do whatever you tell us. Just don't make us face our fears."

Heifetz calls this "flight to authority."[16] It is like the child saying, "I promise I will work really hard to learn to ride this bike. I'll ride for two hours today. But you have to promise never to let go of me." Well, it's obvious that can't work. The child will never learn. But we leaders are faced with this problem all the time.

Think of the Korean pastor. The church faced an adaptive challenge. It absolutely had to move because it was too large for its building, and it absolutely could not move because it had to respect the memories of the martyrs. Faced with such a difficult moment, the congregation could easily have said to the pastor, "You decide; we will do whatever you tell us." But he could not take that deal. Why? First, because the people would not have been able to keep their end of the bargain. If he had decided to move, it would have split the church. But, second, because the choice was not his to make. The whole congregation would need to adapt to the new situation. And he could not decide for them any more than I could decide that my friend was going to quit smoking. Flight to authority cannot work, no matter how tempting it is to shield people from their loss.

So, what do you do when faced with a flight to authority? You do the same thing that I did with my daughter. In Heifetz's phrase, you "fail people's expectations at a rate they can stand."[17] If my daughter had told me she would practice for two hours if I promised not to let go, I would have said to her, "Let's just keep at it." Then I would have run alongside her, holding on as if I had agreed to the bargain. But ever so slowly and carefully, I would have let go for a moment and then grabbed it back—and so on and so on. In other words, I would have kept her focused back on the task.

Let's look back at the Tacoma case and the Korean congregation. In each case the leaders used their authority to construct a holding environment. The EPA did two things to construct a holding environment. They threatened to close the plant; that made the situation uncomfortable enough that people could not ignore the problem. And they convened regular meetings without telling people exactly how they had to change. That made it safe. Likewise, the Korean pastor brought the idea to the church board (who knew that he had the authority simply to decide on his own). That made the situation uncomfortable. Then he said that he would wait for consensus. That made it safe. In each case, the leader created a holding environment. But a holding environment is a fragile thing. It is something that the leader must monitor and nurture—like my grandfather the citrus farmer tending the soil that nourished his trees.

Pacing: Regulating Distress to Maintain the Holding Environment

Heifetz advises that a leader needs to "turn up the heat" or "turn down the heat" to maintain a holding environment. Let me explain.

When someone (or when a group) is feeling overwhelmed, then the leader must turn down the heat so it becomes safe enough for them to experiment with a new way of being. By the same token, when someone (or when a group) is feeling comfortable enough that they can ignore an adaptive challenge, then the leader must turn up the heat so they feel the need to change. The best way to turn up the heat is to make people, in Heifetz's phrase, feel the "pinch of reality."[18] In this phrase, "pinch" does not mean a little bit (as in "a pinch of salt"); it means a small pain (as in "my sister pinched me"). Reality is painful because the person really does need to change. The pinch of reality refers to the negative consequences that come from not changing. If you don't quit smoking, you really will shorten your life span.

A model for how to do this is the Korean pastor we encountered earlier. He turned down the heat (i.e., made it safer and less uncomfortable) by declaring that the board must reach consensus, and then he turned up the heat by making the board feel the pinch of reality. He collected stories about people who circled the neighborhood looking for parking and then gave up. Then he brought those stories to the board. Perhaps he pointed to the congregation's commitment to evangelism and asked how the church could claim to represent Jesus and turn away people who want to worship Jesus. He used specific stories and specific data to keep the board from ignoring the problem. He regulated their distress so that they felt a *productive level of discomfort*. And when they felt both uncomfortable enough that they could not stand still and safe enough that they could experiment with a new way of being, then he knew he was maintaining the holding environment.

The goal in making people feel the pinch of reality is for them to "discover" for themselves their need to change. The elders of the Korean church needed to discover for themselves that the church absolutely had to move. They had to discover that avoiding the problem was the same as turning people away. The leader could not discover that for them. Every month when the board met, he could put new stories before them. But they had to discover the problem. Each elder had to discover for himself that the congregation could not ignore the problem.

But there is a somewhat dangerous decision that comes as people make the discovery that goads them past their denial. *I have seen pastors turn victory into defeat with the ways that they mishandled that moment of discovery.* You will find yourself talking for months, trying to get people to adopt some problem as their own. Finally, someone will come to you at the church and say, "I have made a discovery. I think the church should be doing something about XYZ." And then the person will describe exactly what you've been saying for months, using exactly the language you've been using for months, and that person will have no idea that you ever said it. The person might even be angry at you because "the church should be doing something about this." Don't become defensive. Everything in you will want to say, "Are you kidding me? I've been saying that for months." If you do, you'll ruin everything. *You will make the person feel embarrassed and defensive at just the moment when that thinker is ready to take a new step.*

Here's what I say instead (yes, I've memorized this little phrase because I cannot trust that my instincts will handle the moment very well). I say, "I'm so glad to hear that. It turns out that some other folks in the congregation have had the same idea. Perhaps I can put you in touch with them, and we can work on this together." I will admit, however, that this is easier said than done. I can recall a time when I mishandled such a moment. I was working with an organization as a consultant. For months I had told them that they needed to start keeping data because they were making decisions based on anecdotes rather than facts. The treasurer was blocking this move. Some time later, she told me that she had been thinking about how the church needed to keep better financial data, and she complained that I had not trained her properly. I should have said, "I'm glad to hear that. I think we can work on that together." But that's not what I said. We need to be careful how we handle that moment of discovery.

We turn up the heat by helping people feel the pinch of reality so that they can discover the problem for themselves. How, then, do we turn down the heat? Heifetz points out that one way to make people feel safer is to focus for a brief time on technical problems. So, for example, the dad teaching bike riding could spend time focusing the kid on how to pedal, all the while holding on to the bike. Then the child builds back the confidence to keep pedaling. Or, the Korean pastor could have the board talk about how to re-stripe the existing parking lots so more cars would fit. Re-striping the parking lots will not solve the bigger problem, but it will buy time and build up the board's hopefulness about the problem.

Maintain Disciplined Attention

Adaptive change takes time. A technical problem can often be solved immediately by money and expertise (although some take a long time). But adaptive challenges almost always take time. It takes time for the people who need to change to come to accept that they really do need to change. It takes time to work through the grief process. It takes time to come up with ways of working the problem. It takes time.

Think of the Tacoma case. Each step that the Washington town took required them to face their loss more deeply. They had to recognize that the plant was spewing poison. They had to recognize that the EPA was not going to solve the problem for them. They had to come to stop thinking of a binary choice between either jobs or health. And they had to come up with ways to approach the problem once they decided to pursue both health and jobs. Each of those steps took time because they involved loss; they involved the failure of the town's expectation that the leaders would rescue them and take the problem away from them.

During that period the EPA's job was to keep the people focused on the problem—to keep them from becoming distracted or discouraged. They did this in two ways. They kept threatening to close the plant so that the urgency of the problem never lifted, and they conducted regular meetings so that the people were constantly directed forward.

Maintaining disciplined attention turns out to be the hardest part of adaptive change. For example, in my years of working with congregations through the Fuller Youth Institute, the number one reason congregations failed to make hoped-for changes was that they failed to maintain disciplined attention.

This is where we can remind ourselves of what Pixar called the hungry beast of daily duties. It takes a great deal of energy to lead adaptive change. Leaders often get so distracted by their daily duties that it becomes convenient just to stop focusing on the change. The Korean pastor who used the monthly board meeting to maintain his board's attention could easily have become so caught up in the normal activities of a board meeting that he forgot to focus on the need to move. But he didn't allow himself to become distracted.

This is why we discuss Helen in the appendix at the end of this book. Every leader helping their people needs a Helen. The appendix suggests that you might appoint one of your volunteers (your "Helen") to hold your team's feet to the fire. If I were leading adaptive change, I would appoint a Helen, and I would tell her that her job is to meet with me outside my regular staff meeting and ask me only four questions: (1) When did you meet last with your people on the adaptive challenge? (2) What did you do to maintain the holding environment—to turn up the heat and to turn down the heat? (3) When will you next meet with your people? (4) What do you plan to do to maintain the holding environment at that time?

Give the Work Back to the People, but at a Rate They Can Stand

This is where we must remember that you cannot quit smoking for someone else. The mental model of leadership held by most churches is that leaders decide for the people. They think that a leader, such as the Korean pastor, who does not take the pain away from the people is shirking his responsibility. Let's look more closely at the Tacoma case.

The crucial move was when the EPA decided to conduct community meetings rather than mandate a specific course of action. They decided to create a holding environment where they could turn up the heat with the threat of closing the plant and turn down the heat by not yet closing it. The head of the EPA (William Ruckelshaus) explained his thinking with a quote from Thomas Jefferson: "If we think [the people] are not enlightened enough to exercise control with a wholesome discretion, the remedy is not to take it from them, but to inform their discretion."[19] The EPA leader said, in effect, that only the people could decide which painful choice to make and that it was a leader's job to give them the information necessary to make an enlightened decision.

The public's response to the EPA's decision to create a holding environment was strongly negative. Newspapers across the country saw the EPA (and its leader) as forcing people into a cruel choice between jobs and health. They thought that good leaders take the heat; they don't put it on the people. The EPA leader responded by saying, "People have demanded to be involved and now I have involved them and they say: 'Don't ask that question.' What's the alternative? Don't involve them?"[20] To use Heifetz's language, the public believed in a mental model (a Big Lie?) that said leaders take the pain away; they never make their people face it. But the only way to take the pain away was to decide for them. And no outsider should decide how many jobs are worth how many lives.

The result of giving the work back to the people surprised even the EPA. The EPA expected the community to come to some formula that balanced emissions, health risks, and jobs. But the people eventually came to a different conclusion. They began to push for the diversification of the local economy, especially through retraining the plant's workers. "The idea of diversification, although obvious in retrospect," Heifetz notes, "had not been part of anyone's mindset." Neither "the EPA, industry, labor, environments, [nor] local officials" had thought much about it. "It took the noisy and conflictive process of public workshops, debates in the press, and the mobilization of neighborhoods to generate new ideas."[21]

The EPA leaders used their authority to create a process and not to impose an outcome. Giving the work back to the people at a rate they could stand did two things. It gave the people the power to decide for themselves what was important to them. And it allowed them to generate ideas that the leaders themselves would not have seen. The same thing happened in the Korean congregation. By using his authority to keep the board's attention on the problem, the Korean pastor provided time (and cover) for someone to come up with a solution that could not have come from the leader himself. If we are convinced that "you cannot quit smoking for someone else," then we must give the work back to the people.

----------●----------

We can then summarize Heifetz's insights by working through eight steps. Allow me to list them here and then to illustrate how they work with innovation by applying them through an example we encountered in a previous chapter.

1. Get on the balcony.
2. What kind of change are you facing?
3. Who needs to change? What will it cost them to change?
4. What are you authorized to do?
5. Create a holding environment.
6. Pacing: maintain the holding environment.
7. Maintain disciplined attention.
8. Give the work back to the people.

Summary of Heifetz's Steps for Adaptive Change

Get on the Balcony

Erica, the youth pastor in Florida, decided to teach her middle schoolers to lament. Erica and her ministry partner set aside time to make a plan of action. They agreed to meet regularly. They agreed to engage in systematic listening. They agreed to come to Fuller for an innovation summit.[22] The key insight was to follow the process laid out in chapter 6.

What Kind of Change Are You Facing?

Very quickly they could see that they were trying to change the mental models that people held about youth ministry. That was the major obstacle. But it was not the main goal. The main goal was to change their middle schoolers' mental model of God. Another way to say this is that their people believed Big Lies. The adults believed the lie that youth ministry today should look like youth ministry of a generation ago. And the youth believed the lie that it was wrong (and perhaps dangerous) to express our anger to God. Defeating these Big Lies required the kind of mental model change that is an adaptive challenge.

Who Needs to Change? What Will It Cost Them to Change?

Erica realized that there were at least three groups of people who would need to change if they were going to make the project work. It would cost each group something different; she would need a plan for each one.

1. Young People

   The purpose of the project was to enable the middle schoolers to develop a "grace-based identity," as Erica called it. That would cost them something: they would need to face their fears about talking directly to God about their anger, and they would need to feel the pain of loss that they had been suppressing.

2. Parents

   There were two groups of parents, and each one had to face a change. Some parents were members of the church, and they had to put aside their mental models about the appropriate way to talk to God. Other parents were not part of any church, and they had to recognize the ways their children were growing in faith. And both kinds of parents had to be able to deal with the disruption that might come about when young people start to get in touch with their pain and when they learn to speak to an authority figure (in this case, God) with honesty and anger.

3. Youth Ministry Volunteers

   The adults who volunteer with the youth group would need to recognize a different way of doing youth ministry. Because none of them had engaged in lament earlier, they would experience the awkwardness of temporary incompetence.[23]

What Are You Authorized to Do?

Erica immediately knew what she was authorized to do and what she was not. She had the authority to change what went on under her watch.

1. Young People

    As the youth minister, she had the authority to change the content of the youth group's meetings. That meant she could create a holding environment for the young people when they were meeting.

2. Parents

    She also had the authority to convene a parents' meeting, which meant she had some leverage over parents (but not that much).

3. Youth Ministry Volunteers

    And, of course, she had the authority to convene meetings of her volunteers.

But she did not have the authority to change things under other people's jurisdiction. Specifically, she did not have the authority to engage the whole congregation, nor did she have permission to do anything that might affect the worship service (which is ironic because eventually the congregation invited her and her youth group, during Lent, to lead a portion of the service).

Create a Holding Environment

The most important creative work for Erica went into the decisions about how to construct a holding environment for each of the groups that faced adaptive challenges. Although it is sometimes possible to create one holding environment that serves two groups, Erica had to, in this case, construct separate holding environments for each of the three groups.

1. Young People

    For this group, the holding environment functioned on two levels. At the more general level, the regular youth meeting was a holding environment. The fact that most of the meeting was like any other meeting turned down the heat because any given meeting could seem like no big change. But the fact that she changed a portion of it to focus on lament turned up the heat in that it was different and it invited the young people to face some of their pain.

    At the more specific level, the Mad Libs format of the lament itself was also a holding environment. It turned up the heat because it asked students to write down thoughts and feelings that usually went unexpressed. At the same time, the Mad Libs format turned down the heat because Erica herself provided the format. The students could easily tell themselves that they were not doing anything wrong (even if it meant expressing anger to God) because God's own representative (think "ambassador") was the one who told them to do it.

2. Parents

The holding environment for parents was far more subtle. Erica planted language. She introduced phrases like "God can handle your honesty" and "psalms of lament." Also, she created a shared story of hope by saying that students could express their anger in a controlled way. It gave parents a way to think about how to handle teenage angst. All of that turned up the heat because it was new (and potentially threatening), and it turned down the heat because she herself bore the brunt of the youths' emotional struggle before she sent the young people to their parents. Indeed, the parents eventually asked for a resource that they could use to discuss lament with their kids at home.

At the same time, she used the parents' night as a holding environment. It turned down the heat because it looked like a chance to observe the young people and get to know the volunteers—kind of like every middle school's "Back to School Night." But, on the other hand, it turned up the heat because she invited the parents to participate and discussed ways of talking to God that were likely new to them.

3. Youth Ministry Volunteers

Although a very small team helped Erica do the actual innovating, she did need to train her volunteers and small-group leaders about lament. She conducted a training session for them. Indeed, she not only had to train them about lament but also about listening. She called it "empathy training." You will recall, for example, that she advised her volunteers to control their urges by saying, "Every time you want to speak as you listen, take a sip of water to stop yourself from saying, 'Yeah, but . . .'" She also had them think back on their own experiences as teens, which called up within the volunteers the kinds of feelings that made it easier to empathize ("feeling with . . .") the young people. Indeed, this training became the backbone of the training that Erica took to the parents and eventually to the whole congregation.

I should report, as well, that Erica herself was not always aware that she was creating these layered holding environments. But that is the beauty of working with reinvented practices like lament. They are already anchored in the tradition, which turns down the heat and makes them safe. Yet they are reinvented or new in some way, which turns up the heat. *The practices themselves often become holding environments.*

Pacing: Maintaining the Holding Environment

Erica created a plan for sustained work in innovation by designing the ten-week arc for youth group meetings in advance. She laid out the plan to start with nonthreatening work and to become more and more personal over time. For the first week, she brought in a storyteller to talk about Psalm 22, Psalm 42, Job, and Lamentations. She also had the middle schoolers select song lyrics (from both secular and Christian songs) that expressed their feelings.

As the weeks progressed, each week had a new activity that took them a little deeper into lament. This "paced the process" by gradually turning up the heat. Each week the teens felt a little more comfortable with lament, which turned down the heat. That gave Erica the freedom to introduce something new. For example, she introduced the idea that "You might find as you lament that there is something that you caused." Then she taught them about how to confess when they discovered places where they caused people pain.

Maintain Disciplined Attention

In a similar way, the fact that Erica laid the ten weeks out in advance ensured that she would keep the attention of her people. That is often the easy part. The harder part of maintaining disciplined attention often comes during the creative moments, before the project is introduced to anyone else. For example, when we lead innovation summits with youth ministers, the hardest time for many church teams is the time after the innovation summit (i.e., when they have a prototype) but before they have a plan for how to bring it into their youth group. They celebrate the fact that they have a prototype (which turns on the heat in terms of their own urgency) just at the time they feel the call of other duties in their work (i.e., the hungry beast of daily duties). That is the time that having a "Helen" (an outsider to hold you responsible) can be particularly helpful.

Give the Work Back to the People

Ultimately, Erica was only a gardener who plants and waters. Like my grandfather the citrus rancher, she could only create an environment for growth. The young people themselves had to decide how much or how little they would engage the project. The parents had to decide if they were going to do more than hear about it. And the volunteers had to do the hard work of empathizing. Erica could not do any of that for them any more than she could have quit smoking for one of them. In the end, the work belonged to them (and the Holy Spirit).

How, then, did it all play out? Each week Erica asked the young people to describe in a single word what they were feeling during the youth group meeting. At first, the middle schoolers used words like "sad," "hectic," and "hard." But as the lament project continued, the young people started using words like "progressive," "relatable," and "powerful" to describe the youth group experience. Some even expressed that they were feeling "anger"—which Erica took to be a sign that they were not feeling angry about the youth group but that they were using the process of the youth group to experience and express the anger that they felt as they regularly walked through life.[24]

She also reports that the youth group has grown. It seems that middle schoolers have had such a positive experience that they are inviting friends to join them—and the friends have decided to stick around.

The students reported how their relationship with God has changed as they have been able to express their feelings in honesty before God. "I thought we had to be nice to God," one student said to Erica, "but now I know I can be really honest with him." And another student reported that at first "it was hard to see how love and anger go together," but now "I see how trusting someone even in anger makes deeper relationship."[25]

---------•---------

We started this chapter with the kind of question that all leaders ask at some point, even if it stymies them. *How do you help people change who desperately need to change but desperately don't want to change?* We learned that there is a reason why people don't want to change: people don't resist change; they resist loss. When encountering these adaptive challenges, a leader's duty is to respond with empathy. We create what is called a holding environment—a psychological space uncomfortable enough that our people cannot stand still and safe enough that they can experiment with a new way of being.

It might seem, at first, that this is not the most empathetic way to respond. But then we remember that our people desperately need to change. We as leaders are not imposing the need to change on our people. The world has imposed it. Our friend the smoker really does need to change. The plant in Tacoma really did need to stop poisoning its neighbors. And the congregation in Korea really did need to honor its mission statement. The leaders did not create the need. They only helped their people face the need. The kindest thing that these leaders could do was to create a process—an environment—in which their people could deal with the pain their circumstances had already created and to do it at a rate the people could stand.

Leading adaptive change requires leaders who have the agility to take one faithful step at a time, listening to what they hear and responding to what they read from the people in front of them. Developing that agility can be tricky. That is the subject of the next chapter.

9

The Next Faithful Step

A seminary student named Ingrid came to me because she wanted to invent her own internship in correspondence with her work at a Korean American church. She had a heart for the daughters of immigrants, girls who aspired to go to college. These were the people entrusted to her care. But because Ingrid herself was the child of immigrants from El Salvador, she knew from experience that these girls faced obstacles. Ingrid had done research and knew that providing a mentor who could counsel a girl would double an immigrant teen's chance of staying on track in college. So Ingrid had started a mentoring ministry and mobilized members of the church to work with these girls. Ingrid came to me because she wanted help. Ingrid wanted her fledgling ministry to count as her internship for her degree, and she wanted guidance on how to write a grant so that her denomination would support the ministry.[1]

Ingrid is the wave of the future. She knows that when she graduates from seminary, she cannot count on a church system to create a job for her. No one in her generation can. The Christendom model of preparation and placement has ended, and there is no pipeline for her generation. She knows that she will need to invent a place to minister—whether she ministers inside or outside a church. In short, *her future depends on her capacity for agility.*

The problem, of course, is that seminary education is calibrated for a world that no longer exists; it is not presently designed to develop this capacity for innovation and agility. A generation ago, the goal of a seminary education was to create what one scholar called *"theological camels."*[2] A school pumped a student full of knowledge and then sent the graduate out into the desert, hoping they had learning enough to last a lifetime. For much of the twentieth century, theological camels thrived. Camels are custom-built for a particular environment and exactly the right mode of transportation if you are traveling a predictable route from one oasis to the next. It makes sense that schools were once calibrated for a predictable world.

But the world Ingrid will enter is too unpredictable to count on the camel model of ministry. Camels do not have the adaptability to survive in a changing world. The world Ingrid will enter requires Christian leaders to be agile and imaginative. Although camels are calibrated to thrive in one very specific environment, Ingrid may find that when she reaches the summit of a sand dune, there is no oasis, or even more sand, on the other side; instead, she might enter a rain forest or a barrio. Our graduates will need to respond to changes in the world, changes that they cannot predict. When I was a seminary student twenty-five years ago, no one talked to me about the internet; the World Wide Web as we know it was not created until six months after I graduated. In the same way, there are changes coming in this world that none of us can foresee. The Ingrids of the future need to develop the agility to respond to whatever changes are over the next sand dune.

Let me contrast Ingrid with another graduate. Petra entered ministry as the model candidate. She grew up in a prestigious church and attended a well-known Christian college. Petra breezed through seminary with great grades. She impressed the candidates' committee of her presbytery with her answers to complex theological questions. After graduation, Petra won a plum assignment as an associate pastor at a large church with many staff members—an assignment that put her on track to lead a large congregation of her own one day. I met her because she was the youngest person to participate in a small study group sponsored by her denomination. She was on the fast track. And all this worked great for her, right up until the point where she washed out of ministry in the first few years of that plum assignment. Petra was exactly what seminary education hoped to produce, and that is exactly the problem.

Petra was (and is) tremendously reflective. She remained a part of that denominational study even after she packed her bags, quit the ministry, and moved back to her hometown. Petra took responsibility for her own failings. But, when pressed to see herself as the product of the system that her denomination had created, she wrote a stellar paper on what her experience tells us about preparation for ministry. In her reflections, Petra said that seminary education "is largely based on the academic model, which does not serve the pastor-to-be or the person in the pew." She explained where the "academic model" failed by describing both the seminary and the denominational processes. "The preparation process rewards *textual skills*, but ministry requires *relational skills.* I was told that I was a model candidate. But I realize now that it was because I was good at working with texts. I may have been a good candidate, but the preparation process did not teach me the relational skills necessary for ministry."[3]

She did not have *the agility to connect the texts she read with the people she led.* Indeed, she was taught to put more energy into understanding texts than people. But when she began to lead, she discovered that people are constantly changing and that her job was to find a new reading of Scripture that addressed the lives of the people entrusted to her care. We have seen examples of this in previous chapters. Martin Luther built the Reformation around a new reading of the book of Romans, and Ralph Winter built the contemporary missionary movement around a new reading of Jesus's parting words. But they each did that because they realized that the world had changed—and that people who live in a changing world need new insights from Scripture.

After Petra gave her presentation, we talked further, and she described how these difficulties played out. The longings and losses she experienced in the church position were threaded through a series of role conflicts. As an associate pastor with responsibilities for youth and families, she supervised a youth director, and she reported to a lead pastor.[4] Listening to the youth made her realize that teenagers seemed to need something quite different from what the senior pastor wanted the church to provide. In other words, her congregation was calibrated to serve the needs of youth who no longer existed. Her responsibilities to the teens and to the youth minister clashed with her responsibility to enact what the lead pastor and the church board wanted. The youth minister wanted to serve the youth entrusted to his care, and the lead pastor (and the board) wanted to replicate a ministry from a bygone era. She needed the imagination to create a way to respond to both needs.

Likewise, her role as a pastor competed with her role as a wife and her longing to be a mother. This created tremendous uncertainty. Petra lacked the agility to mediate the role conflict. So she retreated to what she knew best; she wrote and reflected, isolated from people, unsure how to act. She did exactly what her seminary education had prepared her to do, and that was the problem. *Petra did not have the agility to serve the needs of her ever-changing people within the constraints of a traditional congregation.*

The problem, of course, is that we live between Ingrid's future and Petra's past. We have inherited a ministry system designed to produce plodding camels for Christendom. Until that system changes (as a seminary professor, I can point to places where it is changing—especially at my school[5]), the ministry as we know it will be calibrated for a world that no longer exists. *We need a way to instill agility into a community of pastors prepared to minister in a world of predictability that no longer exists.* This chapter is focused on pastors, but the insights apply to any Christian leader who is the product of the American educational system, whether that Christian leader works in a religious setting or a secular business.

----------●----------

This problem of stumbling agility is not restricted to theological education. It is the product of our educational system. Think of the educational system as the place where we lay out our expectations; it is the place where it is easiest to see the world we have calibrated ourselves to serve. In fact, this lack of agility is common in our best graduates, according to Tom Kelley and David Kelley.[6] The Kelley brothers are among the most respected voices in the world of innovation. David Kelley is the founder of two innovation icons: the innovation incubator firm IDEO and the Stanford School of Design (commonly called the d.school). Tom Kelley is a partner at IDEO and has written extensively on innovation. In a recent article, the brothers describe four "chronic fears" that prevent people from exercising the kind of creativity that is necessary for innovation. We will discuss the four phobias in a moment. But before we do, it is important to see the effect that the article had. It sparked a discussion in business schools about the readiness of graduates to do the agile work of innovation.

A business school professor, Hilary Austen, begins one such article by asking, "What do we expect of a good student?"[7] In other words, what is our mental model of success? The article describes the ideal business school student, but it could have been describing Petra or any other model Christian leader. We want "a willing, intelligent mind, diligently applied to coursework. Reliable and rapid recall. A calm, competent response to the pressure of testing. What else? Perhaps a disciplined mindset that assures homework will be turned in on time. The rigor to complete work correctly. An attentive and cooperative attitude in class." These are the characteristics of an ideal student. "In the prevailing model of education," Austen recognizes, "that kind of student will make straight As all the way." Even in the most rigorous programs, "these students will move to the head of the class." Such graduates will then thrive in church interviews because they fit the mental model of a Christian leader that we think will thrive in the world that we think we serve. Petra was just such a student.

Then Austen makes her key point. "The good students, the ones who excel in the current system, are skidding when they hit today's streets." Austen draws the same conclusion about business schools that Petra did about her own experience in theological education. "The trouble with the education system isn't that it isn't doing a good job. It's doing a great job" churning out graduates who embody the ideal that we think the world needs. We pretend that the world is predictable. We think that Christian leaders should create guaranteed outcomes. But *the leaders who crave predictability are stumbling.* And the Kelley brothers can tell us why.

The Kelley brothers identify four fears—they call them "phobias"—that erode creativity and hobble innovation. We fuel these fears when we condition people to expect a predictable world. As we will see, these fears come out not just in our leaders but also in our congregations. They are as follows:

1. The fear of the messy unknown
2. The fear of being judged
3. The fear of the first step
4. The fear of losing control

Let me explain each of the four so that we are clear about the problem. *The fear of the messy unknown* refers to the uncertainty of being faced with a problem that lacks clear parameters. We say that Ingrid needs the agility to invent her future and that Petra needed the imagination to reinvent youth ministry in order to serve the people entrusted to her care within the parameters of a traditional church. But we don't give (indeed, we cannot give) either of them clear parameters for what that would look like. The outcome we expect from them is messy because guidelines are not clear and are unknown because neither Ingrid nor Petra has established examples to emulate.[8]

The fear of being judged means that each of them has to experiment their way to an unknown future in full view of an audience that will react harshly to any misstep. They are each rookies in that they are new to a ministry that they need to invent. We counsel leaders to strive to avoid making their rookie mistakes in public. But they often don't know how to create the white space[9] to experiment on the margins. And they end up making mistakes in public, in environments that do not give them the grace to make the mistakes every rookie makes.

The fear of the first step refers to the fear that comes with thinking that to take one step, a person needs to work out all the steps. Any first step feels like it sets a person on a path that curtails all the other options. But the problem is that the path is not clear. If Ingrid were walking from one oasis to the next, then there would be a well-worn path. But the whole point of talking about agility is to say that there is not a clear path. She will need to blaze her own trail or figure it out as she goes along. And it is much harder to take that first step into the desert when you have no guarantee that there will be an oasis before you run out of water.

Finally, *the fear of losing control* is about the way humans handle fear; we pretend we have control. But none of us really has control. This is a theological statement. We manage our lack of faith by pretending that we have enough control so that we really don't need to rely on God—where "relying on God" means putting ourselves in a situation where we can no longer create our own destinies.

Together these four phobias conspire to create inaction. They mean that the present crop of clergy likely has little experience with agility.

The four fears have something in common, especially for aces like Petra. They push against the strategies that strong students like Petra have developed for dealing with educational projects and assignments. Control is the key for such model students. They want clear expectations, clear deadlines, and clear means with clear ends. They crave the predictability that such clarity creates. But the world that we described for Ingrid specifically precludes this kind of certainty. Petra wants to be a theological camel. She wants to have a clearly defined route between one oasis and the next. When she leaves one waterhole, she wants to know that she has enough learning stored in her hump to get her to the next one. She wants predictability—because she knows that, if she has a predictable set of expectations, she can deliver a predictable (and satisfactory) set of outcomes. *Petra wanted exactly the predictable environment that Ingrid knows she cannot expect.* Petra washed out because the world had changed and she could not adapt. Petra and Ingrid need to innovate; they need to develop agility.

As hard as it is to develop agility, there is one other ability that innovation requires. *Innovation also requires discipline.* We don't normally think of agility and discipline as going together. We caricature agility to the point where we think agile people have no plan, and we distort discipline to mean stubbornly following a plan. Neither is true. Discipline has to do with follow-through, not just planning. Disciplined people can meet their own expectations. They can decide to do something and then have confidence that they will see it through to being done.

Let us add one more example—in addition to Ingrid and Petra. Jean has always had a talent for school. She breezed through high school without having to study all that much. But then she arrived at college. There she found a school filled with people as smart as and smarter than herself. Thus, she experienced a rude awakening. She did not have any real experience with disciplining herself. She would decide that "tomorrow" she would put in the time that she did not put in today. But she could not make herself do it. So she floundered for a while. Eventually she began to think of discipline as a muscle that she had never fully developed, so she began to work the muscle. Over time she was able to trust herself to follow through on a commitment she made to herself.

Agility and discipline are connected. *Preparation makes you agile.* A jazz musician can hop around because she has prepared for hours. A baker can confidently make a recipe he has never seen because he has made all the elements in the past. And a dancer practices elements that he can combine in new and unexpected ways. Experience allows someone to say to himself, "I've seen something like that before, even if I've never seen that exact thing." Or think of athletics. There is a saying in the sports world, "Champions are made in the off-season." The disciplined preparation of the off-season allows an athlete to respond with agility to the unforeseen challenges that come in a difficult game. Preparation allows leaders to develop what we will call "cultivated instincts."

Cultivated Instincts

At first glance, the phrase "cultivated instincts" seems like a contradiction in terms. We normally think of instincts as coming at birth. Baby birds peck their way out of the egg and then open their beaks to the sky. No one told them that the mommy bird would then place wormy morsels in their mouths. In fact, they likely don't really understand the concept of eating. They simply have the animal instinct. They open their mouths, and they survive. That's normally how we talk about instinct. But it's not the only way we describe it.

Let me ask you this. Were you born knowing how to drive a car? Of course not. None of us were. But how many of us can now drive while listening to the radio or carrying on a conversation with our kids or making a mental grocery list—or all three at the same time? We do it instinctively. Let me illustrate what I mean. I live and teach in California, where freeways are a part of life. I ask my students to picture themselves driving on the freeway, and they can all place themselves there instantly. Then I ask them to picture themselves in freeway traffic (another California constant) that is moving at, say, thirty miles per hour because there are so many other cars. Again, they have no problem picturing that. Then I say, "As you are meandering along in sluggish traffic, a cop pulls onto the freeway. What do you do?" Immediately they answer, "We slow down." And everyone laughs. We laugh because there is no threat of a speeding ticket when you are going thirty miles an hour on the freeway. But we are so used to exceeding the speed limit that we all *instinctively* slow down when we see a cop. It's as if the eyes communicate directly to the foot and the foot comes off the gas pedal before the brain even gets involved. Learning agile leadership is like learning to drive. It is a cultivated instinct. It is cultivated because no one was born knowing how to drive. But it is an instinct because experienced leaders are able to act without conscious thought.[10]

Perhaps a better way to talk about cultivated instincts is to think about Maria the nurse. My sister-in-law heard me use this term "cultivated instincts," and she immediately recognized herself and the other nurses she works with every day. Take, for example, her friend Maria. Maria is an intensive care nurse. One day a patient entered the ICU and bantered with the nurses who put her into the bed. She observed aloud that she was not feeling bad enough to be headed to the ICU. So you and I (that is, those of us without cultivated instincts) would think that Maria's patient likely had nothing to fear. But that's not what Maria thought. She *instinctively* ignored the banter and looked at the pallor of the patient's skin and the gloss of her eyes. Maria did not really know she was doing it. It was the years of ICU nursing that kicked in. And what Maria saw worried her. Maria knew that this patient was likely to get really sick really soon. So she got to work preparing for what others could not see coming. The tragic part of this story is that Maria was right. Within a day, her patient was the sickest person in the hospital, and soon thereafter she had died. The pneumonia had set in too far by the time she entered the ICU. Maria's instincts told her what novices could not see. She had cultivated instincts.[11]

There is a common theme between the two examples—learning to drive and being a nurse. *Cultivated instincts teach us what we must notice and what we can safely ignore.*[12] When I was first learning to drive, I was most afraid of the row of cars parked on the side of the road. I was sure that one of them would jump out in front of me when I least expected it. So I drove with my head cocked toward the side of the road. I had not yet learned that the bigger issue was the Buick in front of me. I also thought I had to read every sign. I gave equal attention to "Do Not Enter / Wrong Way" and "Lost Cat, REWARD." Over time, I learned to give great attention to the Wrong Way sign and filter out the Lost Cat sign. That turns out to be an important skill because no one can track all the signs. So we learn which data demand our attention and which data we can safely ignore. That's why Maria the nurse ignored her patient's demeanor (i.e., the laughing and banter) and instead noticed the brown hue in her skin and the film on her eyes. Cultivated instincts help us filter the vast amount of data streaming at us; they teach us what to notice and what we can safely ignore.

That takes us back to the jazz musician, the baker, the dancer, and the athlete. They have agility—they can move gracefully from one thing to the next—because they have cultivated instincts. Preparation has made them agile. They have done the work necessary to respond instinctively.[13]

Agility

Agility is the ability to move deftly from one position to another.[14] This metaphor fits the current climate. We know that society is changing faster than we can accommodate. We know that the old wait-and-copy strategy will no longer work. We know that agile leaders need to learn to take one step at a time. But that is not the mental model that most congregations use when they think about Christian leaders.

Most people want the wrong things from a leader. I remember talking with a committee that was getting ready to interview candidates to be the president of their Christian nonprofit. They were looking for two things in a candidate. They wanted vision (meaning someone who could say, "This is where we are going"), and they wanted a plan (meaning they also wanted the person to say, "And here's how we are going to get there"). In short, they wanted a leader who could tell them the next seven steps that would help them reach their goal.

Now, I understand why we long for such leaders. But there is a problem with that kind of leadership. It won't work—or at least it won't get us the things that matter most. This lay-out-the-steps leadership model works great if you are doing something predictable and unchanging like putting together a bicycle on Christmas Eve. There you want step-by-step instructions tailored for assembling Model Number 1370A—with optional training wheels and tassels for the handlebars. It works because it is a predictable and closed system designed for a very limited situation. You know in advance exactly which parts are there and how they fit together to build Model 1370A. There is no uncertainty, there are no surprises, and there is no need for a backup plan. You can know in advance everything you will ever need to know for your plan to succeed. Or at least that is what they say on the box. As any number of sit-coms will tell you, following the best-laid plan can easily go terribly wrong. Step-by-step instructions only work in a predictable world, and even then only with technical problems. *Adaptive challenges require agility.*

So if leadership is not as predictable as building a bicycle, what is it like? It is like watering and planting. When my daughter Donley was in elementary school, she liked to grow herbs—like sage, lemon balm, and mint. She would buy them in little plastic cups and plant them in clay pots on our patio. When she first learned to grow herbs, we gave her step-by-step instructions. *"First you plant them. Then you water them once a week.*" We gave her a foolproof plan, one that quickly killed her herbs. The problem is that she planted them in the middle of summer. Donley should have watered them far more than once a week when it is regularly one hundred degrees outside. Eventually she learned that her next step after planting depends on the weather. If it is particularly hot outside, she needs to water her herbs a lot. If it is rainy, she has to move them under the awning so they don't drown. And so on. Her goal is not just to plant the herbs. Her goal is to help them grow. So I couldn't give her a step-by-step guide for growing herbs because her next move always depends on what happens after she plants the herbs.

Our goal as Christian leaders is not to put together a ministry like it is a prepackaged bicycle. Our goal is to help God's people grow. Like Paul and Apollos, we plant and water. If our goal is to help people grow, then we cannot follow the lay-out-the-steps model of leadership. What then can a Christian leader do?

I believe that a Christian leader's responsibility is to help God's people take the next faithful step.[15] The temptation is to feel the need to take the next seven steps. But all we can do is take the next faithful step. Indeed, the best process looks something like this: listen, and then take the next faithful step; then listen, and take another faithful step. And so on.

Why is it so important to take one faithful step at a time? Because we can't predict in advance what steps will be necessary. Think, for example, of the congregation that wanted to do the relatively straightforward project of building a fellowship hall on the church property. They expected to form a committee, draw up plans, collect the funds, hire a contractor, and build the hall. But at each step along the way, they discovered things about themselves that made the next faithful step anything but straightforward. Even forming the initial committee proved to be a challenge. It brought up latent controversies between the church staff and the church board about formal control—and buried resentments between wealthy but nominal church families and poor but active members about informal control. Indeed, the pastor was wise enough to see the process for what it was. The next faithful step for the congregation, she wisely realized, was not forming a committee. The next faithful step was dealing with the long-buried resentments over control that needed to be addressed before the congregation was ready to form a committee. If the pastor had stuck to the plan, she never would have helped the congregation take the next faithful step. Building a fellowship hall was a technical problem, but dealing with the control questions was an adaptive challenge.

Indeed, adaptive challenges are never predictable. They always require leaders who are agile. Now don't get me wrong, I do believe that the leader of that congregation had to have a general outline of how the process would go. But she had to hold the process loosely enough to be able to adjust to the needs of each step. Otherwise her congregation could have built the hall, but they would not have grown in faithfulness.

Focusing on the next faithful step is crucial because taking that next step is often painful. And painful steps take time. In fact, it is often tempting to gloss over the painful part (the growing part) in the name of progress. But really, that only helps us if our goals have nothing to do with helping people grow.

We often look for the wrong things in our leaders. We look for people who will tell us where to go and what to do. But what we need are leaders who can help us grow. In short, we need leaders who will help us take the next faithful step.

By this point, I have likely convinced you that you will need to cultivate agility. Now the question is "How?" That is the focus of the rest of the chapter. The rest of the chapter will look at the ways that a leader can grow and develop. The lessons it describes apply to far more than agility. They apply to any instinct that a leader might want to cultivate. Here are positive options that a leader can pursue if they want to develop agility.

Avoid the Blame That Prevents Learning

Renowned Harvard scholar Chris Argyris did an important study of people who (like ministers) spend most of their days helping other people grow and change. He studied them as models for people who work in a range of professions—such as ministers, doctors, and corporate managers. These professionals, he discovered, had a hard time taking the next step toward maturity. Argyris discovered that *we must eliminate what prevents learning before we can learn something really new*. Let me explain what he means.

Over the course of fifteen years, Argyris conducted in-depth studies of management professionals. Almost all of the professionals each had a master's degree from a top university; they were "highly satisfied" with their work. In short, they were the most proficient members of their profession. He asked them about learning—that is, about how they helped organizations get better and about how they themselves improved. He found an interesting pattern that recurred throughout the years. "As long as efforts at learning and change focused on external factors [meaning things outside themselves]," Argyris reported, "the professionals were enthusiastic participants."[16] They liked being a part of what is called, in the parlance of their profession, "continuous improvement"—so long as it was *other people* who had to change. "Yet the moment the quest for continuous improvement turned to the professionals' *own* performance, something went wrong." They balked as soon as Argyris asked them how *they themselves* needed to change. "It wasn't a matter of bad attitude." The professionals were, in principle, committed to improvement. They just weren't comfortable describing their own shortcomings.

"What happened? *The professionals began to feel embarrassed.* They were threatened [and started to] react defensively." They did not want to talk about specific ways that they themselves could improve *because it required them to admit their weaknesses.* They did not want to acknowledge that they had failings because they were afraid they might look bad. So they did what people have done since Adam and Eve got caught in the garden. "They projected the blame for any problems away from themselves and onto what they said were unclear goals, insensitive and unfair leaders, and stupid clients." Argyris regularly met competent and celebrated professionals who said to him, "It's not my fault." He summarized this avoidance behavior by saying that "they looked entirely outside themselves." When confronted with a less-than-perfect performance, these cream-of-the-crop leaders "asserted that they were helpless to act differently— not because of any limitations of their own but because of the limitations of others." They could not learn from their mistakes because they were unwilling to acknowledge that they had done anything wrong in the first place.

We've all met people who could not take responsibility for their own failings, and we've all been that person. I know I have. I remember teaching a seminar for pastors and other leaders. I was using a case study that I have taught perhaps a hundred times. But this group was not reacting to it the way other groups had. Usually the case sparks intense conversation. This time the group seemed, well, a bit bored. I had heard good things about this group from the person who had invited me. She said these were the most theologically reflective pastors in her region. Yet they found my case boring. So what did I do? I mustered my years of experience in teaching and turned it against them. I decided to blame them. "After all," I reasoned silently, "every other group thought this stuff was great. Something must be wrong. So I guess I'll just get through this without embarrassing myself. But, my goodness, these people are disengaged." I was embarrassed. Here I'd been invited to speak to this cream-of-the-crop group of pastors. Yet they could barely muster enough interest to be polite. So, instead of using my experience to understand them, I used it to write them off. I did not want to investigate what was going on because I was afraid I might discover that the cause was my fault. My defensiveness made me timid.

The saddest part of the example was the missed opportunity. I found out later what had happened. Just before I arrived, they had a brief go-around-the-room-and-check-in time. And one of the pastors dropped a bombshell.

She said, "I think I might be gay. I've wondered about this for a long time. Last week I went out on a date with a woman, and I'd like to see her again. I haven't told anyone else. My congregation does not know. My friends and family do not know. Nobody. You are the first ones, and I need your support." There was no time to process this statement—no time to pursue it further because I was standing outside the door. Then I walked in and tried to get their attention.

In retrospect, I realize that they obviously were not bored. They were distracted—and rightly so. Homosexuality was a very controversial issue in this group, and no one was sure of the best way to respond. My abstract case study could not—and should not—compete with the real-life situation playing out in their midst. But here's the sad part. I regularly say that leadership begins with listening, but I never stopped to listen long enough to know what was really happening. When things did not go the way I wanted them to go, I assumed that it was all about me, and I became defensive. They did not respond the way I wanted them to respond, so I wrote them off. I missed an opportunity to learn from the situation because I became defensive. I blamed them, and that stopped the learning cold.

Avoid Unproductive Parallel Conversations

Chris Argyris discovered exactly the same behavior when he observed other professionals as they talked about situations in which they would have to discuss their failings. He observed conversations between these accomplished professionals and their bosses after things did not go well. He wondered if people would be able to acknowledge and explain the mistakes that they had made. Instead, he repeatedly heard frustrating conversations where the professionals learned little. "They talked past each other," he found, "never finding a common language to describe what happened."[17] They could not even acknowledge that there was any way that their behavior could improve. From these observations, Argyris distilled a stereotypical exchange that he called an "unproductive parallel conversation." He cast the exchange so that a professional was talking to his boss. I have shifted the setting of the conversation to drive the point home for pastors, putting the conversation into a congregational setting. It goes like this:

Pastor: My congregation does not want to change.
Questioner: It is the pastor's job to help the congregation to want to change.
Pastor: But the congregation won't listen to me. They think I am wrong.

Questioner: Are there other ways that you might help them see your perspective?

Pastor: Maybe we need more meetings.

Questioner: How will you prepare for these meetings so that they have a different result?

Pastor: We need more communication with the congregation's leadership team.

Questioner: I agree. How will you take the initiative to educate them?

Pastor: Everyone says they are too busy to get together.[18]

An unproductive parallel conversation is a defense mechanism designed to keep the speaker (in this case, the pastor) from having to take responsibility. "The problem with the [pastor's] claims is not that they are wrong," Argyris observed, "but that they aren't useful. By constantly turning the focus away from their own behavior to that of others, the [pastors] bring learning to a grinding halt."[19] The pastor was not willing to acknowledge his own responsibility. He was not willing to see that a good pastor has a responsibility to find a way to communicate to a congregation, even and especially when the congregation does not want to hear the message.

At this point, thoughtful readers may be asking themselves about the logic here. Why would successful people be poor learners? It does not make sense. If we found that underachievers were poor learners, that would make sense. But Argyris argues specifically that smart and successful people have the hardest time learning from mistakes. Why? I am going to linger on this question for a bit because it gets at exactly why pastors who want to take the next step toward agility often have such difficulty doing so. Indeed, it explains why leaders like Petra get trapped by the "four phobias."

Do Not Use Strengths to Cover Weaknesses

Argyris goes back to the very skills that make people successful in our society in order to explain why they are so susceptible to defensive reasoning. People who have a lot of schooling—like ministers—learn early to use their strengths to cover their weaknesses. Our educational system rewards such behavior. I know that I learned to do this early and practiced it often. One of my proudest moments in college involved doing just that. I look back now, and I'm embarrassed because I realize that I was so proud because it felt like I got away with something.

It was in a calculus class called "differential equations." (I was an engineering major.) We learned a variety of ways to solve this particular kind of math problem. Each technique was best suited to a specific kind of problem. Well, I did not really understand all of them. Actually, I did not understand most of them (even now, as I tell the story, I am trying to minimize my failing). Part of the reason was that I was not studying as much as I had in the past. You see, I had just met the girl who would one day be my wife (even now, I want to say, "You see, I had a good excuse"). And I did not want to admit that I was neglecting my studies. But I had one saving strength. I did understand one of the techniques (something called Laplace transforms). So on the final exam, I converted everything to Laplace transforms. I went through complicated machinations to make what would be an easy problem if I'd done my homework into something that I could solve by using the one technique I understood. And I was so proud of myself because I did it. I salvaged a good grade in the class by acing the final exam. What did I learn from that episode? I learned, once again, that I could get by without admitting my mistakes. I learned to use my strength to cover my weakness.

But there is a cost to such a self-satisfied refusal to admit my failings. Two years after I aced that final, I barely passed an upper-division electrical engineering class because I needed to use the techniques that I had never learned in the earlier class. I did not make the connection between the two courses at the time. I rationalized that the class I nearly failed was an elective and that I was not going to be doing that kind of work in my career anyway. I rationalized my failing and pretended that it did not matter. The problem wasn't just that I used a strength to cover a weakness. The problem was my pretending that the weakness never existed in the first place. Because I could not face my weakness, I delayed the damage and made it much worse.

From students and pastors I have heard many similar stories, which help us understand how *the delayed damage of defensive reasoning happens in daily life.* "It's like tennis," one woman said. She was one of those players who couldn't hit a backhand. So instead of practicing to get better at the backhand, she used to run around every shot and hit them all as forehands. But that came at a price, she said. She'd get tired much more quickly than her opponent because she had to run so much farther. And then, when she'd wilt with exhaustion at the end of the game, she'd say to herself that the other player was just in better shape. She delayed the damage by hitting only forehands and then rationalized away the result by congratulating the other player. It's a nice little circle designed to keep the player from taking responsibility for her inability to hit the backhand. In retrospect, she acknowledged that she had a clear motivation for this self-deception. She knew that when she finally admitted to herself that the problem was her backhand, she would need to take more time to practice—which she did not want to do. If the problem was that her opponent was in phenomenal shape, there was nothing she could do. It wasn't her fault. But as soon as she recognized that her own failing was the cause, it became clear to her that she needed to do the hard work to improve. As she told the story, she said that she wasn't ready to acknowledge the problem until she was prepared to work hard at solving it.

The same thing happens, of course, in ministry. Allan was an artist before he became a pastor. As a seminary student, he had taken every course in worship he could find because that's what made his heart sing. He wrote wonderfully poetic liturgies and preached with elegant power. Allan was good at these things because he worked hard at them. He even prepared for the part of the service where he made announcements, thinking of it as the closest thing a pastor ever got to a *Saturday Night Live* monologue. And it worked: his announcements felt smooth and spontaneous, even though he had prepared them with care. There were any number of things that made Allan an excellent pastor.

But Allan hated conflict. A born performer, he wanted everyone to like him. So he avoided Jeri, the cantankerous head of the worship committee. He'd send her an email whenever possible and left phone messages at her home when he knew she was at work. Well, it is easy to predict what happened. One February, he moved the normal communion service from the first Sunday of the month to the second week because he'd scheduled something special for that first Sunday. Jeri did not get the phone message (teenage sons being what they are), and she set up the communion service at the front of the sanctuary. She was, of course, appalled when she discovered too late that the order of worship did not include a Eucharist liturgy. There were tense words before worship, and something little had escalated into something big. Allan predictably blamed Jeri for overreacting to a simple miscommunication. He never understood that the root of the problem had little to do with Jeri. The miscommunication was inevitable because Allan was not willing to embrace his failing and learn how to deal with conflict.

Embrace Your Weaknesses

There are times, however, when people do embrace their weaknesses and learn to get past them. I think of a middle-aged woman named Ann, who had to face her fears when she felt called to become a nurse. Although she described the move as a calling from God, Ann feared school. She "knew" she was not very smart because she had not excelled in high school, but she longed to go where God called her. The epitome of her academic fears was mathematics, which she had avoided since ninth grade. Fortunately, nurses do not have to know math. Or so she thought.

In the midst of nursing school, Ann discovered that nurses need to "calculate meds." If a doctor prescribed a dosage of 0.5 grams and the pharmacy only had an eight-ounce bottle of the medicine, the nurse had to know how to convert grams to ounces. It is a simple math problem, but one that terrified Ann.

So Ann had a choice. She could hide her math weakness and accept that on a few tests she would do poorly—rationalizing that pharmacists usually calculate the dosages anyway. Or she could embrace her weakness and conquer her fear of math. The deciding factor was her intense desire to be a good nurse. It turns out that there was something she feared more than math. Ann could not stand the thought of one day giving a patient the wrong dosage. She had to embrace her weakness. So she asked her son to help her. He was in high school and had long before mastered the simple ratios involved in the calculations. They worked on the problem for a long summer. He would devise problems for her, and she'd struggle to master them. At first, her lack of confidence was a much bigger problem than her arithmetic deficiencies. But over time she became proficient. She passed the courses and became a nurse. But that's not where the story ends.

Ann had learned the lessons so well that she became the math expert on her nursing floor. When others had difficulty converting dosages, they asked for her help. What was once a weakness had become a strength—and the source of a healthy confidence. How had she found the courage to admit her weakness and overcome it? Every time she felt the fear welling up in her, she countered it with her intense desire to be good at the job to which God had called her. Serving the people entrusted to her care was more important than her fear of admitting failure.

Treat Your Failures as an Invitation to Learning

Thus, we would expect that the best way to prevent the delayed damage of defensive reasoning is to acknowledge failure and to work to eliminate it. David Nygren found this to be exactly what happens. He did a study of religious leaders to find out what separated good-but-not-great ones from extraordinary ones. According to his findings, the difference is that extraordinary leaders have the ability to learn from failure.

Nygren coordinated a complicated and comprehensive study of outstanding leaders in religious nonprofit organizations. He looked at a group of professionals similar to the group Argyris studied. Only Nygren asked what characteristics distinguished the very best ones. The key to the study was what is known as a behavioral event interview (BEI), which requires two or three hours of conversation with an interviewer. A researcher (in this case, Nygren) interviews a large body of leaders from throughout the organization or similar organizations (say, the leaders of Roman Catholic religious orders or top administrators in religious hospitals). The leaders have been nominated as either good or outstanding leaders by their peers, but when Nygren does the interviews he does not know which leaders are which. He simply interviews them so that he and his colleagues can analyze their answers. The purpose of the study is to use the answers to show how outstanding leaders see the world differently.[20]

I remember listening to Nygren describe the most striking thing about one such study.[21] He got to the point where he could guess who the outstanding leaders were going to be before he had seen the peer nominations. All he had to do was listen to their answers to the two sets of questions that are the staple of the BEI. He would ask first, "Tell me about a time you were effective at work." Next he would ask the opposite question, about a time that the leader had been ineffective. Then they would repeat the cycle, discussing first a success and then a moment of failure. The BEI plays on how the leaders describe these situations of success and failure. I remember Nygren saying, however, that there was something interesting in the interviews.

I would have thought that the best leaders had the most successes and the worst ones reported the most failures. But it was just the opposite. That's how Nygren could tell the difference before seeing the peer nominations. The best leaders had the most difficulty thinking of a recent event where they had been particularly effective. Meanwhile, the average leaders could think of lots of successes but few failures.

Nygren drew an important lesson from this observation. He said that the difference had to do with how the leaders thought about the events and not with the situations themselves. It had to do with how leaders see the world. A good-as-opposed-to-best leader would describe a situation that was a mixture of good and bad and pronounce it a success. The best leaders would see the mixture as a failure. Let me illustrate what I mean.

Suppose that the leader accomplished what he set out to do but stepped on some toes along the way. The good-not-great leader would conclude, "I had to mend some fences, but in the end I got the job done. It's a success." The best leaders, by contrast, might report, "In the end, I'm not very satisfied with what happened. I may have gotten the result I wanted, but I had to mend a lot of fences when all was said and done. There has to be a way to accomplish this particular goal without hurting people. Next time, I'll have to do a better job monitoring people's feelings." Can you see the difference? The difference is not that the best leaders are pessimists. The difference is that the *best leaders are never satisfied with their performance*. They have a deep-seated longing to get better. The good-but-not-great leader never noticed the opportunity to improve—never acknowledged the weakness embedded in the story about strength. And the excellent leader did not miss the opportunity to get better.[22]

Combine Humility with Self-Confidence

It takes a peculiar combination of confidence and humility for leaders to scrutinize their behavior that way. They have to have confidence, because people who are not self-assured often spend energy hiding their failings—hiding them from others and from themselves. But that confidence must be tempered by enough humility to admit that they will continue to make mistakes.

Jim Collins discovered a similar trait in the best leaders. Just as Nygren hoped to distinguish the best leaders, he attempted to separate good from great companies. Along the way, Collins found that the best companies had "Level V Leadership," as he called it. These leaders combined extreme personal humility with intense organizational will. They were humble about their own abilities and confident about what their organizations could accomplish. This combination of humility and confidence allowed them to do something akin to Nygren's leaders. When Collins's leaders encountered organizational failure, they would take personal responsibility. They would say things like "I'm the one in charge, and I should have seen this problem coming. It's my fault." They didn't blame others (or even bad luck) when things didn't go well; instead, they focused the criticism on themselves. Yet, when those same leaders experienced organizational success, they gave the credit to others. They would say something like this: "We just accomplished something difficult. And we couldn't have done it without Jin-Soo and Tim, who put in the long hours that such an important project requires." They did not take bows or steal the attention. Instead, they put others in the limelight. Collins described it by saying that the best leaders see failure as a mirror and success as a window. The best leaders "look out the window to apportion credit to factors outside themselves when things go well. . . . At the same time, they look in the mirror to apportion responsibility, never blaming bad luck when things go poorly." The best leaders, Collins says, accept personal responsibility for failures and give others credit for successes.[23]

There is thus a common theme that unites the studies done by Argyris, Nygren, and Collins. The best leaders have enough healthy confidence in their own ability (or more precisely, in what God is doing through them) that they can analyze their own behavior and admit their failings. They feel secure enough to accept responsibility and to apportion credit. They embody the self-reflective combination of confidence and humility that Nygren and Collins found in the best leaders and that Argyris discovered was lacking in most others. They avoid the delayed damage of defensive reasoning and instead embrace weakness so that they can overcome it.

See How Perseverance Is as Important as Giftedness

These scholars' insights mean that a leader's attitude is as important as the leader's gifts. We tend to think of leadership as an accumulation of skills and competencies. But the best leaders bring something more. They have a healthy focus on themselves, an attitude that allows them to take responsibility for their failings. Although I don't have Nygren's breadth of experience in identifying the best leaders, I have found that the best students in my classes (i.e., the ones who go on to become the best leaders) and the most impressive pastors I encounter in seminars each share an attitude. In each case, they avoid the temptation to focus on what someone else needs to learn.

Let me explain this temptation to externalize learning. I often hear someone say, "Wow, that was great! I have a friend who really needs to learn that lesson." Or, "Thanks for that talk. I wish my elders were here to hear it." In each case, the reaction to a new lesson is to focus on someone else. It is often a defense mechanism designed to keep learning at arm's length. The best leaders, on the other hand, take a lesson to heart and find a way to change their own behavior as a result of what they've learned.

This temptation to externalize learning is particularly enticing for ministers. After all, it is our job to learn lessons that we can then pass on to other people. I think that one of the holiest moments of a parish pastor's week happens when the pastor is alone in the study, prayerfully considering a biblical text. It is holy when pastors feel the weight of speaking a word from the Lord. We can never lose the sense of privilege and responsibility that comes with being God's messenger. But the responsibility can sometimes have a strange effect on pastors. They begin to act as conduits, allowing the message from God to pass through them without ever penetrating them.

I find that as a teacher I feel this temptation. When something I read or a speaker I hear cuts too close to the bone, I can feel threatened, convicted, or embarrassed. At those moments, I tend to retreat from the discomfort the important lesson causes. I retreat by thinking about people who need to learn the lesson or by picturing myself teaching about the lesson. In short, I minimize the threat to my ego by casting myself as the bearer of the message rather than as its recipient. The by-product of this defense mechanism, unfortunately, is that I minimize my own learning. I spend time thinking about other people precisely so I don't need to think about myself. Leaders who say, "I know someone who needs to learn that lesson," are often hiding from the fact that they need to learn the lesson themselves. They are too intimidated by failure to learn from it.

The ability to learn from failure often comes more naturally to people who have a longing to excel in their calling. Like Ann, the nurse whose love of her vocation was more powerful than her fear of math, they are motivated by a deep-seated sense of privilege and responsibility. I once had a colleague who would often tell a story from the world of psychology that illustrates the power of this longing to develop one's vocation.

Years ago, several studies tried to predict which doctoral students would someday become the best psychologists. They tested a wide variety of traits. And they found that one trait stood out above all the others. It had nothing to do with innate intuition or conspicuous compassion. Instead, they found that the best psychologists turned out to be the ones who had an intense desire to be good psychologists. That relentless desire to improve made them good psychologists. It did not matter how capable (or inept) they were when they started. It did not matter whether or not they had natural gifts for empathetic listening. What mattered is that they kept improving. The most naturally insightful students stalled in their development if they did not have the passion to improve. The most bumbling beginners eventually passed them in proficiency if those beginners kept growing. The key factor in developing agility is a longing to get better. And this, of course, depends on an ability to embrace weakness.

There is another temptation that can come into play here. If one temptation is to ignore our weaknesses, its twin is to obsess about them. Some people read the above and want to cry out that they have some unique disadvantage that disqualifies them from excellence. They allow that deficiency to hide their potential. This is, ironically, just another way to externalize the problem. Pastors who say that something insurmountable prevents them from improving can keep the focus off the issues they can address. Sometimes people use sports analogies to defend themselves. For example, there is a saying in football, "You can't teach speed." And in basketball, they say, "You can't teach height." A player who lacks strength can spend long hours in the weight room to get stronger. And there are various techniques that a coach can teach a player to help them become more skilled. But there are certain qualities in athletics that cannot be taught.

I will acknowledge that the same might be true in ministry. Some people, for example, enter seminary with a natural eloquence. But I think that the question (of what cannot be taught) is less relevant than one might think. I am, for example, a slow, skinny guy who can't jump. But I still play basketball a couple of times a week. I'll never be good enough to carry my team by myself, but I usually find a way to make some contribution to the team. That's the way most vocations work. Few pastors are talented enough to carry a congregation by the brilliance of their gifts (and even if they could, there are theological reasons why that would be inherently dangerous). So most of us are in a position where we need to acknowledge our weaknesses and do the hard work to improve. If I were serious about becoming a better basketball player, I would not try to learn to be faster or taller. I could, however, lift weights to get stronger or practice techniques to become a better shooter.

So we loop back to the question we asked earlier about what is stopping leaders from developing agility. We have come up with at least three lessons that pastors need to learn once they decide to take the next faithful step. Don't cast blame. Acknowledge your own weaknesses and then overcome them. Learn from failure. These are important lessons. But they don't answer the question about what's stopping us. Why do we retreat so easily to defensive reasoning?

Pay Attention to the Theological Roots of Defensive Reasoning

I believe there is a theological root that makes it so hard to accept blame, embrace weakness, and learn from failure. Leaders are especially vulnerable to fear and pride. Fear and pride prevent even the most accomplished Christians from seeing themselves as they really are.

Fear

Fear is a theological problem. Let me illustrate what I mean. I was really nervous during my first year of graduate school. Although I was really proud of the fact that I got accepted at an Ivy League university, I kept wondering when they were going to find out that they had made a mistake. I was sure that I wasn't good enough. And you know what? I wasn't good enough. None of us were. None of us could claim to have an Ivy League education going into the program. The school's reputation was built on how they molded the students they admitted and not on their ability to locate can't-miss students who did not need to be educated in the first place. But all through my first year at Yale, I kept wondering, "When are they going to find out?" I was sure they were going to discover that I did not belong and that they were going to kick me out. So what did I do?

I tried to hide my weaknesses. I spoke boldly, even when I didn't know how much I didn't know. I pretended I knew what people meant when they referenced ideas I'd never heard before. Worst of all, I resented it when someone told me I was wrong. I was scared and tried to cover it up by hiding from my weaknesses. The logic I employed was something like this: "If I admit I am wrong, I will lose credibility. And if I lose credibility, they will make me leave. So I can't let anyone know when I am wrong." This experience became a paradigm for me because it is such a common temptation. My wife and I use the phrase "When are they going to find out?" as shorthand for this anxiety about being in over your head. But how is that a theological problem?

My fear had a theological cause and produced a spiritual effect. I believed I was at Yale because God had called me, just as you probably believe that God called you to the people entrusted to your care. Yet when I encountered difficulty, I asked myself, "What if God called me to the wrong place?" My worry that I did not belong at Yale was tantamount to saying, "I'm not really sure that God called me to this place," or believing that, perhaps, God was mistaken in calling me there.

Naming that theological fear can be quite freeing because a quick look back on my life can refute that fear. I have a long litany of moments when God showed that God will be faithful to me. So at this point, it becomes embarrassingly absurd for me to ask whether or not God can be trusted. That means that every time I feel the When-will-they-find-out? fear welling up in me, I remind myself that I am in the place where God has called me. Since I am in the place where God has called me, it really does not matter whether or not I look bad by admitting I am wrong. God invited me to this place, and a little embarrassment is not going to change that. So I might as well pursue this vocation with all the vigor it deserves.

If the theological cause of my fear is that perhaps God put me in the wrong place, then the spiritual effect is no less insidious. I want so much for God to like me that I often try to do things for God rather than allow God to do them through me. The implication of that logic, of course, is that if I admit my weaknesses, perhaps God will find out about them and stop liking me—or perhaps the people to whom I am called will find out that I am not perfect and stop liking me. I put it that way because the absurdity of the argument is obvious. God knows my weaknesses far more intimately than I ever will—and loves me despite those failings. Pretending to be perfect in front of the people to whom I am called is just another way of casting myself as God, who alone is perfect. Either way, I have a huge investment in maintaining a fiction—a fiction that no one else believes anyway.

There are, thus, two fears at the heart of our unwillingness to admit our weaknesses. We fear that God has not really called us. And we fear that we will lose the love of God and the respect of other people if we let anyone see our failings.

Pride

The other root sin is pride. Theologians like to say that pride is the most basic sin because it allows us to set ourselves up as gods. Even in the Garden of Eden, our first parents ate from the tree so that they could be like God. I must admit that I regularly take the same bite.

Pride manifests itself in at least a couple of particularly insidious ways. First, pride makes me think of myself more highly than I ought. I overinflate my accomplishments and convince myself that I have produced the fruit—rather than God giving the increase. Second, pride makes me think of others as less than myself. I neglect their contributions. It is the opposite of Collins's window and mirror. I let criticism pass through me to others even as I let praise reflect solely on myself. *Pride prevents learning, and arrogance destroys agility.*

The opposite of pride is humility. In leadership, humility manifests itself in ways that tend to surprise Christians. We tend to think of humility as not thinking highly of yourself—when, in fact, it is more appropriate to adapt Romans 12:3 and say, "Do not think of yourself more highly than you ought, but rather with sober judgment, in accordance to the measure of faith God has given you." Humility involves seeing myself as God sees me, as wonderfully able to do all things—but only able to do them through "Christ who strengthens me." Collins writes about the humility that he has observed in the leaders of the best organizations. He found that they combined a personal humility with an almost fanatical confidence about what the people of the organization could do when they worked together.

When I think of such humility, I am reminded of a man named Hugh De Pree. When I became a professor at Fuller Seminary, I came to fill what was called the Hugh De Pree Chair in Leadership Development. So, of course, I wanted to find out about the man for whom my position was named. He had passed away by then, so I read his book.[24] He had been the head of a large corporation called Herman Miller, a company that made some of the most celebrated office furniture. The company really took off while he was president, and he eventually wrote a memoir about his presidency. Now, if you have ever read these memoirs, they tend to follow a certain formula. They say, "This is how I did it." We've all read these kinds of books. Old, wise pastors often write them as well. But there was something different about De Pree's book. It was full of humility. At each turn, he would tell a story about how Herman Miller as a company made some wise or successful move. He would often describe the meeting when the leaders of the company made the key decisions. Yet he tells the story as if he were just a bystander, serendipitously observing what was happening. Over and over, he talks about being surrounded by wonderful people. And he minimizes his own influence as he tells the story. By the end, I realized that he genuinely believed two things: that the company was very special and that his leadership was not. He had an absolute confidence in the company and little personal need to receive credit.

How then is the Christian leader to respond to these dual temptations to pride and fear? These observations about fear and pride are important because they help us see why we have such a temptation to blame others when we fail. But Argyris points out that providing knowledge is not usually enough to get people to embrace their weaknesses. He observed that when he worked with professionals—accomplished adults who genuinely wanted to improve—that "the inevitable response to the observation that somebody is reasoning defensively is yet more defensive reasoning."[25] In other words, reading the last section on accepting blame may make you more willing to embrace weakness, but it is unlikely to make you any more able to accept blame. Knowledge is not enough. What then can help leaders get past the fears that often keep them from taking the next faithful step?

Belonging to God

The antidote to these temptations is theological; it requires a spiritual discovery that creeps into our bones. This theological insight is captured in a famous formulation from the Heidelberg Catechism. "I belong—body and soul, in life and in death—not to myself but to my faithful Savior Jesus Christ." A theology of belonging makes two powerful statements that militate against the temptations that plague leaders. When I say I belong to God, I mean that I am indelibly etched into God's family tree. I cannot be removed or cast out. God has adopted me into God's family. Thus, it is a gift of God and not the result of some heroic act that merits my inclusion in the royal family. I did nothing to become a part of God's family and (here's the best part) I can do nothing to get kicked out of that family. Belonging is the antidote to fear. According to God's promises, I know that nothing can separate any of us from the love that God lavishes on each person in God's family. I know that belonging to God gives me an identity that derives from God's love and specifically not from any action I take to prove myself worthy of that love. In short, I have nothing to fear because I belong to God.

Belonging has another meaning as well. Scripture says, "You have been bought with a price" (1 Cor. 6:20 NASB). In other words, I belong to God in the same way that a vintner owns a piece of land. This fact sometimes offends American sensibilities. We don't like to think of anyone belonging to someone else. But my time is not my own. When that vintner buys a plot of land, he makes that purchase so that the land will become prosperous. He tills the soil, plants the vines, and waters the plants. When he harvests the fruit, the grapes belong to the landowner, who makes something from them that they could never become while still on the vine. I belong to God. I cannot be prideful about what I do. I do not get to choose where to go or what matters most in my life. And I cannot take credit because, as the apostle Paul said, one person may plant the seed, and another water, but "only God . . . makes things grow" (1 Cor. 3:7).

10

Recalibrating Church for the Smartphone Generation

The church as we know it is calibrated for a world that no longer exists. Let us look at one extended example and see how what we have learned might cultivate an innovative congregation and agile leaders. We could focus on any number of issues. But let's take this one. The church as we know it is not calibrated for the smartphone generation. Think back to what life was like for a random American in the nineteenth century. By late in that century, the average American lived in a city and coped with a fragmented life: that meant working in one part of the city, worshiping in another part, and taking the streetcar to a third part of the city to be with their friends. Even a century later, in the 1990s, we lived in a similarly fragmented world. Americans drove their cars to work, to church, and to play. The world of automobiles may have replaced streetcar culture, but there was a way that the worlds were similar. The key to the world of automobile culture was location. You would *go to* work, or *go to* church, or *go to* a friend's house. Even in the 1990s, Americans lived similarly fragmented lives.

The church as we know it is still calibrated for this world divided by location. Look at how we measure devotion. We measure it by attendance—by physical presence in a location. Christians go to church; mature Christians go to a midweek Bible study group. The nineteenth century was a world divided by location. The twentieth century was a world divided by location. And today's church is calibrated for a world divided by location. We expect people to *go to* church.

The millennial generation (and Gen Z behind it), on the other hand, does not live in a world fragmented by location. Look at any group of young adults. The first thing that stands out is that their world revolves around their smartphones. They are quite comfortable being in two places at once. They can watch a ball game while texting a friend or track two group chats with friends in completely different places. Their world is not defined by location. My generation might want to complain about "the young people these days with their phones and their texting," but if we do, then we end up sounding a lot like the old fuddy-duddies that we complained about when we were young. The smartphone generation describes the world as it is. We cannot ask them to stay in a world that is passing away. We will have to recalibrate.

The congregation we will call "Millennial Church" is well-known in its part of its state, as is its pastor.[1] Millennial Church is calibrated for a location-based world that no longer exists, and that fact is prejudicing the way the congregation judges the smartphone generation. The church now has multiple sites, with Sunday morning music happening on each campus and a video of the sermon piped in from the mother church. We will call it "Millennial Church" because the congregation recognizes that most of the people entrusted to its care are young adults—that is, the very generation defined by their smartphones.[2]

Last year the congregation began to post the entire service on its website. That created a problem for church leaders. "Attendance" is down as more and more young adults choose to view the service online. The church leaders (who are not themselves millennials) immediately diagnosed the problem as a lack of commitment from busy (or lazy) millennials. The solution was just as obvious to the leaders as the problem. The millennials needed to *come back to* church. The congregation had constructed a model of ministry where worship happened on Sundays and discipleship happened in midweek small groups. "If the millennials are not coming on Sundays," the leaders reasoned, "then we will be able to get them to *go to* small groups."

Notice how the leaders interpreted the problem (and the solution) by calibrating themselves for a world that is passing away. Their measure of devotion for the congregation is "attendance"—which is about location. Worship means going to church, and discipleship means going to a small group. Millennial Church is still calibrated for a world defined by location, even though they are ministering to a smartphone generation that is no longer subject to location's constraints. The world has changed. Millennial Church will need to recalibrate.

Millennial Church will never stop worshiping God and never give up on discipleship. Think of it in terms of an HMW: If we were a millennial church, how might we recalibrate the congregation's understanding of worship and discipleship for the smartphone generation. Just as a farmer must explore new ways to plant and water, Millennial Church must recognize that they can no longer use the old-fashioned notion of attendance to measure worship and discipleship. Perhaps it might help them to think about other organizations that are recalibrating.

The National Football League is already recalibrating to account for the smartphone generation's new understanding of "attendance." With the advent of high-def pictures, the NFL has come to recognize that fans can often get a better view of the game on their televisions or smartphones. Indeed, in 2017 the Atlanta Falcons opened a new stadium. Why would they spend 1.2 billion dollars when their Georgia Dome was only twenty-five years old? The difference is the fan experience. The new stadium has a circular, giant high-definition television screen high above the field. Dubbed "The Halo," this screen allows fans to have an old-school, communal (and tailgating) experience at the stadium yet also with the up-close view that high-def offers. The NFL had to recognize that there was a flaw built into the old model. The view was not that great from the bleachers. The temptation would be for the NFL owners to use their own experience as the guide for judging how millennials would see their games. It would have been easy—and misguided—for teams to say that bad views were never a problem before and to assume that they would not be a problem in the future. For the smartphone generation, you did not go to a stadium to see a game (the view was better at home); you went to a stadium for the communal experience. Listening to the people they serve taught the Falcons that they had to recalibrate the meaning of attendance— even if it cost the team a billion dollars.

In a similar way, advertisers are adjusting to the smartphone era. "Millennials and Generation Z have [advertisers] perplexed," one observer said. "Young people devour more content in more ways than ever before. They didn't like the old rules, so they changed them. They don't want to pay for 700 cable channels, and they certainly don't want to watch boring commercials for three straight minutes." The author notes that his middle school daughter "leans on Apple TV, Netflix, Hulu, Amazon, and YouTube," all of which she can view on her smartphone. Then she "hops on Instagram, zips through pictures and devours quickie cooking videos. She texts her friends and hangs out with them on Houseparty. This is how she unwinds." Advertisers know that they are not going to lure her and her smartphone generation back to broadcast television. So they have to adapt.[3] That leads the author to his final conclusion—a conclusion that is crucial for those who lead God's people. Anyone who decides, "'I don't like where things are going, they were better for me the old way, we gotta keep the old way!' is doomed to fail." The Atlanta Falcons adapted; advertisers are adapting. The church needs to find a way to recalibrate for the smartphone era.

We in the church are tempted to say, "*Things were better for us the old way.*" And we have lots of examples of people with power resisting change (or failing to embrace it) because they are not the ones who stand to gain from it. For example, in the nineteenth century, medical doctors adopted the innovation of ether, which allowed patients to be unconscious when doctors did surgery and dentists pulled teeth. This was a great innovation because it eased the pain of people who were particularly suffering. But clergymen of the era were against its use in one setting. They opposed giving ether to women in childbirth because the Bible says the pain of childbirth is part of the curse for rebelling in the Garden of Eden.[4] At the same time, those same clergy*men* were embracing technological changes that made other work less burdensome. The whole curse in Genesis says that women will feel pain in childbirth and men will get crops only "by the sweat of [their] brow." In other words, the clergy*men* of that era believed that easing a man's curse of "labor by the sweat of your brow" was acceptable, but easing a woman's curse of "pain in childbirth" was not. The difference, of course, was that the clergy*men* identified with the former but not the latter. If the leaders making decisions in our congregations are the product of the location-based generation, and if the leaders are the ones who created the current model of ministry, then they are likely to say, "Things were better for me the old way." But if those same leaders want to reach the smartphone generation, they need to learn to cultivate agile leaders and innovative congregations.

For Millennial Church, the opportunity is to do more than convince young adults once again to attend Sunday services. The goal is to get them to use the categories of a Sunday morning service (i.e., the practices of the Christian faith) to make spiritual sense of their lives—that is, to create *shared stories of hope* that make spiritual sense of the longings and losses of the people entrusted to their care.

Since leadership begins with listening, we must ask about the longings and losses of the smartphone generation entrusted to the congregation's care. The Fuller Youth Institute has done pioneering work on youth and young adults. In that work, we look especially at three categories when thinking about longing and loss: identity, belonging, and purpose. People's identity is too often in their work. They long to be in community. They want to contribute to a purpose greater than themselves. Yet in the urban high-tech setting where Millennial Church ministers, they often believe the same Big Lie that we saw in Washington, DC: the Big Lie that you can have a meaningful life without community.

As we think about how Millennial Church might innovate a response to the smartphone generation, we also need to think about the practice of worship on Sunday morning and the practice of community in small groups.

Let us start with worship. The model the church wants to preserve is built on a few assumptions about worship. This congregation equates the singing portion of the service with worship—primarily because that is the part of the service directed toward adoration of God. Now, if you were to ask the leaders of the church, they would recognize that the prayers, the offering, and even the greeting of one another are all part of what Romans 12:1 calls the "spiritual service of worship" (NASB). But in the common parlance of the congregation, the singing is called the "worship" part of the service, the group of people who play guitars and drums is called the "worship band," and the ones who sing into the microphones are called the "worship leaders." Indeed, when we talk to the congregation's leaders about the problem of watching the service on the internet, they will usually talk about how the active congregation becomes a passive audience when they watch the singing rather than participate.

This is where we need to examine our assumptions. If the man next to me at church is standing silently with his hands in his pockets while people sing enthusiastically around him, is he participating in worship? I argue that the answer could be yes and it could be no. We would need to know more. Think about a woman who goes to a concert hall to hear the LA Philharmonic. She does not sing—there are no words. Is she "participating"? Well, it depends. I know people who are completely into it yet are silent. And I know people who are passive and bored. But what we have just learned is that the boundary for "participating" is neither physical presence nor vocal participation.

It may be helpful to think about an experience that would resonate for the smartphone generation. Go to a performance of the Broadway show *Hamilton*. No one in the audience sings. But they know the words, they marvel at the choreography, they cry at the end. In short, they participate. The columnist Joe Posnanski, for example, wrote a moving article about taking his daughter, Eliza, to see the musical.[5] Before going to the show, Eliza prepared. She learned all the words, she connected with the *Hamilton* community on Tumblr, she read the "Hamiltome" (the nickname for a thick book all about the making of the show). After the show, she told her friends about it, she repeated messages like "Immigrants, we get the job done," and she hummed the songs throughout the week. She participated in the musical.

So what does it look like to participate in worship? Is it enough to revere God, to be moved by the sermon, and to allow the songs to narrate your week? That sounds to me like participating. There is a saying that claims, "What gets measured gets done." If what we measure is physical presence, then we equate attendance with worship. There is another saying that claims, "[It is] folly to hope for A while rewarding B."[6] We hope for worship while rewarding attendance. If we are going to discover a way to recalibrate for the smartphone generation, we need to find a way to measure what matters most to us and to stop equating worship with physical presence.

Likewise, we need to ask ourselves about what matters most to us with small groups. We assume that midweek small groups promote community and discipleship. But Robert Wuthnow, who is likely the leading scholar documenting American Christianity, has offered a different picture.[7] He found that small groups often do the opposite of what they intend. Instead of promoting depth, they facilitate superficiality. Instead of community, they often promote individualism. To explain this, let me offer a picture that anyone who has spent time in small-group Christianity will find painfully familiar. Imagine that you and I are in a group, and suppose that I respond to the Bible study by spouting my own, dubious interpretation. Or perhaps when we are preparing to pray, I ask the group to pray for me because I have an overbearing and rude boss. How will the group respond? No matter what I say, even if I spout heresy or misrepresent my boss, the group will affirm my saying it. The ethic is to support someone no matter what they say. The result, Wuthnow found, is the opposite of what we intend. There is little depth because people are rarely challenged to go deeper than their own opinions. And there is little community because each person is confirmed in one's own experience. According to Wuthnow's research, the small groups that we cherish often accomplish less than we intend.

My point here is not to disparage small groups. I think that small-group Bible studies can provide great ways to develop the faith. Indeed, small groups have been an important part of my discipleship for almost my entire adult life. Denigrating small groups is not my point. My point, instead, has to do with recalibration—with innovation. *We Christians tend to accept the downside of what we know while scrutinizing the downside of what we don't know.* We discount the disadvantages of small groups and focus on the advantages. At the same time, we focus on the disadvantages of the smartphone generation while discounting the potential advantages. We accept the divided lives that car culture creates while discounting the potential of smartphones for uniting people across distance. If we are going to recalibrate for smartphone culture—if we are going to become calibrated to the world that now exists—we need to recognize the advantages (and the disadvantages) for ministry that come with this new era.

Beyond the practice of worship and the practice of discipleship, there is a third practice that might help Millennial Church recalibrate its ministry for the smartphone generation: the practice of vocation. The apostle Paul reminded the Corinthians that our work begins with God's work in the world. Paul told the Corinthians that God was in the world, "reconciling the world to himself" in Christ Jesus, and has given to us the ministry of reconciliation. Then he says, "We are therefore Christ's ambassadors" (2 Cor. 5:19–20). We have talked about how an ambassador is a citizen of one country who goes to live in another country with the expressed purpose of building relations between the two—in this case, between what Martin Luther called the "kingdom of heaven" and the "kingdom of this earth." Luther tied together the idea of living in two kingdoms with the idea of vocation. "Vocations are located within the kingdom of earth. More precisely, a vocation is the specific call to love one's neighbor which comes to us through the duties which attach to our social place or 'station' within the earthly kingdom."[8] For Luther, one's "station" was attached to one's workplace. Like an ambassador stationed in a particular land, we Christians are appointed to duty in a particular workplace. These are the people entrusted to our care.

A while back, I presented a preliminary version of these ideas to a group of business leaders in Silicon Valley. As we talked about reinventing the practice of vocation to focus on the people entrusted to our care, a young lawyer at a tech firm blurted out, "Do you mean you expect me to care about my employees' personal lives?" I responded, "Yes, I do." Then we had a fruitful discussion about whether Christians bear such a responsibility. But he was not convinced.

A few months later, a book came out that included a much better answer than I gave to the young lawyer's question, even though it is a secular book written for a secular audience. The author, Kim Scott, created the management training courses at Google and then at Apple, and now she mentors the CEOs at places like Twitter and Dropbox. The central idea of the book is that a boss has two responsibilities: to care personally and to challenge directly—and that a boss cannot challenge directly until the boss has cared personally. The young lawyer would have accepted the second duty but not the first.

Scott tells a story to show what it means to care personally for the people entrusted to her care, a story that helps us understand the Christian practice of vocation. She describes a particularly busy day when she was the CEO of a tech startup. Late one night, she had discovered a pricing problem that was so pressing that she canceled all her morning meetings so she could focus on her spreadsheets. But as she walked into the office that next morning, a colleague ran up to her, needing to talk. He was distraught because he had just discovered that he might need a kidney transplant. She sat with him for an hour, calming him over cups of tea. As she walked out his door, she saw an engineer whose son was in the ICU. She took the time to convince him that he belonged at the hospital and not at the office. More tea, more tears. Finally, she encountered a colleague who wanted to tell her some good news; his daughter had just achieved the highest score on a statewide math test. She found time to celebrate with him. The longings and losses of her people had eaten into the time that she wanted to spend on the pricing problem.

Later she discussed the morning with her mentor, complaining that the "emotional babysitting" was getting in the way of the "real work." "This is not babysitting," her mentor replied. "It's called management, and *it is your job!*" Kim Scott then draws the point of the story. "We undervalue the 'emotional labor' of being a boss," she writes, but "this emotional labor is not just part of the job; it's the key to being a good boss."[9] The people are just as much a part of your job as the spreadsheets. Indeed, Scott spends the rest of the book explaining why managers can only challenge directly if they are willing to care personally.

"Do you mean you expect me to care about my employees' personal lives?" the young lawyer asked. Yes, they are not just employees. They are the people entrusted to your care. If you want a job to be more than an occupation—if you want it to be a vocation, a calling where you love your neighbor—then you need to see yourself as planted by God in a setting where you are called to the people entrusted to your care.

So, to summarize, we have two standards that create the parameters helping us think about how Millennial Church might recalibrate its ministry for the smartphone generation. The standards are people and practices—that is, the ever-changing culture and the never-changing gospel. These will help us make spiritual sense of the longings and losses of the people entrusted to our care. The smartphone generation craves meaning for issues of identity, belonging, and purpose. It needs practices like worship, community, and vocation. The practice of worship sets parameters saying that millennials need opportunities to adore God and to adopt the phrases that they will use to narrate their lives. The practices of discipleship and community can only develop if the interactions include the pushback that comes with mutual interaction. The practice of vocation will enable millennials to love their neighbor wherever they are planted on a Tuesday morning or Thursday afternoon by recognizing the people entrusted to their care. Together these insights might allow Millennial Church to recalibrate its ministry according to the ever-changing people and the never-changing gospel.

It turns out that some leaders from Millennial Church were part of an innovation project hosted at Fuller Seminary. They went through the process of brainstorming many ideas described in chapter 6. As part of their brainstorming, they encountered an idea that helped them think creatively about their situation. It is called the "adjacent possible." I will explain what it means and then show how we can use its insights to help us understand how Millennial Church might recalibrate for the smartphone generation.

The term "adjacent possible" comes from Steven Johnson.[10] Think of the image of a house with many rooms. Now let us say that we in the church occupy one or two of those rooms. Most of us, when we seek to discover new ideas, will look in ever-smaller detail at the things in the rooms we already occupy. But the research suggests that innovators pursue a different strategy. They expand their search to different rooms in the house.

In our case, that means learning from areas outside of Christianity or even religion. It means finding some insight from an adjacent room and bringing it back to apply in our area. The respected Stanford scholar Kathleen Eisenhardt (in explaining why all innovation is ultimately meaning-making innovation) describes why innovation is not about thinking outside the box. "Innovation is the result of synthesizing, or bridging, ideas from different domains," she says, calling it "the result of simultaneously thinking in multiple boxes."[11] Rather than pursuing ideas that are truly new, she suggests finding truly new applications for ideas that are well-established in other areas. Let me give two examples that focus on our attempt to recalibrate Millennial Church's small-group ministry for the smartphone generation.

First, we might learn from the realm of online education. In the last twenty years, colleges and universities have pioneered new techniques for extending learning into the world, especially through the internet. For example, the school where I teach (Fuller Seminary) has been offering some degrees online. In that process, we at Fuller created an important distinction that can serve as an *adjacent possible* for Millennial Church.

We originally thought (incorrectly) that the goal of online education was to be "just as good" as in-person education. But as we experimented, we found that online education could do some things better than traditional classroom education. It may be that a smartphone-era small group may be able to do some things better than a traditional location-based small group. Specifically, we at Fuller have come to distinguish between uprooted education and embedded education.

In the traditional model of seminary education, students uproot themselves from their communities and travel across the country to go to a seminary. (Indeed, the very language of theological education assumes a location-based mental model—you *go to* seminary.) For decades, seminaries have understood that it is less than ideal to uproot a person from community in order to teach them about how to lead in community. But we have lived so long with the traditional model's disadvantages that we no longer see them. So we passively accept the contradiction of uprooting someone so that they can learn to lead in community.

By contrast, we at Fuller now talk about embedded education. Online students are not required to uproot themselves from the communities that formed them in order to learn to lead. That affords me as a professor a slate of pedagogical possibilities that would otherwise be impossible. For example, I teach leadership. I can create an expectation that students who are embedded in communities will try out the lessons they are learning in any given week's coursework, and then I can create an assignment that asks them to reflect on what they learned when they took their lessons back to their communities. In the old model, I had to use case studies and other proxies in order to talk about leading in community. For embedded students, I can ask them to reflect on their communities (in all their contextual complexity). Embedded education is better than uprooted education for dealing with life in progress.

The same might be true for a small group. In the traditional model, all the participants uproot themselves from their homes and workplaces and travel to a separate location. Perhaps we can create a model in which the participants engage each other while they are still in, say, their workplace environments (perhaps mediated by smartphones). The embedded small group may afford a kind of learning that would be impossible in an uprooted small group.

Another "adjacent possible" that can teach us about the smartphone generation involves what are called "communities of practice."[12] John Seeley Brown (formerly of Xerox PARC) was commissioned by Xerox to figure out how photocopy technicians learn their craft. The company was spending an enormous amount of money on classes for these tech reps, and managers wanted Brown's team to create an artificial intelligence program. In other words, he was commissioned to do "process innovation."

Brown used a process much like our innovation process. He started by shadowing repair technicians as they worked (i.e., he started listening). Brown found something surprising. He did not need to create a new education program. These tech reps needed to learn from a story and not from a curriculum. When stuck, tech reps did not open a manual. Instead, they sent out a Bat-signal to get a fellow tech rep's help. Together they talked through similar situations they had seen to figure out what to do. What is more, they transferred that knowledge to others because, when they went back to the office, they often sat around playing cribbage and told war stories as they waited for the next call.

The Xerox company's training discouraged them from telling stories. Xerox wanted the reps to do it the traditional way: consult the manual. John Seeley Brown's team suggested just the opposite. They gave them two-way radios (this was before smartphones) so they could constantly be in contact with the experiences of the others.

A community of practice is a group that learns a practice by regularly engaging in storytelling and other informal communication. The church is likely a lot like the Xerox Corporation in that we place the emphasis for a small group on the learning that takes place in a formal Bible study. But we may need to learn from Brown that the most important learning is what happens when a person (embedded in a work setting) calls on others who can share stories from their experience. Xerox thought that uprooting a person to put them into a formal learning space (a classroom) with a standardized curriculum (the manuals) taught people how to be repair technicians. But stories embedded in community were actually far more important. If our goal in the church is to form people for discipleship in the world, we need to recognize that uprooting a person from that world in order to send them to a formal space (a small group) with a standardized curriculum (a lesson plan) might not be the only (or the best) way to form Christians to live faithful lives out in the world.

In conversation with some leaders at Millennial Church, we decided to see if we could create a small-group experience for the smartphone generation that used insights from online education and "communities of practice" to reinvent vocation and community. We then created a prototype for a smartphone small group—one where people did not need to be in the same place to meet.

The prototype the leaders proposed had three parts. First, there is an opening retreat for the participants in the smartphone small group. The purpose of the retreat is to introduce material but also (more importantly) to establish personal connections. This builds on the insight that people are more likely to be vulnerable online with other people once they have met those people in person.

The second part is content and response. Each weekday the participants would receive on their smartphones (through an app like Slack or Trello) content. That content might include lessons on vocation, reflections that use the words from the Sunday morning music, or reflections on (or with) the weekly sermon. The participants should expect to spend about fifteen minutes each day on the material and on constructing a response that they would share with the group. The responses would usually involve answers to questions that focus the content on the people entrusted to their care.

The third aspect of the group is face-to-face prayer and reflection. Each participant meets either once a week in person or twice a week via FaceTime with at least one other person in the small group. The group leaders pay attention especially to people who work in proximity to each other in order to facilitate face-to-face encounters.

This prototype tackles many of the issues that traditional small groups do not presently address. But there is one parameter, however, that the prototype does not yet meet. A community of practice only happens when the people in the community need each other. When the Xerox tech reps got stuck, they would send out the Bat-signal and receive help from other reps. The leaders wanted to allow someone to send out the Bat-signal when they encounter a demanding situation or person in their work setting.

How did the experiment go? The experiment was a good first step, yet it failed at a number of levels. It was a good first step because it did indeed create content that it pushed into the participants' workspaces. But it failed to accomplish some of its other goals. Participants did not meet outside the group for prayer, and no one sent out the Bat-signal. Indeed, the biggest failing was likely the leadership. The couple who had been asked to lead the experiment bowed out because a family issue came up. The leader recruited to replace them did not really have the same level of commitment and was not interested in creating a holding environment that would make it both uncomfortable for people who wanted to avoid meeting and safe enough for people who were anxious about the prototype.

Was it a success or a failure? That depends on what happens next. Most congregations typically treat an experiment as a failure if it does not accomplish every one of its intended goals on the first run. If this congregation does that, they are likely to give up and decide that they cannot innovate small groups for the smartphone generation. But if they recruit and train new leaders and if they try another experiment, they may well get to the point where they can reinvent small groups around the lived experience of the smartphone generation.

In the Bible, the book of Judges shows the people of Israel living out a painful cycle. Many of the stories in the book follow a pattern: the people rebel against God, something bad happens because of it, they cry out to God, God hears and raises a judge, the judge saves the day, the people are grateful (for a while), but then the people rebel. And the cycle starts again. In the last half of the book, the phrase that the author uses to signal that the people are rebelling against God is that everyone "did what was right in their own eyes" (Judg. 17:6; 21:25 NRSV). To emphasize the ways that the people were caught in this destructive cycle, the book even ends with this phrase. It is like ending a story with dot, dot, dot, thus saying that the cycle continues.

Millennial Church is like so many congregations. It is trapped in a cycle. Something happens that teaches them that they must change. They work hard to create something new. They try an experiment. That experiment is both successful and limping. Then the congregation, like the people of Israel in the book of Judges, face a choice. They can let the cycle continue, or they can break the cycle. If Millennial Church decides to try the next round of experiments, it can break the cycle. But if they allow the failings of the experiment to frighten them, the cycle continues.

The church as we know it is calibrated for a world that no longer exists. We need to recalibrate. If we want things to be different, we need to listen to the longings and losses of the people entrusted to our care. We need to reinvent Christian practices to make spiritual sense of those longings and losses. And we will need to express it all as a shared story of hope for the smartphone generation.

APPENDIX

Systematic Listening

1. Who are the people entrusted to your care?

   Decide specifically to whom you and your team will be listening.

2. Set clear metrics.

   Decide how many folks on your team will commit to listening to how many stories from how many people each week. For example, you might say, "The five of us will each conduct two listening sessions each week for four weeks. After each session, we will each write up at least one story of longing and two stories of loss." If you do that, by the end of the month you will have accumulated 120 stories (40 of longing and 80 of loss) from 40 people.

3. Establish accountability.

   For example, you might appoint one of your volunteers (we will call her Helen) to hold your team's feet to the fire. You might say, "Each week we will meet with Helen. Helen does not have to go out to do any of the listening sessions. She does just three things: (1) ensures that we meet; (2) asks each of us in the meeting how many people we met and how many stories we collected; and (3) asks whom we plan to visit next week." When I work with groups, I encourage them to recruit a kind but stern mother, perhaps one whose kids have moved out of the house. Pick someone you don't want to disappoint—someone who will make sure you stay on track and won't accept excuses when you tell her how busy you are.

4. Gather the stories.

At each weekly gathering, read the stories you have been collecting. As the month progresses, take the time to group the stories in themes. What longings stand out? What losses come up again and again? Is there one paradigmatic story that seems to fit the experiences of your people? Ask yourself what you were feeling as you heard the stories and ask yourself how you are being transformed by what you hear. Remember that the purpose of listening is to be transformed so that you can carry your people's longings and losses with you as you engage in recalibrating.

5. Face the Big Lie.

The goal is to describe in a sentence the Big Lie—the story your people tell themselves that prevents them from hearing the gospel of hope and healing. To do that, take out sticky notes and write as many Big Lies as you can recall hearing. Group them together as a team. Then narrow and refine the choices until you can name the Big Lie.

Notes

Preface

1. The idea of mixing and matching options from unrelated fields becomes particularly important for the kind of innovation we will explore. See the discussion at the end of chap. 2, under the heading "Christian Innovation Involves the Innovation of Meaning."

2. The quote is from Alan Kay of Xerox PARC. The project he was describing was his vision for what became the world's first personal computer. Michael Hiltzik, *Dealers of Lightning: Xerox PARC and the Dawn of the Computer Age* (New York: HarperBusiness, 1999), 122.

3. This information is more suitable for journal articles. See, e.g., Scott Cormode, "Innovation That Honors Tradition: The Meaning of Christian Innovation," *Journal of Religious Leadership* 14, no. 2 (2015): 81–102, https://arl-jrl.org/wp-content/uploads/2019/01/Cormode-Innovation-that-Honors-Tradition.pdf.

Chapter 1: How the Church Is Calibrated for a World That No Longer Exists

1. Erica came to Fuller as part of one of three parallel innovation grants at Fuller: Youth Ministry Innovation, Ministry Innovation with Young Adults, and Innovation for Vocation. Together these projects have gathered upward of a hundred congregations to summits on Fuller's campus in Pasadena, California. Each project followed a similar path: the participants engaged in a five-week online training course before coming to Pasadena (one that guided them through a listening project), a three-day summit at Fuller (that eventuated in a project prototype), and a ten-week congregational experiment (guided by a Fuller coach). The Fuller Youth Institute (and especially Caleb Roose and Steve Argue) has been instrumental in these projects.

2. Dwight Zscheile, *The Agile Church: Spirit-Led Innovation in an Uncertain Age* (New York: Morehouse Publishing, 2014), x.

3. This phenomenon is described by Thomas Friedman in his book *Thank You for Being Late: An Optimist's Guide to Thriving in the Age of Accelerations* (New York: Farrar, Straus, & Giroux, 2016).

4. Peter Vaill, *Learning as a Way of Being: Strategies for Survival in a World of Permanent White Water* (San Francisco: Jossey-Bass, 1996).

5. Robert Dabney, "Review of Dr. Girardeau's *Instrumental Music in Public Worship*," *Presbyterian Quarterly* (July 1889), https://www.naphtali.com/articles/worship/dabney-review-of-girardeau-instrumental-music/.

6. L. Gregory Jones, "Traditioned Leadership," *Faith & Leadership*, Jan. 19, 2009, http://www.faithandleadership.com/content/traditioned-innovation.

7. I recognize that the very meaning of "the historic Christian church" is subject to debate. But even those who want to exclude others from the historic faith want to maintain their own specific link with the faith passed on through the generations.

8. The other debilitating temptation is to deceive ourselves that the work of innovation depends on us instead of on God. As we will see, it is the work of the Spirit. We will need to create a process for innovation that neither abandons our responsibility to partner with God in the work of reconciliation nor pretends that human activity is decisive. We do our part and then turn it over to God.

9. This distinction between fatalism and faith goes back to Søren Kierkegaard's *Fear and Trembling*, which was first published in 1843. Indeed, that is why in my prayers I often admit to God that I present things to God with fear and trembling.

10. Although Drucker wrote about the questions many times, the most accessible place to see them together is in the reissued version of his book *The Five Most Important Questions You Will Ever Ask about Your Organization* (San Francisco: Jossey-Bass, 2008). The Drucker Questions have been established as a tool for keeping an organization focused on a common goal. Any enterprise should be able to ask two people in the organization these questions and get similar answers. The questions have become famous enough that they have taken on a life of their own. They show up not only in academic articles but also in magazine pieces, blog posts, and animated videos. The questions are these:
   1. What is your organization's mission?
   2. Who is your customer?
   3. What does your customer value?
   4. What results will your customer use to measure your performance?
   5. What is your plan for providing your customer with value?

11. The church has taken on this apostolic role as ambassador, and thus Paul's assertion about himself and his team ("We are ambassadors") can also be said of we Christians who are sent out into the world to engage in God's reconciling work.

12. The Greek word Paul uses for an "ambassador" refers to an envoy who is sent to speak on behalf of a sovereign. Paul uses this term to emphasize his own authority as the mouthpiece of the God who sent him. But the apostle softens that claim by emphasizing reconciliation. He is thus the envoy of reconciliation who stands between God and the Corinthians, imploring them to accept God's kind offer of reconciling grace. See Paul Barnett, *The Second Epistle to the Corinthians*, New International Commentary of the New Testament (Grand Rapids: Eerdmans, 1997), 307–9.

13. On "reconciliation" as Paul's missional goal, see Murray J. Harris, *The Second Epistle to the Corinthians*, New International Greek Testament Commentary (Grand Rapids: Eerdmans, 2005), 445, 446.

14. For more on this, see Scott Cormode, "Leadership Begins with Listening," Fuller Seminary De Pree Leadership Center, July 17, 2018, https://depree.org/leadership-begins-with-listening.

15. Robert Wuthnow, *The Crisis in the Churches* (New York: Oxford University Press, 1997).

16. Unfortunately, this emphasis on longings and losses can be misinterpreted. As we will see, the focus of our innovation has to be on what God does in the death and resurrection of Jesus Christ. But we start with longings and losses because we are focusing on the human condition. The death and resurrection of Jesus is God's response to the human condition. So our inquiries about longings and losses must always lead us back to the cross. For a very helpful discussion of how our contemporary culture substitutes fulfillment and authenticity for a true understanding of the terrible losses that each human experiences, see Andrew Root, *Faith Formation in a Secular Age* (Grand Rapids: Baker Academic, 2017), 116–51.

17. The best discussion on empathy, as we will see in chap. 3, comes from Brené Brown and her use of Theresa Wiseman's research. The most accessible source is Brown's wonderful little video, "Brené Brown on Empathy," Dec. 10, 2013, https://www.youtube.com/watch?v=1E vwgu369Jw.

18. This quotation and further information in the chapter come from two interviews with Erica—one on Aug. 13, 2018, and the other on Nov. 14, 2018.

19. For a more detailed explanation of this idea, see Scott Cormode, *Making Spiritual Sense* (Nashville: Abingdon, 2006).

20. The precise language of the NIV is as follows: "Let any one of you who is without sin be the first to throw a stone at her" (John 8:7).

21. Please do not let this language about being transformed by story diminish the work of God. A more accurate way to say it is that God transforms people and often does this when they are presented with a story that invites a response.

22. On the ways that these stories define the church, see George Lindbeck, "The Story-Shaped Church," in *Scriptural Authority and Narrative Interpretation*, ed. G. Green and H. Frei (Philadelphia: Fortress, 1987).

23. Ella Saltmarshe, "Using Story to Change Systems," *Stanford Social Innovation Review*, Feb. 20, 2018, https://ssir.org/articles/entry/using_story_to_change_systems.

24. In "Using Story," Saltmarshe points out that "humans have always used stories to make sense out of our chaotic world."

25. Saltmarshe, "Using Story." The quotation from Steinbeck is attributed to an interview he gave in the *Paris Review*.

26. On "ritualized stories," see James K. A. Smith, *Imagining the Kingdom: How Worship Works* (Grand Rapids: Baker Academic, 2013), 108–19.

27. Christine Pohl, *Making Room: Recovering Hospitality as a Christian Tradition* (Grand Rapids: Eerdmans, 1999).

28. The best research on vision comes from James Collins and Jerry Porras, "Building Your Company's Vision," *Harvard Business Review*, September–October 1996, http://www.fusbp .com/pdf/Building%20Companys%20Vision.pdf.

29. On King's theological education and especially on his decision to pursue nonviolence, see Taylor Branch, *Parting the Waters: America in the King Years, 1954–63* (New York: Simon & Schuster, 1988), 69–104.

Chapter 2: The Meaning of Christian Innovation

1. Although some might argue that the first Christian missionary was the Ethiopian eunuch whom Philip encountered in Acts 8.

2. Ralph D. Winter, "The Highest Priority: Cross-Cultural Evangelism," in *Let the Earth Hear His Voice: Official Reference Volume, Papers and Responses; International Congress on World Evangelization, Lausanne, Switzerland* [1974], ed. J. D. Douglas (Minneapolis: World Wide Publications, 1975), 213–25, https://www.lausanne.org/docs/lau1docs/0213.pdf.

3. Winter, "Highest Priority," 214.

4. "Influential Evangelicals," *Time*, Feb. 7, 2005, http://content.time.com/time/specials/pack ages/article/0,28804,1993235_1993243_1993320,00.html.

5. The definition for Christian innovation that I am proposing is consistent with (and a more specific cousin of) the idea that innovation is "a new practice adopted by a community." I emphasize both practices and people in community. Cf. Peter Denning and Robert Dunham, *The Innovator's Way* (Cambridge, MA: MIT Press, 2010), xv.

6. Peter Senge, *The Fifth Discipline* (New York: Currency/Doubleday, 1990), 174–204, esp. 175.

7. Ronald Heifetz and Martin Linsky, *Leadership on the Line* (Boston: Harvard Business Review Press, 2002), 11.

8. Taylor Branch, *Parting the Waters: America in the King Years, 1954–63* (New York: Simon & Schuster, 1989), 143–205.

9. For the text of Martin Luther King Jr.'s speech on Dec. 5, 1955, see https://kinginstitute .stanford.edu/king-papers/documents/mia-mass-meeting-holt-street-baptist-church.

10. Ann Swidler, *Talk of Love: How Culture Matters* (Chicago: University of Chicago Press, 2001), 34.

11. Swidler, *Talk of Love*, 188. She also said, "Deductive logic is not central to the organization of cultural systems" (189).

12. Swidler, *Talk of Love*, 29, 30.

13. Tom Kelley with Jonathan Littman, *The Art of Innovation: Lessons in Creativity from IDEO, America's Leading Design Firm* (New York: Currency/Doubleday, 2001).

14. Tom Kelley and David Kelley, *Creative Confidence* (New York: Crown Business, 2013); see also David Kelley, "How to Build Your Creative Confidence," TED Talk (2012), https://www.ted.com /talks/david_kelley_how_to_build_your_creative_confidence (starting at the 6:02-minute mark).

15. Lara Logan, "How Unconventional Thinking Transformed War-Torn Colombia," *60 Minutes*, Dec. 11, 2016, https://www.cbsnews.com/news/60-minutes-colombia-after-civil-war -lara-logan/.

16. Julian Birkinshaw, John Bessant, and Rick Delbridge, "Finding, Forming, and Performing: Creating Networks for Discontinuous Innovation," *California Management Review* 49, no. 3 (2007): 67–84, esp. 68; online version, with different page numbers, available at http://facultyresearch.london.edu/docs/sim48.pdf.

17. The best summary of the deep structural changes that dominated American Christianity after World War II is Robert Wuthnow, *The Restructuring of American Religion* (Princeton: Princeton University Press, 1990).

18. L. Gregory Jones, "Traditioned Leadership," *Faith & Leadership*, Jan. 19, 2009, http:// www.faithandleadership.com/content/traditioned-innovation.

19. On cultural liturgies, see James K. A. Smith, *Desiring the Kingdom: Worship, Worldview, and Cultural Formation* (Grand Rapids: Baker Academic, 2009), esp. 25; and Smith, *Imagining the Kingdom: How Worship Works* (Grand Rapids: Baker Academic, 2013), 14–21, 108–13. On liturgies as embodied stories, see *Imagining the Kingdom*, 109.

20. Smith, *Desiring the Kingdom*, 26.

21. David Weiss and Claude Legrand helpfully distinguish innovation as a process from innovation as an outcome. Their book emphasizes the process of innovation. There are those as well, such as Scott Anthony, Clark Gilbert, and Mark Johnson, who see innovation as less important than transformation. When an entire organization's purpose and practice undergo a process of innovation, then that adds up to transformation. See Weiss and Legrand, *Innovative Intelligence* (Hoboken, NJ: Wiley, 2011), 5; and Anthony, Gilbert, and Johnson, *Dual Transformation* (Boston: Harvard Business Review Press, 2017), 10.

22. Most of the literature that I quote comes from recent years. For an overview of how scholars wrote about innovation before 2005, see Jan Fagerberg, "Innovation: A Guide to the Literature," in *The Oxford Handbook of Innovation*, ed. Jan Fagerberg, David Mowery, and Richard Nelson (New York: Oxford University Press, 2005), 1–26.

23. There are, however, examples of product innovation among Christians. Creating another translation of Scripture is the creation of a product. The first person to translate the Scriptures into the vernacular of another language was engaging in what we are calling meaning-making innovation. But having one more translation into a certain language does not appreciably change the way that we make meaning.

24. See Jeffery Liker, *The Toyota Way* (Burlington, NC: McGraw-Hill Audio, 2004). Toyota's idea of continuous improvement through "lean" principles has become so important that it now influences many areas of society. See, e.g., John Black, *The Toyota Way to Healthcare Excellence* (Chicago: Health Administration Press, 2016).

25. See Gregory Dees, "The Meaning of Social Entrepreneurship," originally published in 1998 at Stanford, in 2001 reformatted and displayed by Duke University, https://entrepreneurs hip.duke.edu/news-item/the-meaning-of-social-entrepreneurship/.

26. Roger Martin and Sally Osberg, *Getting Beyond Better: How Social Entrepreneurship Works* (Boston: Harvard University Press, 2015), 7–11; see also Martin and Osberg, "Social Entrepreneurship: The Case for Definition," *Stanford Social Innovation Review*, Spring 2007, https://ssir.org/articles/entry/social_entrepreneurship_the_case_for_definition. Although the definitions of Dees (in "Meaning of Social Entrepreneurship") and of Martin and Osberg (in *Getting Beyond Better*) conflict in important ways, it is not uncommon to find them used interchangeably by Christian authors. For examples of how social innovators address large social problems, see Richard Pascale, Jerry Sternin, and Monique Sternin, *The Power of Positive Deviance: How Unlikely Innovators Solve the World's Toughest Problems* (Boston: Harvard Business Press, 2010).

27. The best examples of Christian social innovation are from L. Gregory Jones and Tim Shapiro. Jones distinguishes "social innovation" from "social entrepreneurship." "Social innovation involves the discovery and development of strategies to build, renew, and transform institutions in order to foster human flourishing," while "social entrepreneurship is an activity that focuses on starting new initiatives, and is a subset of a larger focus on social innovation." See Jones, *Christian Social Innovation* (Nashville: Abingdon, 2016), 3–7. See also the "Traditioned Innovation" collection of blog articles at https://www.faithandleadership.com/category /principles-practice-topics/traditioned-innovation; and Tim Shapiro with Kara Faris, *Divergent Church: The Bright Promise of Alternative Faith Communities* (Nashville: Abingdon, 2017).

28. On Schumpeter, see Thomas McCraw, *Prophet of Innovation: Joseph Schumpeter and Creative Destruction* (Cambridge, MA: Harvard University Press, 2007).

29. On "disruptive innovation," see Clayton Christensen's work, starting with *The Innovator's Dilemma: When New Technologies Cause Great Firms to Fail* (Boston: Harvard Business Review Press, 1997). Christensen's approach to higher education is particularly helpful for Christians, as in *The Innovative University* (San Francisco: Jossey-Bass, 2011). Also see Christensen's work on leadership for innovation in Jeff Dyer, Hal Gregersen, and Clayton Christensen, *The Innovator's DNA: Mastering the Five Skills of Disruptive Innovators* (Boston: Harvard Business Review Press, 2011).

30. Julian Birkinshaw of the London School of Economics is the one most associated with the term "discontinuous innovation"; he describes what it is and lists four kinds of research on it: "industry structure," "emerging customer needs," "cognitive barriers," and "internal mechanisms." Birkinshaw, Bessant, and Delbridge, "Finding, Forming," 69. A similar construction comes from Vijay Govindarajan and Chris Trimble on strategic innovation, which "breaks with past practice in at least one of three ways: value-chain design, conceptualization of customer value, and identification of potential customers." Govindarajan and Trimble, "Strategic Innovation and the Science of Learning," *MIT Sloan Management Review* 45, no. 2 (Winter 2004): 67–75, https://sloanreview.mit.edu/article/strategic-innovation-and-the-science-of-learning; cf. Morten T. Hansen and Julian Birkinshaw, "The Innovation Value Chain," *Harvard Business Review*, June 2007, 2–10, https://hbr.org/2007/06/the-innovation-value-chain.

31. Among those who share Schumpeter's commitment to creative destruction, there is a diversity of takes on innovation. For instance, Mohanbir Sawhney, Robert C Wolcott, and Inigo Arroniz list twelve different "dimensions" for innovation, all held together by the idea that "innovation is about new value, not new things." Sawhney, Wolcott, and Arroniz, "The 12 Different Ways for Companies to Innovate," *MIT Sloan Management Review* 47, no 3 (Spring 2006): 75–81, https://sloanreview.mit.edu/article/the-different-ways-for-companies-to-innovate/. Their emphasis develops from Drucker's third question: What does your customer value? In addition to these scholars, prominent practitioners have shaped the conversation. Drucker described innovation as "the effort to create purposeful, focused change in an enterprise's economic or

societal potential." Peter Drucker, "The Discipline of Innovation," *Harvard Business Review*, August 2002, 6; excerpted from Drucker, *Innovation and Entrepreneurship: Practice and Principles* (New York: Harper & Row, 1985). The executives at Google believe that "innovation entails both the production and implementation of novel and useful ideas. . . . For something to be innovative, it needs to be new, surprising, and radically useful." Eric Schmidt and Jonathan Rosenberg, *How Google Works* (New York: Grand Central Publishing, 2014), 206.

32. The diverse viewpoints from the secular literature on innovation do, however, agree that innovation will eventually require a change in organizational culture. See, e.g., Frances Horibe, *Creating the Innovation Culture* (New York: Wiley & Sons, 2001).

33. Paul DiMaggio, "Cultural Entrepreneurship in Nineteenth-Century Boston," *Media, Culture, and Society* 4 (1982): 33–50.

34. Andrew Hargadon, *How Breakthroughs Happen: The Surprising Truth about How Companies Innovate* (Boston: Harvard Business School Press, 2003), xii.

35. Hargadon, *How Breakthroughs Happen*, 31–54. This process is similar to what Paul DiMaggio calls "cultural entrepreneurship." DiMaggio's ideas have more resonance in sociological circles. We will use Hargadon's term because he specifically addresses the goal of innovation, but the ideas go together. In fact, Hargadon learned about creating cultural tools from a band of scholars who quite consciously built upon DiMaggio's original work. So it makes sense that Hargadon discovered cultural processes similar to the ones that DiMaggio first explained. See, esp., DiMaggio, "Cultural Entrepreneurship in Nineteenth-Century Boston"; also see his influential article on the larger question of how culture shapes the way humans process information: DiMaggio, "Culture and Cognition," *Annual Review of Sociology* 23 (August 1997): 263–87.

36. I recognize that I am mixing metaphors when I talk about cultivating tools. But I choose to do this because the process of creating a tool like a hammer is much like that for creating a device. But the process for creating a cultural tool is much more organic; it is more like cultivating a sapling.

37. Hargadon, *How Breakthroughs Happen*, xii.

38. Though there is no room to discuss the topic further, notice that innovation—even innovation that honors tradition—requires both individual innovation and innovative organizations.

39. From the perspective of what neo-institutional scholars call "institutional isomorphism," the blog shapes my thinking through mimetic isomorphism, while my boss is more likely to influence my thinking through normative isomorphism or even sometimes coercive isomorphism. That distinction is important because only a small range of topics can be influenced by normative and coercive means. Neo-institutional organizational theory is closely tied to our interests in cultural innovation because the seminal author in each area is Paul DiMaggio. His work on "cultural entrepreneurship" preceded and strongly influenced Swidler's work on cultural tools. See DiMaggio, "Cultural Entrepreneurship in Nineteenth-Century Boston." On institutional isomorphism, see Paul DiMaggio and Walter Powell, "The Iron Cage Revisited: Institutional Isomorphism and Collective Rationality," in *The New Institutionalism in Organizational Analysis*, ed. W. Powell and P. DiMaggio (Chicago: University of Chicago Press, 1991), 63–82; Roger Friedland and Robert R. Alford, "Bringing Society Back In: Symbols, Practices, and Institutional Contradictions," in Powell and DiMaggio, *New Institutionalism*, 232–63; Harry Stout and Scott Cormode, "Institutions and the Story of American Religion: A Sketch of a Synthesis," in *Sacred Companies*, ed. N. J. Demerath et al. (New York: Oxford University Press, 1998), 62–78; and Scott Cormode, *Making Spiritual Sense* (Nashville: Abingdon, 2006), 109n15.

40. Ann Swidler, "Culture in Action: Symbols and Strategies," *American Sociological Review* 51 (April 1986): 273–86, here 273.

41. One important way to engage this mixing and matching is to explore what Steven Johnson calls the "adjacent possible," an idea he got from Herbert Simon's admonition to explore

the "network of possible wanderings." Steven Johnson, *Where Good Ideas Come From* (New York: Riverhead Books, 2011), 153–55.

42. The literature on culture is filled with mixed and competing metaphors. I will use more than one metaphor, and I will even mix them because that is what the literature has done and that seems to make the whole idea easier to understand. Indeed, in the very first sentence of the abstract of the article where Swidler introduces the idea of a "cultural tool kit," she also refers to them as a "repertoire or 'tool kit' of habits, skills, and styles from which people construct 'strategies of action.'" Swidler, "Culture in Action"; Swidler, *Talk of Love*. Ann Swidler was a coauthor (along with Robert Bellah, Richard Madsen, William Sullivan, and Steven Tipton) of the extremely influential book *Habits of the Heart* (Berkeley: University of California Press, 1985), which lays the groundwork for talking about how culture can shape the most basic human experiences. This book is particularly important because it takes a social science approach to questions that animate what the Western tradition has typically called "the human condition."

43. Swidler, "Culture in Action," 273.

44. Peter Drucker, *Managing in a Time of Great Change* (Boston: Harvard Business Review Press, 2009), 201; cf. Drucker Institute, "The Virtues of Cross-Pollination," Aug. 26, 2011, https://www.drucker.institute/thedx/the-virtues-of-cross-pollination/.

45. This quote and those that follow come from Senge, *Fifth Discipline*, 175–76.

46. Robert Wuthnow, *The Crisis in the Churches* (New York: Oxford University Press, 1997), 6–7.

Chapter 3: Leadership Begins with Listening

1. This situation is a composite of people and congregations.

2. Scott Cormode, *Making Spiritual Sense* (Nashville: Abingdon, 2006).

3. Ann Streaty Wimberly, "Called to Listen: The Imperative Vocation of Listening in Twenty-First Century Communities," *International Review of Mission* 87, no. 346 (July 1998): 331–41, here 332.

4. Barbara Kellerman, *Followership* (Boston: Harvard Business School Press, 2008).

5. Compare with Nancy Tatom Ammerman on the distinction between "niche congregations" and "parish congregations." *Congregation and Community* (New Brunswick, NJ: Rutgers University Press, 1997), 34–36, 384n58.

6. The same is true for my daughter's love of science. One daughter is pursuing a PhD in physics at Ohio State University and working in an area of physics called "condensed matter." I do not understand it. But, during her first year of grad school, I would spend time on Tuesday nights watching YouTube videos so that I could be conversant enough to ask her questions about her work. The sad truth is that the more videos I watched about electron spin and superposition, the less I really understood. But understanding physics was never my goal. Understanding my daughter (and having her feel understood) was the goal.

7. Google focuses its innovative work on its core mission. But the leaders also encourage their engineers to pursue ideas that may not at first appear to be part of the core. They have a mechanism for ensuring that the mission stays at the center. The "Twenty Percent Time" program says that "engineers can spend 20 percent of their time working on whatever they choose, [but the program] is generally misunderstood. It is not about time; it's about freedom," meaning "the sense of freedom that comes from doing what you want to do, not doing what you are told." Eric Schmidt and Jonathan Rosenberg, *How Google Works* (New York: Grand Central Publishing, 2014), 226, 226n182.

8. The Google leaders say, "Our prime directive when it comes to product strategy is to focus on the user." Schmidt and Rosenberg, *How Google Works*, 213.

9. L. Gregory Jones, "Traditioned Leadership," *Faith & Leadership*, Jan. 19, 2009, http://www.faithandleadership.com/content/traditioned-innovation.

10. On the broad appeal and universal application of the good Samaritan story, see Robert Wuthnow, "Along the Road," in *Acts of Compassion* (Princeton: Princeton University Press, 1991), 157–87.

11. The Missional Church Movement has been particularly strong in emphasizing ways congregations can listen to the neighbors who reside in the church's neighborhood. See, e.g., Mark Lau Branson and Nicholas Warnes, eds., *Starting Missional Churches: Life with God in the Neighborhood* (Downers Grove, IL: IVP Books, 2014), and the range of impressive works by Craig Van Gelder, especially his seminal essays in *The Church between Gospel and Culture: The Emerging Mission in North America*, ed. George R. Hunsberger and Craig Van Gelder (Grand Rapids: Eerdmans, 1996).

12. Robert Wuthnow, *The Crisis in the Churches* (New York: Oxford University Press, 1997).

13. See, e.g., the issue of *Fuller* magazine that Fuller Youth Institute executive director Kara Powell edited on "Young People," issue 7, 2016, https://fullerstudio.fuller.edu/issue/issue -seven/; esp. introduction on "identity, belonging, and purpose," https://fullerstudio.fuller.edu /introduction-young-people/.

14. Ta-Nehisi Coates, e.g., documents the longings and losses of African Americans in urban America by weaving his own story into the narrative of American history. His book illustrates that we must listen in order to be transformed. He makes the point that Americans bear a responsibility for American history, and all those who reap the benefits of racism bear the sin that made those benefits possible. Coates, *Between the World and Me* (New York: Spiegel & Grau, 2015), 7–11.

15. If it were a hundred years ago, and I wanted to illustrate the human condition, I would draw on Shakespeare. His most famous writing, e.g., is the "To be or not to be" speech, in which Hamlet contemplates the human condition, asking aloud whether he should kill himself or go on living in spite of the "heartache and the thousand natural shocks that flesh is heir to" (*Hamlet*, act 3, scene 1). But Shakespeare will not do as an example for this generation.

16. Pixar directors think through not just the emotional struggle of the central protagonist; they also look at the other key characters. Indeed, they sometimes portray other characters as foils, whose human condition sets the experience of the central character in relief. For example, *Toy Story 2* revolves around a choice for Woody. But to make that choice clear, Pixar created the characters of Wheezy the Penguin (who was discarded because he had a broken squeaker) and Jessie the Cowgirl (who was abandoned when her beloved owner outgrew her). Ed Catmull of Pixar explains: "With the addition of Wheezy and Jessie, Woody's choice became fraught: he could stay with someone he loves, knowing he will eventually be discarded, or he could flee to a world [i.e., to a museum] where he could be pampered forever, but without the love he was built for. That is a real choice, a real question. The way the creative team phrased it to each other was [this]: Would *you* choose to live forever without love? When you feel the agony of that choice, you have a movie." Catmull, *Creativity, Inc.* (New York: Random House, 2014), 72.

17. The scene is usually available on YouTube. See, e.g., https://www.youtube.com/watch ?v=F2bk_9T482g.

18. Many articles have been published about the bifurcated effect this short sequence had on audiences. Many Anglo viewers expressed confusion because they did not understand that the dumpling-child was a metaphor or a dream. But non-Anglo audiences, especially the children of immigrants, reported becoming teared up, even weeping. See, e.g., Petrana Radulovic, "The Polarized Reactions to Pixar's 'Bao' Are Rooted in Culture," Dec. 18, 2018, https://www.poly gon.com/2018/6/26/17505726/pixar-bao-dumpling-short-reactions.

19. Ed Catmull, "How Pixar Fosters Collective Creativity," *Harvard Business Review*, September 2008, https://hbr.org/2008/09/how-pixar-fosters-collective-creativity.

20. We will return to this idea of loving people by listening to their story when we talk about empathy.

21. He described it this way: "You can preach and lead with greater authority when you know your context; when you know the place and people to whom you minister." Aaron Graham, "Windows on the Church: Session II," presented at Fuller Seminary on the occasion of the inauguration of Mark Labberton as president, Nov. 6, 2013.

22. See Alexia Salvatierra and Peter Heltzel, *Faith-Rooted Organizing* (Downers Grove, IL: InterVarsity, 2014), 66–71.

23. People rarely if ever speak this lie out loud. It stands in the background or as the foundation for their actions. But it is never spoken. Indeed, it often loses its power if spoken aloud. Thus one of the roles of Christians exercising their vocation is to surface the lies prevalent among the people entrusted to their care so that those lies wither in the light of the truth.

24. Graham, "Windows on the Church."

25. Countering this Big Lie is the purpose of Steven Corbett and Brian Fikkert's excellent book *When Helping Hurts* (Chicago: Moody, 2014).

26. This paragraph builds on Chris Argyris's landmark work on the contradictions between a person's "espoused theory" (the beliefs that people claim for their behavior) and their "theory-in-use" (the caveats they attach to those supposed beliefs). See Chris Argyris, "Teaching Smart People How to Learn," *Harvard Business Review*, May–June 1991, 99–109, https://hbr.org/1991/05/teaching-smart-people-how-to-learn?autocomplete=true; on the usefulness of this idea for Christian leaders, see Scott Cormode, "Espoused Theory," 2001, https://www.fuller.edu/next-faithful-step/resources/espoused-theory/.

27. Although I call them "skills" here, a better way to understand them is as "cultivated instincts." See the discussion in chap. 9 under the heading "Cultivated Instincts."

28. I am drawing on Brené Brown's summary of Theresa Wiseman's research documented in *Journal of Advanced Nursing* 23, no. 6 (June 1996): 1062–67, https://www.researchgate.net/publication/227941757_A_concept_analysis_of_empathy. See, e.g., Brown's wonderful little video, "Brené Brown on Empathy," Dec. 10, 2013, https://www.youtube.com/watch?v=1Evwgu369Jw.

29. "Brené Brown on Empathy."

30. Brené Brown, "The Power of Vulnerability," TED Talk, 2011, https://www.ted.com/talks/brene_brown_on_vulnerability?language=en; see also the companion piece, Brown, "Listening to Shame," TED Talk, 2012, https://www.ted.com/talks/brene_brown_listening_to_shame/transcript?language=en.

31. See, e.g., Brad Griffin, "Three Words Every Young Person Wants to Hear," March 17, 2017, https://fulleryouthinstitute.org/blog/three-words.

32. The exact statistic is 87 percent. "What Millennials Want When They Visit Church," Barna Research, March 4, 2015, https://www.barna.com/research/what-millennials-want-when-they-visit-church/.

33. Chimamanda Adichie, "The Danger of a Single Story," TED Talk, 2009, https://www.ted.com/talks/chimamanda_adichie_the_danger_of_a_single_story?language=en (quotation at the 4:37 mark).

34. A good place to start might be Coates, *Between the World and Me.*

35. See Chanequa Walker-Barnes, *Too Heavy a Yoke: Black Women and the Burden of Strength* (Eugene, OR: Cascade, 2014).

36. Almeda Wright has a wonderful book called *The Spiritual Lives of Young African Americans* (New York: Oxford University Press, 2017).

37. A helpful example of how to engage in these conversations is by Teesha Hadra and John Hambrick, *Black and White: Disrupting Racism One Friendship at a Time* (Nashville: Abingdon, 2019).

38. I have been particularly influenced on this topic by a wonderful overview essay that, although older now, provides a progression for how scholars have discussed assimilation. Russell Kazal, "Revisiting Assimilation: The Rise, Fall, and Reappraisal of a Concept in American Ethnic History," *American Historical Review* 100, no. 2 (April 1995): 437–71.

Chapter 4: Making Spiritual Sense

1. Katie Hafner, "Researchers Confront an Epidemic of Loneliness," *New York Times*, Sept. 5, 2016, https://www.nytimes.com/2016/09/06/health/lonliness-aging-health-effects.html.

2. The results of a University of Michigan poll sponsored by AARP. Sarah Elizabeth Adler, "National Poll on Healthy Aging: Many Older Adults Feel Isolated," Mar. 4, 2019, https://www.aarp.org/health/conditions-treatments/info-2019/study-isolation-health-risks.html.

3. Hafner, "Epidemic of Loneliness."

4. Claire Pomeroy, "Loneliness Is Harmful to Our Nation's Health," *Scientific American*, Mar. 20, 2019, https://blogs.scientificamerican.com/observations/loneliness-is-harmful-to-our -nations-health/.

5. "Cigna U.S. Loneliness Index: Survey of 20,000 Americans," by Cigna (health services organization), https://www.multivu.com/players/English/8294451-cigna-us-loneliness-survey /docs/IndexReport_1524069371598-173525450.pdf.

6. Sarah Berger, "Gen Z Is the Loneliest Generation, Survey Reveals, but Working Can Help," CNBC, May 2, 2018, https://www.cnbc.com/2018/05/02/cigna-study-loneliness-is-an-epide mic-gen-z-is-the-worst-off.html.

7. Jane O'Donnell, "Teens Aren't Socializing in the Real World: And That Is Making Them Super Lonely," *USA Today*, Mar. 20, 2019, https://www.usatoday.com/story/news/health/201 9/03/20/teen-loneliness-social-media-cell-phones-suicide-isolation-gaming-cigna/3208845002, citing a study by Jean Twenge, *iGen* (New York: Atria Books, 2018), https://www.cnbc.com /2018/05/02/cigna-study-loneliness-is-an-epidemic-gen-z-is-the-worst-off.html (May 2, 2018).

8. Guy Winch, "The Unexpected Loneliness of Motherhood," *Psychology Today*, Mar. 28, 2017, https://www.psychologytoday.com/us/blog/the-squeaky-wheel/201703/the-unexpected -loneliness-new-mothers; and Wednesday Martin, "The Captivity of Motherhood: Why Moth ers Are Still Lonely," *Atlantic*, July 15, 2015, https://www.theatlantic.com/entertainment/archive /2015/07/the-captivity-of-motherhood/398525/.

9. Sigal Barsade and Hakan Ozcelik, "The Painful Cycle of Employee Loneliness, and How It Hurts Companies," *Harvard Business Review Blog*, Apr. 24, 2018, https://hbr.org/2018/04/the -painful-cycle-of-employee-loneliness-and-how-it-hurts-companies; and Kathryn Vasel, "Why Workplace Loneliness Is Bad for Business," *CNN* Business, Dec. 5, 2018, https://www.cnn.com /2018/12/05/success/workplace-loneliness/index.html.

10. Loneliness is, according to a *Time* magazine interview, "the discrepancy between actual and desired relationships." Jamie Ducharme, "One in Three Seniors Is Lonely," *Time*, Mar. 4, 2019, https://time.com/5541166/loneliness-old-age/.

11. Hafner, "Epidemic of Loneliness."

12. For a more detailed explanation of this idea, see Scott Cormode, *Making Spiritual Sense* (Nashville: Abingdon, 2006).

13. Andre Henry states, "The first task of a prophet is to make the invisible visible." Henry, "Mak ing the Invisible Visible: Prophetic Drama as a Tactic for Social Change," *Fuller* magazine, Winter 2020, fullerstudio.fuller.edu/making-the-invisible-visible-prophetic-drama-and-social-change.

14. Beth Redman and Matt Redman, "Blessed Be Your Name" (Capitol Christian Music Group, 2002), https://www.lyrics.com/lyric/5758033/Matt+Redman.

15. Max De Pree, *Leadership Is an Art* (New York: Dell, 1989), 11.

16. Karl Weick had in mind the ways organizations think when he wrote that. Weick, "En actment Processes in Organizations" (1977), reprinted in *Making Sense of the Organization* (Malden, MA: Blackwell Publishers, 2001), 189. He goes on to say, "Organizations talk to themselves . . . in order to clarify their surroundings and learn more about them" (189). But, as Swidler will show us, the concept applies as well to individuals.

17. On the importance of making things "discussable," see Scott Cormode, "Mixed Messages Cause Chaos," 2019, https://www.fuller.edu/next-faithful-step/resources/mixed-messages-cause

-chaos/; and Cormode, "Make Mixed Messages Discussable," 2019, https://www.fuller.edu/next-faithful-step/resources/make-mixed-messages-discussable/.

18. This is why Chris Argyris implores leaders to separate directly observable data from the interpretations that we attach to them. He tells leaders to treat their interpretations as hypotheses to be tested rather than as observations to be believed. Chris Argyris, "Good Communication That Blocks Learning," *Harvard Business Review*, July–August 1994, 77–85, https://hbr.org/1994/07/good-communication-that-blocks-learning; and Argyris, "Teaching Smart People How to Learn," *Harvard Business Review*, May–June 1991, 99–109, https://hbr.org/1991/05/teaching-smart-people-how-to-learn?autocomplete=true.

19. My discussion of almsgiving in early Christianity is shaped by two authors: David Downs and Helen Rhee. See Downs, *Alms: Charity, Reward, and Atonement in Early Christianity* (Waco: Baylor University Press, 2016); Rhee, *Loving the Poor, Saving the Rich: Wealth, Poverty, and Early Christian Formation* (Grand Rapids: Baker Academic, 2012); and Rhee, ed., *Wealth and Poverty in Early Christianity* (Minneapolis: Fortress, 2017).

20. My understanding of enactment is strongly shaped by Karl Weick. See the section on "Enactment" in Weick, *Making Sense*, 176–236.

21. I am very much taken with the structure that Andrew Root calls "kenotic stories" or stories that "take the xyz shape." What he means is this: stories that follow a pattern of "although [x] not [y] but [z]." The paradigmatic story is "although [Jesus existed as God] he did not [regard equality with God a thing to be grasped] but [emptied himself]." I would argue that the practices we describe here can each be described as a kenotic story. For example, hospitality says, "Although [I am an insider] I do not [claim the privileges of being an insider just for myself] but [share those privileges with outsiders]." Or vocation says, "Although [I have gifts] I do not [use those gifts to serve myself] but [use those gifts to serve others]." This becomes what Root calls "the narrative shape of ministry." Andrew Root, *Faith Formation in a Secular Age* (Grand Rapids: Baker Academic, 2017), 166–71, 208–10, here 166. While the paradigm is his, the bracketed examples are my own.

22. This section on practices draws on a portion of my earlier book *Making Spiritual Sense*, 96–107.

23. MacIntyre's writing is itself rather opaque. So much of the material that I will quote to explain his ideas comes from his students and others who have used his work to good effect. You will understand why it is necessary to rely so heavily on his interpreters when I give you his definition of a social practice: "any coherent and complex form of socially established cooperative human activity through which goods internal to that form of activity are realized in the course of trying to achieve those standards of excellence which are appropriate to, and partially definitive of, that form of activity, with the result that human powers to achieve excellence, and human conceptions of the ends and goods involved, are systematically extended." Alasdair MacIntyre, *After Virtue*, 2nd ed. (Notre Dame, IN: University of Notre Dame Press, 1984), 187.

24. The concept of "practice" has slightly different meanings in the various scholarly traditions. Religious educators, for instance, distinguish between the terms "theory" and "practice," especially emphasizing the fallacy of assuming that theory always precedes practice. Sociologists also have a different take on the word "practice." They see "'practice' as [any] unconscious, embodied, or habitual action, contrasted with articulated, conscious ideas." The quote is from Ann Swidler, *Talk of Love: How Culture Matters* (Chicago: University of Chicago Press, 2001), 191, but she references Stephen Turner and others as well. Other important sociological discussions of "practice" come from Michel Foucault—who emphasizes the ways practices replicate and reinforce power structures—and Pierre Bourdieu, who insists that "practice has a logic which is not that of the logician." See, e.g., Michel Foucault, *The History of Sexuality*, vol. 1, *An Introduction* (New York: Pantheon, 1978); Pierre Bourdieu, *The Logic of Practice* (Stanford, CA: Stanford University Press, 1990), quoted in Swidler, *Talk of Love*, 192. See also Robert

Wuthnow et al., *Cultural Analysis: The Work of Peter L. Berger, Mary Douglas, Michel Foucault, and Jürgen Habermas* (Boston: Routledge & Kegan Paul, 1984); Stephen Turner, *The Social Theory of Practices: Tradition, Tacit Knowledge, and Presuppositions* (Chicago: University of Chicago Press, 1994); on "logics," see Roger Friedland and Robert Alford, "Bringing Society Back In: Symbols, Practices, and Institutional Centralizations," in *The New Institutionalism*, ed. W. Powell and P. DiMaggio (Chicago: University of Chicago Press, 1991), 223–62; on an application of Friedland and Alford's notion of "institutional logics" to the world of faith, see Harry S. Stout and Scott Cormode, "Institutions and the Story of American History: A Sketch of a Synthesis," in *Sacred Companies*, ed. N. J. Demerath et al. (New York: Oxford University Press, 1998), 62–78.

25. In the last twenty years there has been a particularly interesting scholarly conversation about practices. Starting with MacIntyre and Dykstra, it continued with a number of interesting books. Several have particularly shaped my thinking (in addition to those quoted in this chapter): Dorothy Bass, ed., *Practicing Our Faith* (San Francisco: Jossey-Bass, 1997); Miroslav Volf and Dorothy Bass, eds., *Practicing Theology: Beliefs and Practices in Christian Life* (Grand Rapids: Eerdmans, 2002); Christine Pohl, *Making Room: Recovering Hospitality as a Christian Tradition* (Grand Rapids: Eerdmans, 1999); Pohl, *Living in Community: Cultivating Practices That Sustain Us* (Grand Rapids: Eerdmans, 2012); L. Gregory Jones, *Embodying Forgiveness* (Grand Rapids: Eerdmans, 1995); Benjamin Conner, *Practicing Witness: A Missional Vision of Christian Practices* (Grand Rapids: Eerdmans, 2011); Frank Rogers, *Practicing Compassion* (Nashville: Upper Room Books, 2015); and Bonnie Miller-McLemore, *In the Midst of Chaos: Caring for Children as a Spiritual Practice* (San Francisco: Jossey-Bass, 2011).

26. Or, as Craig Dykstra puts it, "Practice is not the activity of a single person. . . . It is participation in the larger practice of a community and a tradition." Dykstra, "Reconceiving Practice," in *Shifting Boundaries: Contextual Approaches to Theological Education*, ed. Barbara Wheeler and Edward Farley (Louisville: Westminster/John Knox, 1991), 35–66, here 41.

27. The most famous form of this radically individualized spirituality has come to be called "Sheilaism." It is so named because Robert Bellah and his coauthors write about a woman who describes her faith by referring to herself. "My faith has carried me along," she said. "It's Sheilaism. Just my own little voice." Then, when asked to define this faith, she said, "It's just try to love yourself and be gentle with yourself. You know, I guess, take care of each other." Bellah et al., *Habits of the Heart* (Berkeley: University of California Press, 1985), 221. See also Wade Clark Roof, *A Generation of Seekers: The Spiritual Journeys of the Baby Boom Generation* (New York: HarperSanFrancisco, 1993), emphasizing the contemporary tendency for some to say that they are "spiritual but not religious."

28. Dykstra, "Reconceiving Practice," 47 (emphasis added).

29. It is important, of course, to recognize that practices can become trapped by tradition. The community of faith must reinvent and reinvigorate a practice with each new generation. This debate mirrors the biblical balance that avoids the poles of legalism and antinomianism. John Calvin, according to the historian William Bouwsma, describes this as walking between the labyrinth and the abyss. The labyrinth represents the overdependence on rules, law, and tradition. He does not use the term the way some contemporary Christians talk of "walking the labyrinth." Instead, he refers to a place where the walls close in and the way out is hidden behind layers of confusing passages. The abyss, on the other hand, represents the lack of boundaries and guidance. It refers to the feeling of never-ending free fall that comes when one cannot get oriented and is left to conjure one's own construction of God and the world. I argue that people who participate in Christian practices are constantly walking between the labyrinth of stale traditionalism and the abyss of traditionlessness. Bouwsma, *John Calvin: A Sixteenth-Century Portrait* (New York: Oxford University Press, 1988), 45–48.

30. Robert Wuthnow has proposed a framework for spirituality based on practice in *After Heaven: Spirituality in America since the 1950s* (Berkeley: University of California Press, 1998).

He observes that "a traditional spirituality of inhabiting sacred places has given way to a new spirituality of seeking. . . . People have been losing faith in a metaphysic that can make them feel at home in the universe and that they increasingly negotiate among competing glimpses of the sacred, seeking partial knowledge and practical wisdom" (3). To this group, he proposes "the idea of a practice-oriented spirituality" (168).

31. Mark Labberton, "The Ongoing Story of Fuller Seminary: Roots in Orthodoxy, Branches in Innovation," *Theology, News and Notes*, Spring 2014, https://fullerstudio.fuller.edu/the-ongoing-story-of-fuller-theological-seminary-roots-in-orthodoxy-branches-in-innovation/.

32. Indeed, Rembrandt has at least three different versions of this scene, all from different perspectives but all showing the Samaritan removing the injured man from the horse and entrusting him to the innkeeper's care. On the ways that contemporary Americans interpret the good Samaritan parable (and on Rembrandt's renditions), see Robert Wuthnow, "Along the Road," in *Acts of Compassion: Caring for Others and Helping Ourselves* (Princeton: Princeton University Press, 1991), 157–87.

33. I especially have in mind here Craig Dykstra's seminal article on "reconceiving practices." In it, he says, "Our identities as persons are constituted by practices and the knowledge and relationships they mediate. . . . Communal life is constituted by practices. Communities do not just engage in practices; in a sense, they are practices." Dykstra, "Reconceiving Practice," 47.

34. For a deeply moving account of a father taking his daughter to see the play, see Joe Posnanski, "Hamilton," Dec. 31, 2016, https://sportsworld.nbcsports.com/hamilton/.

35. Alisdair MacIntyre has defined a virtue as "an acquired human quality the possession and exercise of which tends to enable us to achieve those goods which are internal to practices and the lack of which effectively prevents us from achieving any such goods." MacIntyre, *After Virtue*, 191.

36. Miroslav Volf, "Theology for a Way of Life," in *Practicing Theology*, 250, 251. Three articles from that same volume make similar points: Craig Dykstra and Dorothy Bass, "A Theological Understanding of Christian Practices"; Amy Plantinga Pauw, "Attending to the Gaps between Beliefs and Practices"; and Kathryn Tanner, "Theological Reflection and Christian Practices."

37. Brad Kallenberg, "The Master Argument of MacIntyre's *After Virtue*," in *Virtues and Practices in the Christian Tradition: Ethics after MacIntyre* (Notre Dame, IN: University of Notre Dame Press, 2003), 7–29, here 22.

38. Kallenberg, "Master Argument," 21.

39. Jeffrey Stout, *Ethics after Babel: The Languages of Morals and Their Discontents* (Boston: Beacon, 1988), 271.

40. This is why the practices cannot be separated from the tradition. The "standards of excellence . . . require soul-searching theological conversations with others." Another name for those soul-searching conversations sustained over time is the Christian tradition. Craig Dykstra and Dorothy Bass, "Times of Yearning, Practices of Faith," in Bass, *Practicing Our Faith*, 1–12, here 7.

41. Kallenberg, "Master Argument," 21.

42. Lauren Winner argues that some "mistakes" are not mistakes in that some "deformations of the practices are part of the practices themselves." *The Dangers of Christian Practice: On Wayward Gifts, Characteristic Damage, and Sin* (New Haven: Yale University Press, 2018), 16. This means that distortion is inevitable because it results from the "characteristic damage" of the fall. For example, if hospitality is treating outsiders like insiders, examples of characteristic damage would involve handing out the privileges in order to accrue benefit (a distortion), expecting thanks and perhaps even reward for showing hospitality (then it becomes an exchange or transaction), and wanting to retain special-insider status (i.e., being the first among equals).

43. I see compassion as empathy in action.

44. Thomas Jeavons and Rebekah Burch Basinger, *Growing Givers' Hearts* (San Francisco: Jossey-Bass, 2000), 20.

45. Wells quotes respected theatrical writer Keith Johnstone:
People trying to be original always arrive at the same boring old answers. . . . An artist who is inspired is being *obvious*. He's not making any decisions, he's not weighing one idea against another. Experienced improvisers know that if they have attained a state of relaxed awareness, they can trust themselves to be obvious. . . . The practices and disciplines of Christian discipleship aim to give the Christian the same state of relaxed awareness, so that they have the freedom—indeed, the skill—to "be obvious" in what might otherwise seem an anxious crisis. (Keith Johnstone, *Impro: Improvisation and the Theatre* [New York: Routledge & Kegan Paul, 1979], as quoted in Samuel Wells, *Improvisation: The Drama of Christian Ethics* [Grand Rapids: Brazos, 2004], 81)

46. Practices work as what I describe in chap. 9 as "cultivated instincts." They are ways of living that do not come naturally but that, over time, can become second nature. A significant part of cultivating instincts is learning what to notice and what can safely be ignored. See Scott Cormode, "Constructing Faithful Action: Inculcating a Method for Constructive Ministry," *Journal of Religious Leadership* 3 (Spring 2004): 221–76, https://arl-jrl.org/wp-content/uploads/2016/01/Cormode-Constructing-Faithful-Action-Inculcating-a-Method-for-Reflective-Ministry.pdf.

47. Wells, *Improvisation*, 12 (emphasis added).

48. Wells, *Improvisation*, 12. He goes on to say, "The moral life is more about . . . the long period of preparation [than] the tiny episode of implementation" (73), and "When one comes to a moment of crisis, one depends on the habits one has already formed" (76).

49. Dallas Willard, *The Divine Conspiracy* (San Francisco: HarperSanFrancisco, 1998), 35–60.

50. Tara John, "How the World's First Loneliness Minister Will Tackle the 'Sad Reality of Modern Life,'" *Time*, Apr. 25, 2018, http://time.com/5248016/tracey-crouch-uk-loneliness-minister/.

51. Newspaper and magazine articles point to the study, done in 2015, by Nicole Valtorta et al., "Loneliness and Social Isolation as Risk Factors for Coronary Heart Disease and Stroke," *Heart* 102 (Apr. 18, 2016): 1009–16, https://heart.bmj.com/content/heartjnl/102/13/1009.full.pdf.

52. Rhitu Chatterjee, "Americans Are a Lonely Lot, and Young People Bear the Heaviest Burden," NPR, May 1, 2018, https://www.npr.org/sections/health-shots/2018/05/01/606588504/americans-are-a-lonely-lot-and-young-people-bear-the-heaviest-burden.

53. Vivek Murthy, "Work and the Loneliness Epidemic," *Harvard Business Review: The Big Idea*, September 2017, https://hbr.org/cover-story/2017/09/work-and-the-loneliness-epidemic.

54. I recognize that there is a movement among some to say that Christians are being "persecuted" here in the United States. But in my judgment, society still rewards upstanding persons with benefits far more than it persecutes them. (This is a key argument in Max Weber's classic work *The Protestant Ethic and the Spirit of Capitalism* [1905], trans. and updated by S. Kalberg (New York: Oxford University Press, 2011).

55. Bryant Myers, *Walking with the Poor* (Maryknoll, NY: Orbis, 2011).

56. See some caveats in Steven Corbett and Brian Fikkert's *When Helping Hurts* (Chicago: Moody, 2014).

57. This is a key insight of Kara Powell and Chap Clark, *Sticky Faith: Everyday Ideas to Build Lasting Faith in Your Kids* (Grand Rapids: Zondervan, 2011).

58. Miroslav Volf, *Exclusion and Embrace: A Theological Exploration of Identity, Otherness, and Reconciliation* (Nashville: Abingdon, 1996), 129.

59. A celebrated theologian of the early church (Gregory of Nazianzus) described the incarnation by saying that for your sake Jesus became a stranger in a strange land. Thus the God who hosts us humans also made himself subject to our hospitality. Gregory of Nazianzus, "Oration on Holy Baptism," cited in Pohl, *Making Room*, 33.

60. Rhee, *Loving the Poor*, esp. "Wealth, Poverty, and Koinonia," 103–38.

61. Pohl, *Making Room*, 17–19; and Pohl, *Living in Community*, 159–76.

62. The Fuller Youth Institute found that this experience of "warm community" was integral to churches that are growing young (i.e., that are proficient in reaching young people). Kara Powell, Jake Mulder, and Brad Griffin, *Growing Young* (Grand Rapids: Baker Books, 2016), 163–95.

63. I have been particularly influenced on this topic by a wonderful overview essay that, although older now, provides a progression for how scholars have discussed assimilation. Russell Kazal, "Revisiting Assimilation: The Rise, Fall, and Reappraisal of a Concept in American Ethnic History," *American Historical Review* 100, no. 2 (April 1995): 437–71.

Chapter 5: Reinvented Practices as Shared Stories of Hope

1. Karl Weick, "Small Wins: Redefining the Scale of Social Problems," *American Psychologist* 39, no. 1 (January 1984): 40–49, https://homepages.se.edu/cvonbergen/files/2013/01/Small -Wins_Redefining-the-Scale-of-Social-Problems.pdf.

2. See Kara Powell and Chap Clark, *Sticky Faith: Everyday Ideas to Build Lasting Faith in Your Kids* (Grand Rapids: Zondervan, 2011); and Kara Powell, Jake Mulder, and Brad Griffin, *Growing Young* (Grand Rapids: Baker Books, 2016).

3. Powell, Mulder, and Griffin tell this story in *Growing Young*, 211–12.

4. Timothy Keller's book *Every Good Endeavor* is particularly important for our discussion because he ties together Karl Weick's notion of sensemaking, Alasdair MacIntyre's understanding of practices, and our emphasis on the story that defines a person. See esp. chap. 9, "A New Story for Work," which opens with the assertion, "People cannot make sense of anything without attaching it to a story." Keller, *Every Good Endeavor: Connecting Your Work to God's Work* (New York: Dutton, 2012), 155.

5. There has been a robust and interesting scholarly discussion of vocation in the last two decades. The best books are by Labberton, Hardy, Keller, and Volf (see notes below). Other important insights come from Steven Garber, *The Fabric of Faithfulness* (Downers Grove, IL: IVP Books, 2007); Garber, *Visions of Vocation* (Downers Grove, IL: IVP Books, 2014); Amy Sherman, *Kingdom Calling* (Downers Grove, IL: IVP Books, 2011); Douglas Schuurman, *Vocation* (Grand Rapids: Eerdmans, 2004); and Kathleen Cahalan and Douglas Schuurman, eds., *Calling in Today's World: Voices from Eight Faith Perspectives* (Grand Rapids: Eerdmans, 2016).

6. Lee Hardy, *The Fabric of This World: Inquiries into Calling, Career Choice, and the Design of Human Work* (Grand Rapids: Eerdmans, 1990), 46.

7. Mark Labberton's book *Called* (Downers Grove, IL: IVP Books, 2014) is particularly articulate in explaining how the first calling placed on any Christian is the call to discipleship.

8. Quoted in Hardy, *Fabric of This World*, 51. Miroslav Volf argues that Luther inappropriately intertwines a calling with a job—creating what Jürgen Moltmann calls "the consecration of the *vocational-occupational structure*." Volf, *Work in the Spirit* (New York: Oxford University Press, 1991), 107–8; quoting Moltmann, *On Human Dignity* (Philadelphia: Fortress, 1984), 47. William Placher points out that Luther's notion of station is rooted in a static view of society that relates women and peasants to marginal status and baptizes a wealthy man's standing. We thus need to reference his work but shift the usage of the word "station" so that it takes on a more contemporary meaning, allowing for social mobility. Thus we draw inspiration from Luther without adopting all his assumptions. See Placher, *Callings* (Grand Rapids: Eerdmans, 2005), 206.

9. *Tin Toy* (1988) is usually available on YouTube. See, e.g., https://www.youtube.com /watch?v=ffIZSAZRzDA.

10. Kate Harris, "Motherhood as Vocation," https://washingtoninst.org/motherhood-as -vocation/; cf. Harris, "Navigating the Challenges of Career, Motherhood, and Identity," https:// vimeo.com/121758875.

11. The idea that mission is ultimately about the people we serve is at the heart of what has come to be called the Missional Church Movement. The movement traces its roots to the

writing of Lesslie Newbigin in the 1980s and Darrell Guder in the 1990s. It then expanded with the work of Craig Van Gelder, Alan Roxburgh, Mark Lau Branson, and (of late) Dwight Zscheile. Lesslie Newbigin said at the beginning of the movement, "The task of ministry is to lead the congregation as a whole in a mission to the community as a whole, to claim its whole public life, as well as the personal lives of all its people, for God's rule." Newbigin, *The Gospel in a Pluralistic Society* (Grand Rapids: Eerdmans, 1989), 238. Other titles on the subject by these scholars include Darrell Guder, *The Continuing Conversion of the Church* (Grand Rapids: Eerdmans, 2000); Darrell Guder et al., eds., *Missional Church* (Grand Rapids: Eerdmans, 1998); Craig Van Gelder, *The Ministry of the Missional Church* (Grand Rapids: Baker Books, 2007); and Alan Roxburgh and Scott Boren, *Introducing the Missional Church* (Grand Rapids: Baker Books, 2009).

12. This resonates deeply with Atul Gawande's reflections on becoming a surgeon. No one is talented enough or gifted enough to put a knife in another person's flesh. Strengths get you started, but ultimately, serving a people entrusted to your care involves cultivating areas that do not come naturally. See Atul Gawande, "The Learning Curve," *New Yorker*, Jan. 28, 2002, https://www.newyorker.com/magazine/2002/01/28/the-learning-curve.

13. Walter Brueggemann, "The Liturgy of Abundance, the Myth of Scarcity," *Christian Century*, Mar. 24–31, 1999, https://www.religion-online.org/article/the-liturgy-of-abundance -the-myth-of-scarcity/.

14. Miroslav Volf, *Free of Charge* (Grand Rapids: Zondervan, 2005), esp. chap. 1, "God the Giver."

Chapter 6: A Process for Innovation

1. Andrew Hargadon, *How Breakthroughs Happen: The Surprising Truth about How Companies Innovate* (Boston: Harvard Business School Press, 2003), 7.

2. Linda Hill, Greg Brandeau, Emily Truelove, and Kent Lineback, "Collective Genius," *Harvard Business Review*, June 2014, 94–102, https://hbr.org/2014/06/collective-genius. They also observe that "direction-setting leadership can work well when the solution to a problem is known and straightforward."

3. Julian Birkinshaw, Cyril Bouquet, and J.-L. Barsoux, "The 5 Myths of Innovation," *MIT Sloan Management Review* 52, no. 2 (Winter 2011): 43–50, https://sloanreview.mit.edu/article /the-5-myths-of-innovation/.

4. Albert Einstein, quoted in Walter Isaacson, *Innovators: How a Group of Hackers, Geniuses, and Geeks Created the Digital Revolution* (New York: Simon & Schuster, 2014), 68.

5. Isaacson, *Innovators*, 84.

6. Isaacson uses this agricultural imagery: "What may seem like creative leaps—the Eureka moment—are actually the result of an evolutionary process that occurs when ideas . . . ripen." *Innovators*, 91.

7. For others who use agricultural metaphors to describe a systems approach to innovation, see Vijay Govindarajan and Chris Trimble, "Strategic Innovation and the Science of Learning," *Sloan Management Review* 45, no. 2 (Winter 2004): 67–75, https://sloanreview.mit.edu/article /strategic-innovation-and-the-science-of-learning/; and Eric Schmidt and Jonathan Rosenberg, *How Google Works* (New York: Grand Central Publishing, 2014), esp. 207, 240.

8. See, e.g., Linda A. Hill, Greg Brandeau, Emily Truelove, and Kent Lineback, *Collective Genius: The Art and Practice of Leading Innovation* (Boston: Harvard Business Review Press, 2014), 138.

9. Quoted in Hargadon, *How Breakthroughs Happen*, 3.

10. Hill et al., *Collective Genius*, 18.

11. Respected scholar Kathleen Eisenhardt argues that "innovation is inherently serendipitous and almost impossible to predict." Thus the seed that you think will grow into the towering

redwood is likely not the one that shoots up. So it is more advantageous to have many saplings than it is to have just one. Eisenhardt, foreword to Hargadon, *How Breakthroughs Happen*, vii.

12. This work of nurturing ideas is so crucial to innovation that Vijay Govindarajan and Chris Trimble have created a cottage industry of articles and books describing this nurturing of immature ideas as "the other side of innovation." See Govindarajan and Trimble, *The Other Side of Innovation* (Boston: Harvard Business Review Press, 2010); Govindarajan and Trimble, *10 Rules for Strategic Innovators* (Boston: Harvard Business School Press, 2005); and Govindarajan and Trimble, *Beyond the Idea* (New York: St. Martin's Press, 2013).

13. Schmidt and Rosenberg, *How Google Works*, 209–10; they are quoting James C. Collins and Jerry I. Porras, *Built to Last* (New York: HarperBusiness, 1994).

14. Edward Farley, "Interpreting Situations: An Inquiry into the Nature of Practical Theology," in *Formation and Reflection: The Promise of Practical Theology*, ed. Lewis S. Mudge and James N. Poling (Philadelphia: Fortress, 1987), 1–26.

15. Luke Timothy Johnson, *Scripture and Discernment: Decision Making in the Church* (Nashville: Abingdon, 1996), esp. the opening chapter on "Definitions."

16. Ruth Haley Barton, *Pursuing God's Will Together: A Discernment Practice for Leadership Groups* (Downers Grove, IL: IVP Books, 2012), 10.

17. Danny Morris and Charles Olsen, *Discerning God's Will Together* (Lanham, MD: Rowman & Littlefield, 2012); Elizabeth Liebert, *The Soul of Discernment* (Louisville: Westminster John Knox, 2015); Elizabeth Liebart, *The Way of Discernment* (Louisville: Westminster John Knox, 2008); and Mark Yaconelli, *Contemplative Youth Ministry* (Grand Rapids: Zondervan, 2006), esp. 243.

18. Johnson, *Scripture and Discernment*, 110.

19. Ellen T. Charry, *By the Renewing of Your Minds: The Pastoral Function of Christian Doctrine* (New York: Oxford University Press, 1997), 4–5, 9, and 133.

20. See, e.g., the myriad perspectives for approaching the topic that are captured in Bonnie Miller-McLemore, ed., *The Wiley-Blackwell Companion to Practical Theology* (Malden, MA: Wiley-Blackwell, 2014); and Kathleen Cahalan and Gordon Mikoski, eds., *Opening the Field of Practical Theology* (Lanham, MD: Rowman & Littlefield, 2014).

21. Scott Cormode, "Constructing Faithful Action: Inculcating a Method for Reflective Ministry," *Journal of Religious Leadership* 3, no. 1 (Spring 2004): 221–76.

22. Branson and Martínez prefer to call it a spiral to emphasize the ways that the process never stops. I will gladly grant their point. See Mark Lau Branson and Juan Martínez, *Churches, Cultures and Leadership: A Practical Theology of Congregations and Ethnicities* (Downers Grove, IL: IVP Academic, 2011), esp. chap. 1.

23. Thomas Groome's process has five nodes. See Thomas H. Groome, "Theology on Our Feet: A Revisionist Pedagogy for Healing the Gap between Academia and Ecclesia," in *Formation and Reflection: The Promise of Practical Theology*, ed. Lewis S. Mudge and James N. Poling (Philadelphia: Fortress, 1987), 55–78; Groome, *Sharing Faith* (San Francisco: HarperSanFrancisco, 1991).

24. Richard Osmer, *Practical Theology: An Introduction* (Grand Rapids: Eerdmans, 2008).

25. I see the seminal summaries of practical theology to be Don Browning, *A Fundamental Practical Theology* (Minneapolis: Fortress, 1995); Groome, *Sharing Faith*; Branson and Martínez, *Churches, Cultures and Leadership*; Osmer, *Practical Theology*; and Andrew Root, *Christopraxis: A Practical Theology of the Cross* (Minneapolis: Fortess, 2014). For an African American perspective, see Dale Andrews and Robert London Smith, eds. *Black Practical Theology* (Waco: Baylor University Press, 2015). For an Asian American perspective, see Courtney T. Goto, "Asian American Practical Theologies," in Cahalan and Mikoski, *Opening the Field*, 31–44. For a Hispanic perspective, see Hosffman Ospino, "US Latino/a Practical Theology," in Cahalan and Mikoski, *Opening the Field*, 233–50.

26. Practical theologians who write from the perspective of marginalized communities helpfully emphasize that this listening needs to take into account the specific context. For example, African American theologians Dale Andrews and Robert London Smith Jr. write, "We locate the starting point of doing practical theology in the experiences, practices, and worldviews of persons and communities of faith, especially when change, conflict, crises, neglect, and ignorance arises." "Prophetic Praxis for Black Practical Theology," in *Black Practical Theology*, ed. Dale P. Andrews and Robert London Smith Jr. (Waco: Baylor University Press, 2015), 11.

27. This quote and the other summarizing questions come from Osmer, *Practical Theology*, 4.

28. IDEO has written a summary of their process and placed it on the internet: *The Field Guide to Human-Centered Design* (San Francisco: IDEO.org, 2015), http://www.designkit.org/resources/1.

29. The Google version of the process is summarized in Jake Knapp, *Sprint: How to Solve Big Problems and Test New Ideas in Just Five Days* (New York: Simon & Schuster, 2016).

30. Thank you to Macy Davis of the Fuller Youth Institute for creating the graphic.

31. About 65 of 150 (43 percent) of the psalms are laments.

32. The contemporary recovery of lament traces its roots back to an article by Walter Brueggemann, "The Costly Loss of Lament," *Journal for the Study of the Old Testament* 36 (1986): 57–71. The best recent summary comes from John Witvliet, "What about Liturgical Lament?," Jan. 17, 2016, http://www.academia.edu/20220148/Reflections_on_Lament_in_Christian_Worship.

33. Walter Brueggemann, *Psalmist's Cry: Scripts for Embracing Lament* (n.p.: House Studio, 2010).

34. IDEO runs a website for crowd-sourcing answers to vexing innovation questions, with each question phrased as a "How might we . . . ?" One question that IDEO asked, "How might we fight food waste?" became a case study for large-scale crowd-sourced innovation. See https://www.openideo.com/content/fighting-food-waste-together.

35. Knapp, *Sprint*, 73–80; see also IDEO, *Field Guide*, 85; see also Google's Design Sprint Kit, available for free at https://designsprintkit.withgoogle.com/.

36. Johnson, *Scripture and Discernment*, 109–19.

37. When I teach the rules to my students, I summarize what I call "Scott's Four Rules for Writing" this way: Every sentence has a main idea, but only one. Every paragraph has a main idea, but only one. Every paper has a main idea, but only one. And every paragraph in the paper must relate directly to the paper's main idea.

38. In reading my advisers' award-winning work, I noticed that they broke some of the grammar rules that I had been taught. For example, to ensure that each sentence had only one simple and direct point, they often started sentences with words like "And . . . ," "But . . . ," and "So . . ." I was always taught to combine the sentences that started with such words. But I noticed that their writing had a momentum that others' essays lacked. So I have adopted their habit—to many a copyeditor's chagrin.

39. Malcolm Gladwell has shown that "the capacity to practice" is a hallmark of people who become excellent, and Angela Duckworth uses the same phrase to describe people who develop grit. Gladwell, *Outliers* (New York: Little, Brown, 2008); and Duckworth, *Grit* (New York: Scribner, 2016).

40. We are all aware of (and look down our noses at) churches that accept attendance as a proxy for spiritual growth.

41. James Collins, *Good to Great and the Social Sectors* (New York: HarperCollins, 2005), 14.

42. John Goldingay, "John Goldingay on Lament," Apr. 25, 2016, https://www.youtube.com/watch?v=dXyuLxqAw88.

43. "The work of discernment has to do with building the *community identity* as such rather than with the praise or condemnation of an *individual's behavior*." Johnson, *Scripture and Discernment*, 119 (emphasis in original).

44. "Brené Brown on Empathy," Dec. 10, 2013, https://www.youtube.com/watch?v=1Evw gu369Jw; on its connection to innovation. See also Tom Kelley and David Kelley, *Creative Confidence* (New York: Crown Business, 2013), 21, 22, 85–89.

45. Kelley and Kelley, *Creative Confidence*, 123.

46. Knapp, *Sprint*, 111–13; for an internet tutorial, see https://designsprintkit.withgoogle .com/methods/sketch/crazy-8s/.

47. Patrick Miller, *They Cried to the Lord: The Form and Theology of Biblical Prayer* (Minneapolis: Fortress, 1994), 57, 337–57; cf. Bruce Waltke, James Houston, and Ericka Moore, *The Psalms as Christian Lament: A Historical Commentary* (Grand Rapids: Eerdmans, 2014); and Glenn Pemberton, *Hurting with God: Learning to Lament with the Psalms* (Abilene, TX: Abilene Christian University Press, 2012).

48. John Goldingay has written extensively on the psalms of lament, but his most accessible insights are posted in videos and podcasts generated from Fuller Studio at Fuller Seminary; e.g., "John Goldingay Teaches Psalms of Protest," 2016, https://fullerstudio.fuller.edu/psalms -protest/; and "John Goldingay on Lament," 2014, https://youtube.com/watch?v=dXyuLxq Aw88.

49. "John Goldingay on Lament."

50. Soong-Chan Rah, *Prophetic Lament: A Call for Justice in Troubled Times* (Downers Grove, IL: IVP Books, 2015); and Rah, "Let the People Lament," Feb. 28, 2016, https://www.you tube.com/watch?v=U6-z-DbVqF4.

51. Leslie C. Allen, *A Liturgy of Grief: A Personal Commentary on Lamentations* (Grand Rapids: Baker Academic, 2011).

52. See illustrations in Knapp, *Sprint*, 111–13, or online at https://designsprintkit.withgoogle .com/methods/sketch/crazy-8s/.

53. I recognize that worship does not always come from a place of joy—or even from feelings alone. But since in this chapter I am dealing with feelings of longing and loss, I am emphasizing feelings in worship.

54. At the design firm IDEO, they have something called Boyle's Law, named for Dennis Boyle, who proclaims, "Never go to a meeting without a prototype." Tom Kelley with Jonathan Littman, *The Art of Innovation: Lessons in Creativity from IDEO, America's Leading Design Firm* (New York: Currency/Doubleday, 2001), 106.

55. These are quotations from the report Erica wrote to summarize her listening.

56. This quotation and further information in the chapter come from two interviews with Erica—one on Aug. 13, 2018, and the other on Nov. 14, 2018.

57. "Brené Brown on Empathy."

58. Holding environments will be discussed in chap. 8.

Chapter 7: Organizing for Innovation

1. Cf. Walter Isaacson, *Innovators: How a Group of Hackers, Geniuses, and Geeks Created the Digital Revolution* (New York: Simon & Schuster, 2014), 35.

2. One CEO used a different metaphor to make the same point. "My job," he said, "is to set the stage, not to perform on it." Linda A. Hill, Greg Brandeau, Emily Truelove, and Kent Lineback, *Collective Genius: The Art and Practice of Leading Innovation* (Boston: Harvard Business Review Press, 2014), 3.

3. It's not clear that Drucker actually said this. But the head of Ford Motor Company (Mark Fields), in a famous statement, attributed the quote to Drucker; now the collective lore associates the statement with him. On the accepted place of the quotation, see Bernard Ross, "Culture Eats Strategy for Breakfast," 2020, https://www.managementcentre.co.uk/culture -eats-strategy-for-breakfast/.

4. Linda Hill, Greg Brandeau, Emily Truelove, and Kent Lineback, "Collective Genius," *Harvard Business Review*, June 2014, 4–10, http://www.capss.org/uploaded/2014_Redesign

/Leadership_Development/Institutes/images_2015-2016/Deeper_Dive_2015/session_1_hand outs/Collective_Genius.pdf.

5. "Innovation usually emerges when a diverse people collaborate to generate a wide-ranging portfolio of ideas, when they then refine and even evolve into new ideas through give-and-take and often-heated debates." Hill et al., "Collective Genius," 5.

6. Hill et al., "Collective Genius," 6.

7. For more on the ways that purpose creates identity, see James Collins and Jerry Porras, "Building Your Company's Vision," *Harvard Business Review*, September–October 1996, http:// www.fusbp.com/pdf/Building%20Companys%20Vision.pdf; and Scott Cormode, *Making Spiritual Sense* (Nashville: Abingdon, 2006), 81–83.

8. Robert Wuthnow, *The Crisis in the Churches* (New York: Oxford University Press, 1997).

9. We must recognize that our ultimate purpose focuses on the worship of God and the forming of God's people. We work that out, however, by serving the people God entrusts to our care. So, for the purposes of this chapter, we will focus on those people, knowing that we can never lose sight of the fact that our planting and watering is merely our way of partnering in the work God has always been doing.

10. We are not looking at the values that the congregations espouse; we are looking at the values in use. On Chris Argyris's distinction between "espoused theory" and "theory-in-use," see Scott Cormode, "Espoused Theory," 1999, https://www.fuller.edu/next-faithful-step /resources/espoused-theory/.

11. On the connection between values and identity, see Cormode, *Making Spiritual Sense*, 77–81.

12. I should say something about this term "amorphous problem." The reason "learning" is such an important value is that the organization cannot really understand the problem while trying to solve it. The organization can understand the goal (i.e., make spiritual sense of the human condition experienced by the people entrusted to its care). Each time it attempts an innovation, it learns a bit more about the longings and losses of its people. Thus the organization never fully understands its final goal—just as Google never fully understands the experience of its user.

13. Hill et al., "Collective Genius," 5.

14. Tom Kelley and David Kelley, *Creative Confidence* (New York: Crown Business, 2014).

15. Julian Birkinshaw, Cyril Bouquet, and J.-L. Barsoux, "The 5 Myths of Innovation," *MIT Sloan Management Review* 52, no. 2 (Winter 2011): 43–50, https://sloanreview.mit.edu /article/the-5-myths-of-innovation/. As we will see in chap. 9, it is important when bringing in outsiders not to socialize the outsiders too quickly. There are plenty of examples of the mixed messages that religious organizations deliver when they hire someone because they have a different point of view and then judge them based on the degree to which they conform to the very standards they were meant to disturb. This applies, say, to Christian nonprofits that hire a nonwhite person and then expect them to see things from a white perspective. It also applies to Christian colleges that bring in someone to represent an interdisciplinary perspective and then judge them on the degree to which they think like everyone else. Likewise, congregations will sometimes want to "invite people from the neighborhood," yet with the unspoken understanding that they expect the people who visit to look, act, and think like the congregation's old-timers.

16. Kathleen Eisenhardt, foreword to *How Breakthroughs Happen*, by Andrew Hargadon (Boston: Harvard Business School Press, 2003), viii.

17. Starting in the 1980s, much of the scholarship on theological education has bemoaned the "fragmentation" of the theological curriculum. Yet, by all accounts, the disciplines (and their attendant courses) still operate independently. Indeed, a department's worth at many schools is measured by the degree to which it can act as a silo, with areas that cannot or do not operate as silos complaining that they lack status. This is important because one of the reasons why the movement toward integration in theological education stalled is that "interdisciplinary" work was seen as a threat to the status of departments that saw themselves as

traditionally underappreciated. This meant that professors tended to see integration as a veiled means for departments that traditionally had high status to swallow those that traditionally had low status. So what started out as a way to honor diversity (by integrating diverse voices from across the curriculum) came to be seen as a threat to diversity (because people assumed that any collaboration between bodies with unequal status will always benefit those with power). Edward Farley began the discussion of fragmentation in 1983 with the publication of *Theologia: The Fragmentation and Unity of Theological Education* (Philadelphia: Fortress). See also Edward Farley, "Why Seminaries Don't Change: A Reflection on Faculty Specialization," *Christian Century*, February 5–12, 1997, 133–43; and David Kelsey and Barbara Wheeler, "New Ground: The Foundations and Future of the Theological Education Debate," in *Theology and the Interhuman: Essays in Honor of Edward Farley*, ed. Robert R. Williams (Valley Forge, PA: Trinity Press International, 1995), esp. 186–87. The history of the debate that Farley initiated is summarized in Conrad Cherry, *Hurrying toward Zion: Universities, Divinity Schools, and American Protestantism* (Bloomington: Indiana University Press, 1995), esp. chap. 4; and esp. in David H. Kelsey, *Between Athens and Berlin: The Theological Education Debate* (Grand Rapids: Eerdmans, 1993).

18. The best illustrations of how silos ultimately marginalize diverse voices come from the women who work together at the Center for Gender and Organization (CGO), coordinated by Simmons College in Boston. What they say about the experience of women also explains much about the experiences of people of color and of others who labor within a dominant ethos. In multiple articles and books, they have shown that the idea of "valuing the feminine" by creating a separate (i.e., silo for) space for women only isolates them. It gives the appearance of honoring women's concerns while allowing the rest of the organization to engage in business as usual. They show how the silo space strategy was a phase that organizations passed through (esp. in the 1970s) but one that did not serve the cause of gender equity. Instead, these scholars argue that the best way to rectify the inequities for women in the workplace is to change the culture of corporations. That can only happen, they say, through engagement rather than isolation. The irony is that the people who most opposed the integration process were the women who controlled the "women's departments." They confused their individual loss of power with a loss of power for the group they were supposed to represent. For a compilation of CGO's work, see http://www.simmons.edu/about-simmons/centers-organizations-and-institutes/cgo. For a summary of the massive literature on gender and organization, see two overview articles by CGO participants Robin Ely of Harvard, Debra Meyerson of Stanford, and Marta Calas and Linda Smircich of the University of Massachusetts: Robin Ely and Debra Meyerson, "Theories of Gender in Organizations," in *Research in Organizational Behavior*, ed. Barry M. Staw and Robert I. Sutton (Greenwich, CT: JAI Press, 2000), 22:103–51; and Marta Calas and Linda Smircich, "From 'The Woman's Point of View': Feminist Approaches to Organization Studies," in *Handbook of Organization Studies*, ed. Stewart Clegg, Cynthia Hardy, and Walter R. Nord (Thousand Oaks, CA: Sage Publications, 1996), 218–57; on ethnicity, cf. Stella Nkomo and Taylor Cox, "Diverse Identities in Organizations," in Clegg et al., *Handbook*, 338–56; for resources on how to implement cultural change that supports gender equality in the workplace without resorting to marginalizing silos, see Debra Meyerson, *Tempered Radicals: How Everyday Leaders Inspire Change at Work* (Boston: Harvard Business School Press, 2003); Joyce Fletcher, *Disappearing Acts: Gender, Power, and Relational Practice at Work* (Cambridge, MA: MIT Press, 2001); and three books by Deborah Kolb of the Harvard Program on Negotiations: Kolb, *Everyday Negotiations: Navigating the Hidden Agendas of Bargaining* (San Francisco: Jossey-Bass, 2003); Kolb, *Her Place at the Table: A Woman's Guide to Managing Five Key Challenges to Leadership Success* (San Francisco: Jossey-Bass, 2010); and Kolb, *Negotiating at Work: Turning Small Wins into Big Successes* (San Francisco: Jossey-Bass, 2015).

19. Mark Granovetter, "The Strength of Weak Ties," *American Journal of Sociology* 78, no. 6 (May 1973): 1360–80.

20. Eric Schmidt and Jonathan Rosenberg, *How Google Works* (New York: Grand Central Publishing, 2014), 213–14.

21. Ironically, Google gave up this commitment over time. In 2015, they modified the language to say, "Do the right thing." Then in 2018, they removed the "Don't be evil" commitment altogether. The point I am trying to make is that planting language can strongly shape your congregational culture. Google found it inconvenient to live up to its values and thus changed the values. Kate Conger, "Google Removes 'Don't Be Evil' Clause from Its Code of Conduct," *Gizmodo*, May 18, 2018, https://gizmodo.com/google-removes-nearly-all-mentions-of-dont-be-evil-from-1826153393.

22. Schmidt and Rosenberg, *How Google Works*, 64, 65.

23. Schmidt and Rosenberg, *How Google Works*, 234–40, quotes from 238–40.

24. It is clear that the only way to produce innovation is to build on experiments. Therefore we need to revisit our "mental model" of an experiment to see how it plays out in Christian organizations. Govindarajan and Trimble list five criteria for good experiments: (1) results are available quickly, (2) results are unambiguous, (3) experiments can be isolated from outside influences, (4) experiments are inexpensive, and (5) experiments are repeatable. All this is well and good if you are making devices. But back in 1974 Cohen and March showed that some organizations live under conditions of "ambiguity"—including churches and schools. In those organizations, it is impossible to follow these five criteria because (1) there is a lag in how means lead to ends so results cannot be available quickly; (2) results are, by definition, never unambiguous; (3) forces interact so that experiments can never be isolated from outside influences; and (4) situations are so complicated that no result is repeatable. So we will not be able to follow the "scientific method" when talking about experimentation. See Vijay Govindarajan and Chris Trimble, "Strategic Innovation and the Science of Learning," *MIT Sloan Management Review* 45, no. 2, (Winter 2004): 67–75, https://sloanreview.mit.edu/article/strategic-innovation-and-the-science-of-learning/; Michael Cohen and James March, *Leadership and Ambiguity*, 2nd ed. (Boston: Harvard Business School Press, 1986); on the implications of ambiguity for religious organizations, see Scott Cormode, "Multi-Layered Leadership: The Christian Leader as Builder, Shepherd, and Gardener," *Journal of Religious Leadership* 1, no. 2 (Fall 2002): 69–104.

25. This is a complicated quotation. It appears in many studies of innovation. But the quote is likely apocryphal in the sense that Edison did not "invent" the incandescent light bulb. I continue to use the quote, however, because its core is true. Edison did improve the light bulb to the point of innovation, and Edison did go through an enormous number of failed attempts before getting the innovative result that we celebrate. For a detailed description of Edison's innovative prowess (as well as a debunking of the myths we attach to Edison), see Hargadon, *How Breakthroughs Happen*, esp. 7.

26. Birkinshaw et al., "5 Myths," 45.

27. Peter Senge, *The Fifth Discipline* (New York: Currency/Doubleday, 1990). "Over the long run, superior performance depends on superior learning," writes Senge in "The Leader's New Work: Building Learning Organizations," *MIT Sloan Management Review* 32, no 1 (Fall 1990): 7–23, https://sloanreview.mit.edu/article/the-leaders-new-work-building-learning-organizations/.

28. Govindarajan and Trimble, "Strategic Innovation."

29. The fact that we learn more from failure than from success has been an accepted part of the disciplines of organizational behavior and organizational psychology at least since Karl Weick's pioneering work in the 1960s. For a summary of his work, see Karl Weick, *Social Psychology of Organizing*, 2nd ed. (New York: McGraw-Hill, 1979); and his compendium: Weick, *Sensemaking in Organizations* (Thousand Oaks, CA: Sage Publications, 1995). See also Chris Argyris on how leaders who avoid learning from mistakes end up avoiding learning, which he explores in the seminal book he coauthored with Donald A. Schon, *Theory in Practice: Increasing Professional Effectiveness* (San Francisco: Jossey-Bass, 1992).

30. "Ambiguity" is a particularly important organizational term. Later we will discuss the technical definition. The seminal work on this is Cohen and March, *Leadership and Ambiguity*.

31. Kelley and Kelley, *Creative Confidence*, 48, 49. Diego Rodriguez publishes many of his ideas in his influential *Metacool* blog (http://metacool.com). See esp. his 2009 series on 21 Principles of Innovation.

32. Govindarajan and Trimble, "Strategic Innovation."

33. Jules Goddard, Julian Birkinshaw, and Tony Eccles, "Uncommon Sense: How to Turn Distinctive Beliefs into Action," *MIT Sloan Management Review* 53, no. 3 (Spring 2012): 33–39, https://sloanreview.mit.edu/article/uncommon-sense-how-to-turn-distinctive-beliefs-into-action/.

34. On Google's commitment to "focus on the user," see Schmidt and Rosenberg, *How Google Works*, 5, 212–16; for the science of "user experience," see Jakob Nielsen, *Designing Web Usability* (Indianapolis: New Riders, 2000) and his extremely influential website useit .com (now housed at http://www.nngroup.com/articles/ as part of his consultancy practice, The Nielsen-Norman Group).

35. On sticky faith, see Kara Powell and Chap Clark, *Sticky Faith: Everyday Ideas to Build Lasting Faith in Your Kids* (Grand Rapids: Zondervan, 2011); Kara Powell and Brad Griffin, *The Sticky Faith Launch Kit* (Fuller Youth Institute, 2013); and https://fulleryouthinstitute .org/sticky-faith/what-is-sticky-faith.

36. Esp. see the work of the Center for Gender in Organizations, https://www.simmons.edu /academics/research/cgo/publications.

37. The wise Christian leader Max De Pree calls this "temporary incompetence." He argues that all leaders experience temporary incompetence when they try something new or innovative. De Pree, *Leadership Jazz* (New York: Currency/Doubleday, 1992), 43–44.

38. They also quote Steve Jobs, who reportedly said, "Real artists ship." Google says, "New ideas are never perfect right out of the chute, and you don't have time to wait until they get there. Create a product, ship it, see how it does, design and implement improvements, and push it back out." Schmidt and Rosenberg, *How Google Works*, 234.

39. See Atul Gawande, "The Education of a Knife," in *Complications* (New York: Penguin Books, 2002).

40. Ed Catmull, *Creativity, Inc.* (New York: Random House, 2014), 70–76.

41. Terry Gross, Interview with Director Pete Docter, *Fresh Air*, June 10, 2015, https://www.npr.org/2015/06/10/413273007/its-all-in-your-head-director-pete-docter-gets-emotional -in-inside-out.

42. Catmull, *Creativity, Inc.*, 45–65, and 66.

43. For more on the power of "candor" in organizational culture, see the wonderful book by Kim Scott, *Radical Candor* (New York: St. Martin's Press, 2017).

44. Catmull, *Creativity, Inc.*, 86.

45. Robert Kegan and Lisa Lahey have pointed out that the reason most people and most organizations do not change is because they cannot handle these competing commitments. They say, e.g., that a man may be committed to losing weight, but he is more committed to eating well. The greater commitment prevents progress on the lesser one. When our organizational commitment to avoiding conflict outweighs our commitment to honest conversation, then we know that candor will never prevail. See Robert Kegan and Lisa Laskow Lahey, *Immunity to Change* (Boston: Harvard Business Press, 2009); and Kegan and Lahey, *How the Way We Talk Can Change the Way We Act* (San Francisco: Jossey-Bass, 2001).

46. Chris Argyris shows how mixed messages create what he tongue-in-cheek calls "Four Easy Steps to Chaos." Argyris, "Skilled Incompetence."

47. Note that Catmull was not asking for candor in all things—only in storytelling. The overriding purpose of the story was so important that the key people in the organization were relentless in "stripping a plot down to its emotional load-bearing sequences and then rebuilding it from the ground up." That can only work when the entire creative team is allowed to speak with candor. For Christian organizations, if our overriding purpose is to make spiritual sense

of the human condition experienced by the people entrusted to our care, then that is the place where we must have candor. Catmull, *Creativity, Inc.*, 56.

48. Catmull, *Creativity, Inc.*, 131.

49. Catmull, *Creativity, Inc.*, 132 (emphasis in original).

50. The management structure of successful organizations is calibrated to be what Vijay Govindarajan and Chris Trimble describe as "a Performance Engine" that pursues goals with ruthless efficiency. Their ruthless engine is Catmull's hungry beast. Govindarajan and Trimble, *Beyond the Idea* (New York: St. Martin's Press, 2013), 7.

51. Catmull, *Creativity, Inc.*, 132.

52. Catmull, *Creativity, Inc.*, 133.

53. Catmull notes that it is particularly important to protect people who are speaking with candor to senior leaders. He illustrates this by talking about what happened when Pixar merged with Disney Animation, which had a hierarchical culture that penalized people for speaking truth to authorities. Eventually, Catmull and Lasseter gathered the Disney employees and "stressed that no one at Disney needed to wait for permission to come up with solutions. What is the point of hiring smart people, we asked, if you don't empower them to fix what's broken? For too long, a culture of fear had stymied those who wanted to step outside Disney's accepted protocols." Catmull, *Creativity, Inc.*, 264.

54. It is not surprising that Pixar illustrates these points. Pixar was one of the organizations that Hill et al. studied for *Collective Genius*. Indeed, one of Hill's coauthors (Greg Brandeau) is the former chief technology officer for Pixar.

55. On Pixar and mental models, see Catmull's discussion of Pixar's movie *Inside Out*. In discussing the movie, Catmull says, "We are meaning-making creatures" who use "mental models" to make sense of the world. And "when human beings see things that challenge our mental models, we tend not just to resist them but to ignore them." He emphasizes, "Our mental models are not reality." But once a "flawed mental model . . . gets in our head, it is difficult to change." Catmull, *Creativity, Inc.*, 178–82; see also 225.

56. Catmull, *Creativity, Inc.*, 86, 87.

57. Catmull, *Creativity, Inc.*, 88, 89.

58. Catmull, *Creativity, Inc.*, 92, 93.

59. Ronald Heifetz, *Leadership without Easy Answers* (Cambridge, MA: Belknap Press of Harvard University Press, 1994); and Ronald Heifetz and Donald Laurie, "The Work of Leadership," *Harvard Business Review*, January–February 1997, 124–34, http://www.nhcue.edu.tw/~aca/fte/95-2/4.pdf. On the application of these holding environments to religious organizations, see Cormode, "Multi-Layered Leadership."

60. Hayagreeva Rao, Robert Sutton, and Allen P. Webb, "Innovation Lessons from Pixar: An Interview with Oscar-Winning Director Brad Bird," *McKinsey Quarterly*, April 2008, http://www.mckinsey.com/insights/innovation/innovation_lessons_from_pixar_an_interview_with_oscar-winning_director_brad_bird (emphasis in original).

61. Brad Bird gave an example of how important it is to handle such confrontational candor. By letting an angry person confront him and taking that person's anger not as an affront but as an expression of passion, Bird was able to turn the tide and create what we will later call a momentum-changing small win. But he could only do that because it was appropriate—indeed welcome—for someone to confront him. When Bird became director of *Ratatouille*, the project had been in development for five years but had significant problems. Right after he became director, Bird gathered the people who had invested the most time into the movie up to that point. At that point in the production, all of the rats were designed to walk on two legs because the creators were worried that the audience might be repulsed by scurrying rats. Bird thought it unwise and he wanted to reconstruct the rats, even though it would be expensive. He said,

> "We have to get them so that they walk on all fours. And Remy, the protagonist rat, has to be able to walk not only on all fours but up on two legs." Everybody said, "Ugh!"

because they had spent a year making the rats look good walking on two legs. . . . One of the guys challenged me. He said, "I want to know why you're doing this." Now, I had gone into this film reluctantly. It's not what I was looking to do after *The Incredibles*. And there was a part of me that wanted to say, "Because I'm the director, that's why. Do *you* want to take this problematic thing over?" But I stopped and thought for a second. I thought, these guys have been sent down blind alleys for a couple of years. They want to know that I'm not doing anything lightly and that if I'm going to make them do a bunch more work, it's for a reason. So I said, "This movie is about a rat who wants to enter the human world. We have to make that a visual choice for the character. If you have all of the rats walking on two legs, there's no separation between him and the other rats. If we have this separation as a visual device, we can see the character make his transformation and choose to be on two legs, and he can become more or less ratty, depending on his emotional state. That brings the audience into the character's mind." I spent six minutes saying all this, and the guy was initially scowling. But gradually the scowl went away, and he said, "OK." Once I gave that answer, everyone felt, "OK, we're on this ship and we're going toward a definite destination." (quoted in Rao, Sutton, and Webb, "Innovation Lessons from Pixar")

62. Catmull, *Creativity, Inc.*, 101.

63. This commitment to candor is so strong that it even affected the most famously strong personality in Silicon Valley, Steve Jobs. He was known for arguing so passionately for his perspective that he created what people called a "reality distortion field" that made people agree with him even when they thought he was wrong. When that did not work, he was notorious for pulling rank. At least, that is how he operated at Apple. Steve Jobs owned Pixar. He could have commanded people to make any story changes he wanted. But, according to Catmull, Jobs "didn't believe that his instincts were better than the people here, so he stayed out. That's how much candor matters at Pixar: It overrides hierarchy." Catmull, *Creativity, Inc.*, 100. On the "reality distortion field," see Walter Isaacson, *Steve Jobs* (New York: Little, Brown, 2011).

64. Like all the cases that I use in my teaching, it is fictionalized so that no one's mistakes are open to public scrutiny.

Chapter 8: Innovation and Change

1. Ronald Heifetz, *Leadership without Easy Answers* (Cambridge, MA: Belknap Press of Harvard University Press, 1994), 88–95.

2. Heifetz, *Leadership without Easy Answers*, 91.

3. Heifetz, *Leadership without Easy Answers*, 92.

4. The parent company closed the plant as much for economic reasons having to do with the price of ore as they did for environmental reasons. But they certainly blamed the EPA just the same, and the scapegoating worked. One worker is quoted as saying, "It's the EPA's fault." Heifetz, *Leadership without Easy Answers*, 94.

5. Doug Sutherland, county executive, quoted in Heifetz, *Leadership without Easy Answers*, 95, 308n20.

6. This story is based on a situation from one of my doctor-of-ministry students. I have modified it slightly. See Scott Cormode, "Multi-Layered Leadership: The Christian Leader as Builder, Shepherd, and Gardener," *Journal of Religious Leadership* 1, no. 2 (Fall 2002): 69–104.

7. Ronald A. Heifetz and Marty Linsky, *Leadership on the Line: Staying Alive through the Dangers of Leading* (Boston: Harvard Business School Press, 2002), chap. 3, "Get on the Balcony."

8. Ronald Heifetz and Donald Laurie, "The Work of Leadership," *Harvard Business Review*, January–February 1997, 124–34, http://www.nhcue.edu.tw/~aca/fte/95-2/4.pdf.

9. Heifetz and Linsky, *Leadership on the Line*, 60–69.

10. Heifetz and Laurie, "Work of Leadership," 124.

11. Heifetz and Linsky, *Leadership on the Line*, 11.

12. I recognize that this is not the only perspective, nor even the best perspective, on grief. But because it is so well known, it provides an easy window on people going through grief.

13. I also recognize that these are not really "stages" in that someone can easily bounce back and forth through each of these without necessarily following them in any order.

14. Heifetz, *Leadership without Easy Answers*, 69.

15. Heifetz gets the language of "holding environment" from psychology. D. W. Winnicott used the term to talk about the relationship between a mother and an infant. Psychologists adopted the term to describe the relationship between a therapist and a client. Heifetz, a trained psychiatrist, then brought that idea into organizational settings and summarizes it this way: "The therapist 'holds' the patient in a process of developmental learning in a way that has some similarities to the way that a mother and father hold their newborn and maturing children." Heifetz, *Leadership without Easy Answers*, 104. Winnicott's influence is discussed in Heifetz and Linsky, *Leadership on the Line*, 101–3 and 238n1.

16. Heifetz and Laurie, "Work of Leadership," 128.

17. Heifetz, *Leadership without Easy Answers*, 83.

18. Heifetz and Laurie, "Work of Leadership," 128.

19. Heifetz, *Leadership without Easy Answers*, 91.

20. Heifetz, *Leadership without Easy Answers*, 92.

21. Heifetz, *Leadership without Easy Answers*, 94.

22. We at Fuller Seminary have hosted three parallel projects on innovation: Youth Ministry Innovation, Ministry Innovations with Young Adults, and Innovation for Vocation. For each project, we host annual summits where churches send teams to work through innovation projects. Over the years, we have had over a hundred congregations in these summits.

23. You will recall that "temporary incompetence" is the phrase that Max De Pree uses to describe the stumbling awkwardness that we all feel when we engage in some activity for the first time. Max De Pree, *Leadership Jazz* (New York: Currency/Doubleday, 1992), 43.

24. The information provided here is from an interview with Erica that took place on Nov. 14, 2018.

25. This quotation is from a phone interview with Erica that took place on Aug. 13, 2018.

Chapter 9: The Next Faithful Step

1. Scott Cormode, "Educating for Agility," *Theology, News, and Notes*, Spring 2014, 34–35, https://digitalcommons.fuller.edu/tnn/174/ + download.

2. The phrase comes from James O'Donnell, a leading scholar of historic Christianity who specializes in Augustine. In the early 1990s, when O'Donnell was an early leader in the area of teaching with technology, the Lilly Endowment commissioned him to write a paper on how the coming rise of technology should influence theological education. The paper came out in 1996, before most seminaries had websites or even email. O'Donnell chose to write about the vulnerabilities of theological education and the potential for technology to address those vulnerabilities. Sadly, the vulnerabilities remain. James O'Donnell, "High-Tech Christianity," unpublished paper commissioned by the Lilly Endowment and Auburn Theological Seminary and presented in various venues. After O'Donnell's move to Georgetown, it was lodged at http://faculty.georgetown.edu/jod/texts/lilly.html (March 1996).

3. "Petra" is a pseudonym. These reflections come from a talk she gave to our national study group. When I asked for a copy of her remarks, she sent me the manuscript: "An Analysis of the Preparation for Ministry for the Presbyterian Church USA: An Appeal for Flesh and Blood." Emphasis in original.

4. This role conflict is a classic example of the "middle manager's dilemma." The essence of the dilemma is that middle managers have more responsibility than they have authority. For an intriguing discussion of how the trend toward "flat organizations" exacerbates the middle

manager's dilemma, see this article by esteemed Stanford scholar Harold J. Leavitt in Harvard Business School's *Working Knowledge* series: "The Plight of Middle Managers," Dec. 13, 2004, http://hbswk.hbs.edu/archive/4537.html.

5. At Fuller Seminary, we have created a course (called IS500: Practices of Vocation) that teaches what we call "vocational agility." It is typically the first course that a master's student takes at Fuller.

6. The following paragraphs discuss the Kelley brothers' book *Creative Confidence* (New York: Crown Business, 2014), which is summarized in a number of shorter venues, including Kelley and Kelley, "Reclaim Your Creative Confidence," *Harvard Business Review*, December 2012, 1–5; Kelley and Kelley, "Creative Confidence: The Path from Blank Page to Insight," *Rotman Management*, Winter 2014, 17–21; and David Kelley, "How to Build Your Creative Confidence," TED Talk, 2012, http://www.ted.com/talks/david_kelley_how_to_build _your_creative_confidence?language=en.

7. Hilary Austen, "The Educator's Dilemma: Engaging Students in Knowledge Creation," *Rotman Management*, Fall 2013, 23–27. This quotation and those that follow are from p. 23 of this article.

8. Some organizations live under conditions that scholars call "ambiguity." There is a technical definition for the term. Ambiguity exists when three conditions are in play: (1) Unclear goals: These are goals that are unclarified, like our goal of spiritual growth, which cannot be measured precisely. (2) Uncertain means: The means we use to reach our ends cannot guarantee we accomplish our goals. (3) Multiple constituencies: If you have unclear goals and uncertain means, then your goals and the effectiveness of your methods will have to be interpreted. And if you have multiple constituencies, then you will have multiple interpreters (and multiple interpretations). Together these three conditions add up to "ambiguity." And because scholars know that ambiguity reigns in organizations like churches and schools, we know that Christian leaders will have to face these messy unknowns on a daily basis. See Cohen and March, *Leadership and Ambiguity*; see also Cormode, "Multi-layered Leadership," 81–84.

9. Mark Maletz and Nitin Nohria, "Managing in White Space," *Harvard Business Review*, February 2001, 102–11.

10. Although I first wrote about cultivated instincts over twenty years ago, I see significant resonance with James K. A. Smith's work on cultural liturgies. See, for example, his discussion of "mindless healthy eating" in *Imagining the Kingdom* (Grand Rapids: Baker Academic, 2013), 10.

11. See Smith on "the feel for the game" in *Imagining the Kingdom*, 87.

12. See Smith on "sanctified perception" in *Imagining the Kingdom*, 101, 102, and 151–69.

13. Christian practices are ritualized stories. They work like the scales that a musician practices to improve her playing or the drills an athlete uses to hone his skills. On "ritualized stories," see Smith, *Imagining the Kingdom*, 108–19.

14. Normally, one might expect a section here on the leadership skills necessary for innovation. Indeed, the skills for agility are different from the skills for innovation. But the skills for innovation are the skills necessary to engage in innovation without having a process. The whole point of this book has been to create a process that enables people who have not necessarily cultivated the skills for innovation to engage in Christian innovation. For example, "associating" is considered a necessary skill for innovators (where associating means the ability to connect seemingly unrelated questions from different fields). The process of listening and reflecting on reinvented practices (and perhaps even reinventing those practices) creates a context for bringing together questions and perspectives from different contexts. If leaders are working the process described in this book, then they will need the much more easily cultivated skill of agility. That is what this section is about. If a reader is interested in the skills for innovation, see Jeffrey Dyer, Hal Gregersen, and Clayton Christensen, "The Innovator's DNA," *Harvard Business Review*, December 2009, 2–8, https://hbr.org/2009/12/the-innovators-dna.

15. Scott Cormode, "Constructing Faithful Action," *Journal of Religious Leadership* 3, no. 1 (Spring 2004): 221–76.

16. The quoted material from Argyris here and immediately following is from "Teaching Smart People How to Learn," May–June 1991, 99–109, https://hbr.org/1991/05/teaching-smart -people-how-to-learn?autocomplete=true.

17. Argyris, "Teaching Smart People."

18. Argyris, "Teaching Smart People."

19. Argyris, "Teaching Smart People."

20. Nygren describes one such study in David J. Nygren, Miriam D. Ukeritis, David C. McClelland, and Julia L. Hickman, "Outstanding Leadership in Religious Nonprofit Organizations: Leadership Competencies in Roman Catholic Religious Orders," *Nonprofit Management & Leadership* 4, no. 4 (Summer 1994): 375–91.

21. I have heard David J. Nygren present this material twice, both under the auspices of the Yale Program on Non-Profit Organizations: in Washington, DC, at Catholic University in 1996; then in Chicago in September 2000. The following reflections are from my notes on those two wonderful presentations.

22. I remember Nygren saying that the best leaders can seem a bit obsessive. They are constantly picking apart their past performances. He acknowledged that sometimes it goes to extremes and that some leaders can never enjoy the calling that God has given them.

23. James Collins, *Good to Great: Why Some Companies Make the Leap—and Others Don't* (New York: HarperBusiness, 2001), 35.

24. Hugh De Pree, *Business as Unusual* (Zeeland, MI: Herman Miller, 1986).

25. Argyris, "Teaching Smart People."

Chapter 10: Recalibrating Church for the Smartphone Generation

1. I am not calling the congregation by its real name to protect its anonymity.

2. According to a 2016 report by the Nielsen rating service, 97 percent of American millennials have smartphones: http://www.nielsen.com/us/en/insights/news/2016/millennials-are-top -smartphone-users.html.

3. Bill Simmons, *The Ringer*, Sept. 29, 2017, https://www.theringer.com/nfl/2017/9/29/163 87550/donald-trump-protest-nfl-nba-colin-kaepernick-week-4-nfl-picks.

4. Atul Gawande, "Slow Ideas," *New Yorker*, July 29, 2013, https://www.newyorker.com /magazine/2013/07/29/slow-ideas.

5. Joe Posnanski, "Hamilton," Dec. 31, 2016, http://sportsworld.nbcsports.com/hamilton/.

6. Steven Kerr, "On the Folly of Hoping for A, While Rewarding B," in *The Organizational Behavior Reader*, ed. David A. Kolb, Joyce Osland, and Irwin M. Rubin, 6th ed., 548–61 (Englewood Cliffs, NJ: Prentice Hall, 1995).

7. Robert Wuthnow, *Sharing the Journey: Support Groups and America's New Quest for Community* (New York: Free Press, 1994); and Wuthnow, *"I Come Away Stronger": How Small Groups Are Shaping American Religion* (Grand Rapids: Eerdmans, 1994).

8. The quotation is from Lee Hardy's summary of Luther in *The Fabric of This World* (Grand Rapids: Eerdmans, 1990), 46.

9. Kim Scott, *Radical Candor* (New York: St. Martin's Press, 2017), 3–5.

10. Steven Johnson, *Where Good Ideas Come From* (New York: Riverhead Trade Books, 2011).

11. Kathleen Eisenhardt, foreword to *How Breakthroughs Happen: The Surprising Truth about How Companies Innovate*, by Andrew Hargadon (Boston: Harvard Business School Press, 2003), viii.

12. Chris Turner, "What Are 'Communities of Practice'?," in *The Dance of Change: The Challenges to Sustaining Momentum in a Learning Organization*, by Peter M. Senge et al. (New York: Currency/Doubleday, 1999), 477–80; Jean Lave and Etienne Wenger, *Situated Learning:*

Legitimate Peripheral Participation (New York: Cambridge University Press, 1991); see also Etienne Wenger, *Communities of Practice: Learning, Meaning and Identity* (New York: Cambridge University Press, 1998), summaries: https://www.cambridge.org/core/books/communities -of-practice/724C22A03B12D11DFC345EEF0AD3F22A; and Thomas Stewart, "The Invisible Keys to Success: Shadowy Groups Called Communities of Practice Are Where Learning and Growth Happen," *Fortune*, Aug. 5, 1996, https://money.cnn.com/magazines/fortune/fortune _archive/1996/08/05/215440/index.htm; cf. Fred Kofman and Peter M. Senge, "Communities of Commitment: The Heart of Learning Organizations," *Organizational Dynamics* 22 (Autumn 1993): 5–23, http://leeds-faculty.colorado.edu/larsenk/learnorg/kof_sen.html.

Index

CPSIA information can be obtained
at www.ICGtesting.com
Printed in the USA
LVHW021516300721
694023LV00002B/179